The *Regula* as a Rhetorical Device in Roman Law

Legal History Library

VOLUME 71

The titles published in this series are listed at *brill.com/lhl*

The *Regula* as a Rhetorical Device in Roman Law

By

Olga Tellegen-Couperus and Jan Willem Tellegen

BRILL | NIJHOFF

LEIDEN | BOSTON

Cover illustration: A classical-style bust of Cato Major, also known as Cato the Elder. Generated by the authors via DALL·E OpenAI on May 29th, 2024.

Library of Congress Cataloging-in-Publication Data

Names: Tellegen-Couperus, O. E. (Olga Eveline), author. | Tellegen, J.W. (Jan Willem) author.
Title: The *regula* as a rhetorical device in Roman law / by Olga Tellegen-Couperus and Jan Willem Tellegen.
Description: Leiden ; Boston : Brill, 2025. | Series: Legal history library; volume 71 | Includes bibliographical references and index. | Summary: "The main part of our book presents our novel exegesis of twenty texts from title D. 50.17 *De diversis regulis iuris antiqui*. To Romanists, this may come as a surprise because they usually associate that title with general rules of law only, not with rhetoric. Our unconventional choice is the result of a concerted reading of Cicero's *Topica* and Justinian's *Digest*. It started with Trebatius, the jurist for whom Cicero wrote his *Topica* and some of whose responsa have been preserved in the *Digest*: we noticed that in one responsum he used two unmistakable rhetorical devices: a topos and a thesis."
Identifiers: LCCN 2024037749 | ISBN 9789004711013 (hardback) | ISBN 9789004711020 (ebook)
Subjects: LCSH: Rhetorical argumentation (Roman law) | Law, Ancient. | Cicero.
Classification: LCC KJA100 .T45 2025 | DDC 340.5/4–dc23/eng/20240814
LC record available at https://lccn.loc.gov/2024037749

Typeface for the Latin, Greek, and Cyrillic scripts: "Brill". See and download: brill.com/brill-typeface.

ISSN 1874-1793
ISBN 978-90-04-71101-3 (hardback)
ISBN 978-90-04-71102-0 (e-book)
DOI 10.1163/9789004711020

Contents

ORATIO REBUS DUBIIS INVENTA EST

T. LIVIUS, *Ab urbe condita* 3.56.3

Preface

The title of this book may likely raise a few eyebrows, since in Romanist literature the *regula* is commonly regarded as an established principle, rule even, of Roman law – most decidedly not as a rhetorical device. For more than two decades, and perhaps a little defiantly, we have consistently argued that in Roman antiquity law and rhetoric were in fact closely connected and that the texts of the Roman jurists that found their way into Justinian's Digest can often be better understood when viewed as arguments used to win over a judge or a jury. In this book, we offer compelling evidence for our proposition: more than a few *regulae* in title D. 50.17 and elsewhere are arguments that were originally crafted for a specific case, are based on commonplaces, *topoi*, and are worded in general terms, as *theseis*.

This 'symbiotic' understanding of the role of rhetoric in Roman law reinforces our equally unorthodox view of Roman law itself: more than being a system of legal rules based on logic (if it even is that), it is a *Fundgrube* of arguments that can be used in contentious matters – of which there are, then as now, many. Legal dilemmas are seldom easy to solve; usually, both sides to a conflict present arguments that appear reasonable and just. In such a situation, a jurist perforce resorts to rhetoric to buttress their client's claim or defence. This novel perspective brings Roman law much closer to real life and adds to its fascination.

We hope that our book will help Romanists to recognise rhetorical devices when construing texts on Roman law and that it will inspire Classicists to use texts from Roman law when illustrating how rhetorical devices work in practice.

When we were writing this book, we received encouragement, advice, and help from others. We are grateful to them all and to some in particular. Randall Lesaffer gave us some useful pointers on the scope and direction of our book and initiated contact with the publisher. Our warm and very special thanks go to Dick Broeren. Supported at stages by Ineke Sijtsma-van der Kruk, his colleague of many years, he gave generously of his time to assist us in editing and revising our draft texts. We believe the book is the better for it.

Olga Tellegen-Couperus and Jan Willem Tellegen
Utrecht, April 2024

CHAPTER 1

Introduction

1 The Research Topic: The Use of *topoi* and *theseis* in Legal Argumentation

We think it is time for a rethink of the role of rhetoric in Roman legal argumentation. A Roman orator preparing his speech would run over a list of rhetorical commonplaces (*topoi*) from which he could draw arguments and then express them in general terms (*theseis*), as Cicero relates:

> Orator, 47 Faciet igitur hic noster – non enim declamatorem aliquem de ludo aut rabulam de foro, sed doctissimum et perfectissimum quaerimus – ut, quoniam loci certi traduntur, percurrat omnis, utatur aptis, generatim dicat[.]
>
> Therefore our orator – it is not a mere declaimer in a school that we seek, or a ranter in the forum, but a scholarly and finished speaker – our orator finding certain definite places enumerated, will run rapidly over them all, select those which fit the subject, and then speak in general terms.[1]

This is what one would expect an orator to do. But would a Roman *jurist* also use *topoi* and *theseis* when substantiating his opinion, his *responsum*, about a thorny legal problem? Modern scholarship of Roman law has not given this question its due, because the *communis opinio* has for a very long time been that Roman jurists were very different from orators and were indifferent to rhetoric.[2] For well over twenty years, we have argued to the contrary: that the Roman jurists were not all that different from the orators and were well acquainted with rhetoric. We have found support for our view in Cicero's works, in Gaius' Institutes, and in the main source of Roman law, Justinian's Digest.[3] In this book, we turn our attention to the question of whether the Roman jurists used *topoi* and *theseis* when formulating an argument in a legal

1 Text and translation by Hubbell (1949), slightly adapted.

2 Similarly, e.g., Schulz (1946) 54–55. Less rigorously, Wieacker (1988) 667–669, Babusiaux (2011) 13–15, Stagl (2013) 2, and Kacprzak (2016) 200–201.

3 This has enabled us to shed new light on much-debated issues, such as, most recently, the *voluntas testatoris*, Tellegen-Couperus and Tellegen (2016).

 | DOI:10.1163/9789004711020_002

discussion.[4] In his *Topica*, which he wrote at the request of the jurist Trebatius, Cicero assumes they did.[5] If Cicero's assumption is correct, it should be possible to find evidence of *topoi* and *theseis* in Justinian's Digest and, in turn, to illuminate how the jurists worked as well as, more generally, the relationship between Roman law and rhetoric.

As *topoi* and *theseis* are argument schemes, it stands to reason to concentrate on those texts in the Digest that contain arguments. Horak estimated that about one third of the Digest texts do; in his view, the reason why arguments are missing in the other two thirds is that, over the centuries between their first documentation and their final compilation in the Digest, many *responsa* were shortened.[6] The commonly held view, however, as first expressed by Schulz, is that the Roman jurists as a rule did not include arguments in their *responsa*, but relied on their own or another jurist's authority.[7] Moreover, it is generally assumed (also by Horak) that when the Roman jurists included arguments, they only used legal arguments based on logic.[8] But here sometimes problems arise, such as when arguments are put forward that do not logically fit the perceived system of Roman law or that are even entirely unrelated to law. Various explanations for these anomalies have been offered, a recurring one being that the text in question had been interpolated by Justinian's compilers, but they all overlook the possibility that these arguments are rhetorical arguments.

A main reason why Romanists by and large do not give serious consideration to the idea of a Roman jurist using *topoi* and *theseis* is that they are unfamiliar with rhetoric. Even though both belong to the *Altertumswissenschaft* (science of antiquity), Roman law and rhetoric are commonly regarded as belonging to different disciplines and are therefore mostly studied separately, by Romanists and Classicists respectively. The law and rhetoric divide finds its origins in 19th-century German historical narratives, as Cunningham has recently described in detail.[9] At the time, the jurists of the Historical School constructed a system of modern civil law which they perceived as a science that was based on ancient Roman law, and Roman law itself consequently also came to be viewed as a science. This took rhetoric out of the equation; it was

4 The terms *topos* and *thesis* refer to the content and the wording, respectively, of an argument. We use the Greek terms throughout because these are more familiar than the ones in Latin (*locus* and *propositio*) and English (place and proposition).

5 See Chapter 2.

6 Horak (1969) 289–292. Similarly, Kaiser (2015) 128–130.

7 Schulz (1946) 124–125.

8 Horak (1969) 40–44.

9 Cunningham (2018) 11–35.

not a science but an *ars*, a skill, for which lawyers were presumed to have had little use. Having been raised on this divide, Romanists have largely ignored rhetoric and have not identified *topoi* and *theseis* in the Digest.

Classicists, on the other hand, have traditionally been more interested in Roman philology and literature than in Roman law. Roughly half of Cicero's works – a commanding source of knowledge on Roman rhetoric and, especially, argumentation – deals with legal practice, such as his forensic speeches and his books *De oratore* and *Topica*, but Classicists tend to pay scant attention to the legal dimension of these works. In publications on rhetoric, they usually ignore Justinian's Digest and therefore also miss out on the rhetorical devices that we believe are in evidence in these texts.[10]

In this chapter, we first describe how the concept of legal science is used in Romanist literature and with what consequences (Section 2). Then, after establishing that there is no continuity between ancient and modern Roman law (Section 3), we turn to Romanist research into the relationship between law and rhetoric from the 20th century onwards (Section 4). In the final section we explain how we set about identifying twenty *regulae* in D. 50.17 that we believe are based on two rhetorical devices: *topoi* and *theseis* (Section 5).

2 Roman Law and Legal Science

In the past two centuries, the view that Roman law and rhetoric belong to separate, mutually exclusive disciplines has become a paradigm of Roman law research. An essential assumption of this paradigm is that Roman law was an autonomous science based on logic. This of course raises the question what Romanists mean by science. There is an abundance of literature on the question whether law is a science, but there is little discussion about the criterion or criteria for qualifying Roman law as a science.[11] Two paradigmatic definitions are those proposed by Kaser and Horak. Kaser describes the evolution of Roman law as a science as follows:[12]

---

10 E.g., Kennedy (1972) 7–18 deals with judicial oratory but only fleetingly mentions 'that by the first century BC technical legal advice was secured by a patron or a client from a jurisconsult, a professional legal authority' (p. 14). Corbett (1990) 136–139 discusses some special topics for judicial discourse but only refers to Greek sources. In his *Introduction to Classical Legal Rhetoric*, Frost (2005) overlooks the Roman jurists and their work. There are exceptions, e.g., Frier (1985), Crook (1995), and Reinhardt (2003) who refer to the Digest and to Gaius' Institutes but still contrast law and rhetoric.

11 For an overview, see Tuori (2007) 22–25.

12 Kaser (1967) 164.

> Zum Wesen einer solchen [Wissenschaft, TC&T] gehört die Entwicklung inhaltlich genau bestimmter und von einander abgegrenzter juristische Begriffe und ihre Ordnung und Abstimmung aufeinander in einem von der Sachlogik bestimmter System.

The main source of Roman law that might be expected to use such a system would be Justinian's Digest. But that is not what the Digest does; for the most part, it follows the order of the *Edictum Perpetuum*, the final version of the praetorian edict as edited in the second century AD by the jurist Salvius Iulianus. In the preface to his reconstruction of the Edict, Lenel explains that it followed the formulary procedure and that its system had grown by association over a long period of time.[13] While Kaser concedes that Justinian's Digest is casuistic and that it lacks a system based on *Sachlogik*, he assumes that Gaius' Institutes did have such a system, consisting of three parts (the law of persons, the law of property, and the law of procedure), and that it was based on the concept of subjective rights. This explanation has become leading, but we do not subscribe to it. Elsewhere, one of us has argued that the concept of subjective rights was unknown to Roman law and that Gaius when constructing his Institutes probably used the law of procedure.[14]

The second modern-day definition of science to be applied to Roman law was provided by Horak in his famous monograph *Rationes decidendi*. He describes legal science as follows:

> Zwei Merkmale nun werden allgemein für notwendig angesehen, damit man von Wissenschaft sprechen kann: erstens eine gewisse *Systematik*, und zweitens ein gewisser *Begründungszusammenhang*. Beide stehen in enger Wechselwirkung.[15]

This description differs from Kaser's in that Horak also requires a context of justification, that is to say, argumentation through deduction from a certain premise. But Horak, too, finds himself deadlocked because, when examining about 300 Digest texts dating from the late Republic and containing an

13 Lenel (1927) 14–17. According to Schulz (1946) 151, 'Mommsen called this edictal order a disorder', adding that 'certainly it is anything but a masterpiece of systematization.'

14 Tellegen (1994) 52–55. See also Tellegen-Couperus and Tellegen (2013) 37–40. *Ius quod ad personas pertinet* may refer to the question of who can start proceedings, *ius quod ad res pertinet* to what can be the object of proceedings, and *ius quod ad actiones pertinet* to what remedies are available.

15 Horak (1969) 10.

argumentation, he can qualify only a small number of them as scientific, and even these are dubious.[16] Yet to him, other ways of argumentation, for instance based on *topoi*, are not at all relevant to legal science.

The perception that Roman law was a science and that therefore Roman law and rhetoric were two separate disciplines has had three far-reaching consequences. The first one is that Romanists have long supposed that the jurists and the orators had different ways of working: the jurists developed their science in a completely disinterested way, only wanting to serve the truth, whereas the orators were not interested in the truth. Assuming that truth is unambiguous, a jurist aimed to find the one correct solution to a legal problem.[17] An orator assumed that legal problems could be solved in more than one way, and it was his job to find a solution that was in his client's interest and to make a persuasive case on his client's behalf. This perceived separation makes it almost impossible for Romanists to imagine that Roman jurists would use *topoi* and *theseis* to sway a praetor or a judge.

The second after-effect of regarding Roman law and rhetoric as separate disciplines is that a distinction is made between legal and rhetorical sources, the criterion being the author. Legal sources, so the narrative runs, were written by jurists and therefore present reliable data on Roman law; the rhetorical sources, having been written by orators, are legally unreliable and therefore hardly relevant to understanding Roman law.[18] This rigid separation takes no account of the fact that some legal sources are also rhetorical, and vice versa. As a result, bizarrely we think, Justinian's Digest is exclusively considered a legal source, and Cicero's works are solely valued as non-legal or literary sources.[19]

The third carry-over of the perceived law-rhetoric split is the misapprehension of the continuity between Roman law in antiquity and Roman law in the new era. A textbook example of this misunderstanding can be found in Kaser's description of the renaissance of Roman law in the introduction to his *Römische Rechtsgeschichte*:[20]

16 Elsewhere, we have demonstrated that the text which according to Horak contains the best 'Begründung', D. 43.19.3 pr., is not based on a certain premise and does therefore not present a case of legal science. See Tellegen-Couperus and Tellegen (2013) 45–48.

17 For a critical overview, see Thomas (2014).

18 An exception is Stagl (2013), who convincingly explains that the *Declamationes Minores*, which are attributed to Quintilian, may be an important source of Roman law.

19 E.g., Horak (1969), Kaser (1971), and, more recently, Tuori (2007) and Babusiaux (2011). Yet, Giaro (2007) and Schiavone (2012), e.g., do not distinguish between types of sources.

20 Kaser (1967) 11. Similarly, Rainer (2014) 1.

> Die Wiedergeburt des römischen Rechts im Mittelalter ist vielmehr eine Neuentdeckung der römischen Rechtswissenschaft, deren wichtigste Ergebnisse am Ende seiner antiken Entwicklung im “Corpus iuris civilis”, einem grossen Sammelwerk mit Gesetzeskraft aus dem 6. Jh. n. Chr., zusammengetragen worden waren.

Kaser asserts that what was rediscovered in the twelfth century was Roman legal science as it had been summarised in Justinian's codification. In other words, both ancient Roman law and Roman law of modern times were a science, and the history of Roman law was in fact the history of Roman legal science. But how could the medieval scholars who discovered the Digest possibly identify Roman law as a legal science? They did not find a clear-cut system. Nor did they know Gaius' Institutes, because its manuscript was not discovered until 1806. Moreover, they lacked a reliable reconstruction of the praetorian edict; Lenel's only appeared in 1883.

To date and to our knowledge, no primary sources have come to light corroborating the assumption that the Romans were familiar with the concept of ‘legal science’. True, the Justinian codification was the end of ancient Roman law as well as the starting point of modern Roman law, but as a common element it is hardly relevant. The Roman jurists never knew Justinian's Digest, whereas to modern scholarship it is the principal source of ancient Roman law. That is why we think any continuity there is between ancient and modern Roman law cannot be reliably predicated on the notion of ancient Roman law as a science: it was not a science, and neither was it cleanly severed from rhetoric. Yet modern-day Roman law scholarship tends to regard Roman law as a science and to ignore rhetoric. To understand how this separation took root in the collective scholarly mind requires taking a closer look at the two histories of Roman law and the 600-year interim.

3 The Two Histories of Roman Law

Ancient Roman law, *le droit Romain Romain*, applied roughly from 500 BC to 500 AD, modern Roman law, or *das heutige römische Recht* as it later came to be called, roughly from 1100 to 1900. In the 600 years between these two periods, the political landscape of Western Europe changed dramatically, and so did the world of law.

For ancient Roman law, the last two centuries BC were a crucial period. Two events coincided: a new procedure for civil litigation, the formulary procedure, was introduced, and Greek rhetoric gained a foothold in Rome. We believe that together these two events set going the evolution of a modern and flexible body of private law that was unique in antiquity. Both jurists and orators contributed to this evolution by giving legal advice and publishing their *responsa*, and by acting as advocates and publishing their speeches. Of these *responsa*, relatively few have survived, and that only indirectly, but relatively many rhetorical sources have survived, including about thirty forensic speeches by Cicero and his *De oratore* and *Topica*.

In the first two centuries AD, jurists and orators appear to have 'specialised', with jurists mainly giving and publishing legal advice and orators primarily acting as advocates. Still, rhetoric continued to have value for the jurists just as legal knowledge continued to be relevant to the orators. This was stressed by Quintilian – the first professor of general rhetoric in western Europe to be paid by the state – in his *Institutio oratoria*,[21] and it is also obvious in Gaius' Institutes, the only source of Roman law to have been preserved directly.[22] The political turbulence of the third century AD changed the jurists' activities in that they no longer published their *responsa*. Imperial legislation became the primary source of law, but the jurists and the orators continued to work together and contribute to the development of late Roman law.[23] And until the fifth century AD, the rhetorical works of Cicero and Quintilian played a central role in education. The fall of the Western Roman Empire put an end to that as well.

The history of western Europe between 500 and 1100 is extraordinarily complex. It was marked by the confrontation and interaction between the Greek-Roman culture, the Judeo-Christian culture, and the Germanic and Celtic cultures.[24] Retaining much of their native ways of life, the Germanic and Celtic tribes that had settled within the borders of the Roman empire also adopted elements of Roman culture. Two of these elements played a crucial role: Christianity and the written word. All over western Europe, abbeys and monasteries were founded, and in their schools written texts from antiquity were preserved and copied. These texts included not only the Bible and works of the Church Fathers, but also those of pagan authors, such as Cicero's *De oratore* and *Attic Nights* by Aulus Gellius.[25] From a legal point of view, western

21 Quintilian, *Inst. Or.* 12.3. Cf. Tellegen-Couperus (2021) 272–275. The Letters of Pliny the Younger also show that its author – although known as an *orator* – had extensive legal knowledge. See Tellegen (1982).

22 Gaius' description of the controversies between the Sabinian and Proculian schools shows that he was familiar with rhetoric. On these controversies, Leesen (2010).

23 Humfress (2007) 11–28, particularly 19.

24 See Lesaffer (2009) 123–193 with bibliography.

25 For an overview, see Reynolds and Wilson (1991) 95–106.

Europe resembled a patchwork quilt: each tribe, each nation had its own customary law, whereas Roman law continued to be applied to the Romanised indigenous population. In the seventh and eighth centuries, Germanic law and Roman law merged, if to varying degrees: in the south, Roman law was dominant, in the north Germanic law. Moreover, other legal systems developed: feudal law and canon law. As a result, several legal systems existed side by side, applying to different sections of the population. In the sixth century, during the short Byzantine occupation of Italy, a manuscript of the then recently published collection of fundamental Roman legal texts, compiled by order of the Byzantine Emperor Justinian and today known as the *Corpus iuris civilis*, was offered to the Pope in Rome. It was not until 500 years later, around 1070, that this manuscript was rediscovered in Pisa.

It was then that the second history of Roman law began. It differed essentially from the first history in being highly theoretical and for regarding Roman law as a science – although the latter feature did not become manifest for quite some time. The medieval jurists regarded the *Justinian* codification and the preserved texts of canon law as the sources of an ideal law, and they assumed that scholasticism would enable them to discover it.[26] The idea of Roman law as a science did not arise until the sixteenth century, in the minds of French humanists such as Donellus. In Stein's words, '[Donellus] assumed that Justinian's law must be logical even though it did not appear to be so, and applied himself to identifying what he conceived to be its underlying rational structure.'[27] In the seventeenth and eighteenth centuries, the civil law came to be organised in various ways, reflecting the influence of Natural Law and the Enlightenment. On the European continent, this resulted in codification, for example in Austria and France, and the French Civil Code served as a model for the Dutch, Belgian, Italian, and Spanish civil codes. The final step in the 'scientification' of Roman law was taken by the founder of the German Historical School, Friedrich Carl von Savigny. Starting from the work of the second-century AD jurists, he tried to ascertain the central principles of Roman law and created the new scientific system of present-day Roman law, *das heutige römische Recht*.[28] It was not until the middle of the nineteenth century, when the Historical School began to exert its influence all over Europe and beyond,[29] that modern Roman law became completely separated from ancient Roman law and, by extension, from rhetoric.

26 Lesaffer (2009) 239–261, 283. See also Mayali (2015).

27 Stein (1999) 80.

28 Lesaffer (2009) 372–471.

29 Stein (1999) 123.

Up to that point, there had been ample room for rhetoric. The Italian humanists of the fifteenth century rediscovered Cicero's and Quintilian's rhetorical works and used them as a standard for correct Latin. In the middle of the seventeenth century, rhetoric came to be viewed as relevant to jurists, too: in 1674, the Roman advocate and cardinal Giovanni Battista De Luca published a treatise on the use of rhetorical techniques in legal practice, *Dello stile legale*.[30] In France, Germany, and the Netherlands, the eighteenth and early nineteenth centuries saw the publication of various works on forensic eloquence,[31] all of which contained numerous references to Cicero and Quintilian. It was Mommsen who changed all this: an admirer of Julius Caesar, he despised Cicero and actively sought to tarnish his reputation.[32] The jurists of the Historical School, who already disregarded rhetoric, proved susceptible to Mommsen's 'smear campaign' and it was not long before rhetoric disappeared from the law school curricula.

4 Romanist Research

These developments also had an impact on research in Roman law. By 1900, when civil law had at long last been codified in Germany, too, modern Roman law ceased to be directly applicable and it consequently lost its practical relevance. Yet everywhere in continental Europe, it was still regarded as the basis of modern civil law and it was still taught at the universities. The same happened in research: on the one hand Roman law turned into an object of historical-philological studies such as Lenel's groundbreaking work, but on the other hand it was (and is to this day) viewed as the basis of modern civil law.[33] Scholars searching for the origin of a rule from a modern codification would consult Justinian law or would try to reconstruct the legal rule in question as stemming from 'classical' law.[34] The by now undisputed tenets were that ancient Roman law was a science, that just like in modern law there was only

30 Rossi (2003) 82–88.

31 Van der Linden (1827) 13–14 mentions Gin, *De l'eloquence du barreau*, Paris (1767), K.S. Zacharia, *Anleitung zur gerichtlichen Beredsamkeit*, Heidelberg (1810), and several other works.

32 Mommsen (1856) 619–621. See our comment in Tellegen and Tellegen-Couperus (2004) 70–75.

33 Cf. Zimmermann (1996) preface IX–XI.

34 The qualification 'classical' stems from the 19th century and refers to the time from Augustus to Diocletian, according to Schulz (1946) 99.

one correct solution to every legal problem, and that the Roman jurist could find that solution on the basis of his scientific legal knowledge.

A twentieth century proponent of this view was Schulz. In his *History of Roman Legal Science*, he sketches the rise of Roman legal science in the late Republic and gives the lead role to the jurist Quintus Mucius Scaevola,[35] arguing that Scaevola's *libri XVIII de iure civili* had laid the basis for the system of Roman law that had been used in Gaius' Institutes and that had formed the basis of private law on the European continent. Schulz's view continues to hold sway, as appears for instance from a recent book by Schiavone, *The Invention of Law in the West*.[36]

This approach to Roman law has led to insurmountable problems in explaining both legal and rhetorical sources. In Justinian's Digest, for example, different solutions for one and the same problem are given, sometimes proffered by different jurists but sometimes even by one and the same jurist.[37] Of course, such irregularities do not fit the view that for every legal problem there is only one correct solution, and many a Romanist has felt compelled to bring legal sources of antiquity in line with precepts of modern legal science, mixing up the tradition of a text and its interpretation.[38] And as such adaptations are essentially 'deregulated', chaos ensues. It is true that in the twentieth century textual criticism lost some of its vigour but the tendency to harmonise contradictory texts remains very much alive.[39] At the same time, other approaches to classical Roman law have come into vogue, one being forensic rhetoric.[40] In his handbook on the history of Roman law, Franz Wieacker even devotes a whole chapter to *Gerichtsrhetorik*, but he restricts its scope to the *status* theory, ignoring the core component of rhetoric, argumentation theory.[41] The Romanist mindset, it would appear, struggles to tune in to the idea that a Roman jurist might want and even try to persuade his audience of his solution

35 Schulz (1946) 94–96. Also, e.g., Frier (1985) 155–171. More differentiated, Stein (1999) 16–17.

36 Schiavone (2012) 177–244.

37 Kaser (1972) 21 qualifies this as *ius controversum*, an expression which he thinks (p. 21) only occurs in the work of Cicero and other non-legal authors, but which according to Schwarz (1951) 207–208 was avoided by the jurists because they regarded it as incompatible with the dignity of law. See also Bretone (2009) 763–772.

38 On the so-termed interpolation hunt, i.e., the tracing of supposed changes in the texts of the classical jurists made by the compilers of Justinian's Digest, see Kaser (1972) and Wieacker (1988) 154–182. Kaiser (2015) 128–130 reveals a genuine interpolation.

39 See, e.g., the exegesis of D. 50.17.4, 7, 35, 64, 88, 113, 180, 192.1, and 195 in Chapters 4–10.

40 Two other approaches, 'law and society' and 'principle and pragmatism', are described in two edited volumes by Du Plessis (2013) 1–2 and Spagnolo and Sampson (2020) respectively.

41 Wieacker (1988) 669–675.

to a particular legal problem at least in part by means of rhetoric – which is, after all, the art of persuasion.

The exegesis of rhetorical sources of antiquity – which often refer to Roman law – has continued to vex Romanists.[42] Various attempts have been made to harmonise these sources with the idea of Roman law being a science. Sometimes, they have been dismissed as inferior, sometimes they have been altered. We believe harmonisation efforts driven by the traditional law-rhetoric divide are not conducive to efficacious exegesis because in our experience legal and rhetorical sources are usually best interpreted together.

There are hopeful signs that things are turning around. In 2009, Lovato organised an *incontro di studio* on the theme of *Tra retorica e diritto*. In five contributions, various topics were discussed, such as the origin and history of the *regulae iuris*, the development of the law of evidence from the late Republic to the early third century AD, the use of other jurists' opinions as an argument, the use of logic and dialectic by the Roman jurists, and the similarities and differences between Quintilian's *Institutio oratoria* and Gaius' Institutes.[43] These contributions are interesting indeed, but except for the third paper they do not deal with the Roman jurists using rhetoric.

That particular topic is the subject of Leesen's monograph, also published in 2009. In *Gaius meets Cicero. Law and Rhetoric in the School Controversies*, Leesen analyses the twenty-two school controversies mentioned in Gaius' Institutes and demonstrates that, in each controversy, the representatives of the Sabinian and Proculian schools 'operated the argumentation theory of the *topica* to construct and argue their legal opinion.'[44]

Two years later, Babusiaux published her monograph *Papinians* Quaestiones. *Zur rhetorischen Methode eines spätklassischen Juristen*. The rhetorical character of Papinian's *Quaestiones* has raised more doubts about its authenticity than almost any other work of Roman law.[45] Now that viewing a seemingly inconsistent text as interpolated by Justinian's compilers is no longer a foregone conclusion, Babusiaux turns to classical rhetoric to analyse this work.[46]

42 A classic example is the *causa Curiana*, which is known only through Cicero's works. We return to this case in Chapter 3.

43 The contributions by Carla Masi Doria, Salvatore Puliatti, Emanuele Stolfi, and Renato Quadrato were published in Lovato (2011), which also includes a summary of the fourth paper, by Antonio Mantello. Already in 2001, one of us had organised an international conference for jurists and linguists at Tilburg (the Netherlands) on the theme 'Quintilian and the Law'; the papers were published in Tellegen-Couperus (2003).

44 Leesen (2010) 329.

45 Babusiaux (2011) 8–13.

46 Babusiaux (2011) 15.

She proceeds on the assumption that Papinian wrote *Quaestiones* at the time of the Second Sophistic when, after the example of the Greek Sophists, education in dialectics and rhetoric was highly prized. Babusiaux thinks that Papinian, as a member of the emperor's *consilium* and as the author of the rescripts issued in the emperor's name, will have been well versed in rhetoric. While we are not convinced by her approach, we do share her conclusion that, not only in Papinian's commentary on the imperial constitutions but also when he renders the opinions of other jurists and his own views, the rhetorical and legal argumentations are closely connected and that only together can they properly explain the texts in question.[47] What if this were also true of Papinian's other works and of those of other Roman jurists?

More recently still, in his PhD thesis *Law, Rhetoric and Science. Historical Narratives in Roman Law*, Cunningham claims that jurists and orators were very often the same, or similar people, engaged in the same, or similar activities, that Cicero was not an outsider to the legal world of the jurists, and that Republican Roman law developed from rhetorical argument.[48] We agree. But we demur at Cunningham's apparent implication that this development is manifest mainly or only in legal procedure, more precisely, in the *in iure* stage of the formulary procedure, and that the praetor, 'informed by topical, rhetorical arguments which appealed to socially understood values in Roman society [such as *aequitas* and *pietas*, TC&T] modified the law according to how persuaded he was by the value in these arguments.'[49] We think this is too limited a scope since rhetorical argumentation is relevant in any discussion on dubious legal matters, not in specific legal procedures only.

5 Our Research

To borrow two of Kuhn's famed phrases, we believe it is time for a 'paradigm shift', to move away from the 'normal science' of regarding Roman law and rhetoric as unrelated to viewing Roman law as living in symbiosis with rhetoric.[50]

---

47 Babusiaux (2011) 22–23 and 63–64 explains Papinian's comment on the imperial constitutions on the basis of the *status* theory, and his discussions of other jurists' opinions and his own views by referring to topics and dialectics. This approach is remarkable because in rhetorical theory *status* and topics serve completely different purposes.

48 Cunningham (2018) 45–79; 146–157. He describes *bonorum possessio* and the *querela inofficiosi testamenti* as examples of legal innovation based on rhetorical appeals to the principles of *aequitas* and *pietas* respectively. See also Cunningham (2020).

49 Cunningham (2018) 146.

50 Kuhn (1996).

For this fundamental change, there is a powerful argument in Cicero's *De officiis*, where he states *Atque huic arti* [i.e., *scientia iuris*, TC&T] *finitima est dicendi* [*gravior*] *facultas et gratior et ornatior*: knowledge of the law is closely related to the more popular and more distinguished gift of eloquence.[51] Being versed in the law could certainly further a person's career (by helping the people or individual citizens solve legal problems), but pairing legal competence with eloquence could give it a boost. In practical terms, this meant pleading for or against a case and convincing a magistrate or a judge of the rightness of a particular point of view. This relationship between rhetoric and law must have left its traces in the sources of Roman law, and we therefore assume that these sources can be better understood by taking rhetoric into account.

To ascertain whether the Roman jurists used *topoi* and *theseis* when formulating an argument in a legal discussion, we restricted ourselves (as far as possible) to the first history of Roman law, and we studied both Roman legal sources and Roman rhetorical sources. That constitutes something of a break with past research because, as we set out earlier, Romanists and Classicists seldom take cognisance of each other's scholarly pursuits. By studying Justinian's Digest and Cicero's rhetorical works in relation to one another, we straddled both domains.

The main part of our book presents our novel exegesis of twenty texts from title D. 50.17 *De diversis regulis iuris antiqui.* To Romanists, this may come as a surprise because they usually associate that title with general rules of law only, not with rhetoric. Our unconventional choice is the result of a concerted reading of Cicero's *Topica* and Justinian's Digest.

It started with Trebatius, the jurist for whom Cicero wrote his *Topica* and some of whose *responsa* have been preserved in the Digest: we noticed that in one *responsum* he used two unmistakable rhetorical devices, a *topos* and a *thesis*. Our subsequent perusal of Cicero's *Topica* is the subject of Chapter 2. What makes *Topica* special is that Cicero wrote it for legal practice. By giving examples, he explains how the various *topoi* can be put to good use and how a *thesis* can make an argument more convincing. Even so, these examples, and Cicero's *Topica* generally, are often viewed as legally and rhetorically irrelevant, and as a professional jurist, Trebatius, it is felt, would certainly have had no need of them. We disagree and we submit that (1) a much-criticised example in *Topica* was appropriate both legally and rhetorically, and (2) in a particular

---

51 *De officiis* 2.66. Kunkel (1967) 38–40 fully quotes and comments on the preceding section (2.65) about the *scientia iuris* but he ignores 2.66 about rhetoric.

case mentioned in the Digest, Trebatius – conceivably inspired by *Topica* – used a topical argument and formulated it in general terms, as a *thesis.*

In Chapter 3, we turn to Quintus Mucius Scaevola *pontifex* and wonder whether this alleged founder of Roman legal science might not have done the same. Scaevola was one of the advocates in the *causa Curiana*, a famous trial known only through Cicero's works. Predictably, Romanist interpretations of Scaevola's performance are uniquely linked to his reputation as a jurist. We think this is a predisposed interpretation and that Scaevola commanded admiration for his ingenious use of rhetoric, too. Scaevola also gave *responsa*, a small number of which have been preserved in the Digest, and in one of these he appears to have used the *topos in maiore minus inest*. This *topos*, which is formulated as a *thesis* and which stems from Aristotle's *Rhetorike*, also figures in seven cases included in title D. 50.17 *De diversis regulis iuris antiqui*.

For us, the big question then was whether title D. 50.17 contains similar rhetorical arguments. A rhetorical argument used in legal argumentation can only be properly recognised as such in its legal context. Using Lenel's *Palingenesia iuris civilis*, we were able to trace this context in the *leges geminatae* of twenty *regulae*. Our exegesis of them forms the main part of this book (Chapters 4–10). As we observed above, Romanists habitually discuss these *regulae* in the light of the second history of Roman law, which is why they cannot recognise them as rhetorical arguments, but having stepped away from that particular perspective, we show not only that these twenty *regulae* are indeed *topoi* formulated in general terms, but also that each of them is meant to apply to one particular case only. This makes them *theseis* in the sense of Cicero's *Topica*.

In Chapter 11, we put our findings to the test by examining the first text in D. 50.17, which introduces the *regula* concept. In Romanist literature, D. 50.17.1 has been interpreted in very different ways, usually in connection with the *regula Catoniana*, which is not mentioned in D. 50.17 but which is pre-eminently regarded as a legal rule. We establish that the *regula* in D. 50.17.1 matches the other *regulae* in this title we discuss: they, as well as the *regula Catoniana*, are rhetorical arguments formulated in general terms but intended for one specific case only.

In concluding our book (Chapter 12), we argue that, in thorny questions, the Roman jurists were not averse to using rhetorical arguments to strengthen their *responsa*. Their *auctoritas* as jurists was not always enough to convince the praetor or the judge, and sometimes they even expediently preferred rhetorical arguments to strictly legal ones. Against this backdrop of legal pragmatism and of revisiting the traditional, exclusive view of Roman law as a science, the *responsa* in question can be understood more easily and more fully than has so far been the case. Rather than being poles apart, Roman law and rhetoric were two sides of the same coin – legal practice – and we believe they should be appreciated and studied as such.

CHAPTER 2

Cicero's *Topica* and Trebatius Testa

If, as we believe, in Roman antiquity law and rhetoric lived in symbiosis, it stands to reason to assume that the Roman jurists used rhetorical devices in their *responsa*. At first glance, it may seem difficult to find support for this assumption, not least because of the five traditional canons of rhetoric (*inventio, dispositio, elocutio, memoria*, and *actio*) the last two solely concern delivery by an orator, that is to say, speaking. Yet the first three can clearly add to the persuasiveness of written text, too. In a legal context, they can be seen to work to great effect in the forensic speeches delivered and published by Cicero as well as in the published *responsa* of Roman jurists, particularly in the argumentation of the latter type of legal text. It was there that a jurist had two tasks to accomplish. First, as part of *inventio*, he needed to find a convincing argument; here the *topos* was essential. And second, as part of *elocutio*, he had to formulate the argument in such a way that it would be even more convincing; here the *thesis* was useful. For all that, though, Romanists do not commonly show awareness of the potential relevance of these rhetorical elements to legal texts. One reason for this oversight is that Romanists by and large do not distinguish between the first and the second histories of Roman law (see Chapter 1). Another reason has to do with the background of other researchers of Roman history, especially those that study classical rhetoric: they are often schooled in philosophy or philology, or indeed rhetoric, but not in law and that does not predispose them to study the use of rhetoric by the Roman jurists.[1] These blind spots, if we may be forgiven for calling them that, could conceivably render their interpretations of Roman legal texts incomplete. That liability alone is sufficient reason for us to explore the posited law-rhetoric symbiosis. It also makes sense to do so, because Cicero's rhetorical works abound in references to law.

It is one of these works, *Topica*, that is of great value to our research, not only because it is a rich and detailed source of information on the *topos* and the *thesis*, but also because in it Cicero describes these two concepts in a way novel to his contemporaries and because he unquestionably wrote it for Roman jurists, notably C. Trebatius Testa. These striking features notwithstanding, Cicero's

1 See, e.g., Kennedy (1972) and Rubinelli (2009).

 | DOI:10.1163/9789004711020_003

Topica has generally attracted scant attention in modern literature[2] and scholarly approval of it has been scantier yet. Viehweg, for example, in 1953 compared it to Aristotle's *Topike*, and while he believed that Cicero's work had been more influential, he held Aristotle's *Topike* to be far superior.[3] But in later decades even this sparing praise met with resistance among Romanists. Horak, for instance, readily concurred that Cicero's *Topica* was not in the same league as Aristotle's *Topike*, but he insisted that scientifically *topoi* had had little to offer to the Roman jurists.[4] Other Romanists found fault with Cicero's *Topica* for being of inferior quality in terms of both law and rhetoric; Schmidlin and Watson came to this conclusion on the basis of their interpretations of a single passage from *Topica*.[5] Given these Romanists' disparagement of this work, it is perhaps understandable that none of them wondered whether *Topica* had been of use to Trebatius, but it is regrettable they did not. It also obviously leaves a blank to be filled, because Cicero expressly wrote it for Trebatius' benefit.[6]

The standing of this work has since improved somewhat. In 2003, Reinhardt, a Classicist, published a new edition of *Topica* with an introduction, a translation, and a commentary. In the introduction he explains that Cicero's idea of rhetorical invention was outside the mainstream in two ways: Cicero assigned a prominent role to the location of arguments and reasons (*topoi*), and he argued that the *status* theory be applied to general questions, *theseis*. For the latter, Reinhardt even coins the term 'thetical rhetoric' to summarise Cicero's view that 'discussions of legal cases should be informed by a consideration of the wider issues raised by them'.[7] Still, in his discussion of the legal aspect of Cicero's *Topica*, Reinhardt adheres to the commonly held view on Roman legal science and the contrast between Roman law and rhetoric; he even distinguishes between rhetorical and legal invention, stating that 'a jurist will normally look at a case in an impartial way, i.e., he will start from a contradictory pair of propositions rather than from an intended conclusion, and only

2 The only modern monograph on Cicero's *Topica* was by Riposati (1947) and his study mainly attends to the rhetorical and philosophical aspects of *Topica*.

3 In *Topik und Jurisprudenz*. We refer to its fifth edition (1974).

4 Horak (1969) 47–48. Similarly, Nörr (1977) 48.

5 Schmidlin (1970) 199–200 and Watson (1971) 57–58.

6 To more easily distinguish between the method of *topica* and Cicero's treatise *Topica*, we use 'topics' throughout to refer to the rhetorical method for inventing arguments. For a specific category of argumentation identified through this method we use *topos* (pl. *topoi*).

7 Reinhardt (2003) 3–7, particularly 7. (Curiously, if on an unrelated subject, the *index locorum* lists Justinian's Digest as a work of Diogenes Laertius).

then reach a conclusion.'[8] Not surprisingly, he, too, does not inquire whether Trebatius might have used Cicero's *Topica* in his *responsa*.

Presuming that he did is not wishful thinking or idle speculation: in her monograph on the law schools of the early Empire, Leesen demonstrated that, in their controversies, the Sabinians and the Proculians used *topoi* as described by Cicero to support their respective points of view.[9] Babusiaux' monograph on the rhetorical method of Papinian in his *Quaestiones* explores a similar avenue.[10] Kacprzak used Cicero's *Topica* to investigate the connection between logic and jurisprudence in the late Republic.[11] And referring to Reinhardt's new edition of Cicero's *Topica*, Thomas recently concluded that 'if the late Republican legal development is re-assessed without the myth of antagonism between jurists and orators, but rather in the context of increased specialisation within the legal profession, the *Topica* would receive not only a different reception, but another evaluation as well.'[12]

We here aim to contribute to such a reappraisal by trying to answer the question whether Cicero's *Topica* is likely to have inspired Trebatius to use *topoi* and *theseis* in his *responsa*. To that end, we first describe these two concepts (Section 1). We then turn to Cicero's *Topica* itself to identify its purpose and construction (Section 2). Next, we make a short but worthwhile detour. Cicero's *Topica* is traditionally compared with Aristotle's early work *Topike* (and unfavourably so) and we want to assess whether there is merit to this comparison: could Cicero's *Topica* in fact have been inspired by another of Aristotle's works (Section 3)? Next, we tackle the issue whether Cicero really dealt so poorly with law and rhetoric as Schmidlin and Watson say he did by discussing their interpretations of *Topica* 21 (Section 4). Finally, we present one of Trebatius' *responsa* in which we believe he used a *topos* and a *thesis* (Section 5). With these markers in place, we hope to more confidently rate the potential utility of Cicero's *Topica* to Trebatius' written legal advice.

8 Reinhardt (2003) 53–72 at 66. He adds that the jurist 'may have to consider legal statutes pertinent to the case under discussion' and that 'his choice of an argument for one or another pole of the contradictory pair represented by the *quaestio iuris* will not necessarily be guided by the quest for plausibility – indeed, he would not hesitate to offer a *prima facie* vastly implausible argument – but by the diverse set of ideas which determines legal decisions.' No sources are referenced here.

9 Leesen (2010). The *thesis* fell outside the scope of her research.

10 Babusiaux (2011).

11 Kacprzak (2012).

12 Thomas (2016) 21.

1 *Topos* and *Thesis*

Of the two notions central to this study, the first, *topos* (Latin: *locus*), originated in early Greek rhetoric around 450 BC. The literal meaning of the word is 'place', and the rhetoricians used it to indicate the location where the orator could find arguments and other information that could be apposite to his speech.[13] Aristotle is widely credited with systematically describing the *topoi*, first in his *Topike* and later in his *Rhetorike*. In *Topike* he placed the use of *topoi* in the context of philosophical debate, and in *Rhetorike* he discussed their use in political, forensic, and demonstrative speeches. What Aristotle's observations show is that a *topos* could serve various functions, even concurrently, and that it was broadly applicable over a wide range of subject areas, including, if not especially, legal practice. While not explicitly defining a *topos*, Aristotle characterises it as '[a heading] under which many enthymemes fall.'[14] The word *enthymeme* usually has the meaning of abbreviated syllogism,[15] but it can also be used more widely to mean any type of argument, and it is to this wider meaning that Aristotle referred in his generic characterisation of *topos*. Cicero's description of this notion is consistent with Aristotle's: 'Accordingly, we may define a topic as the region of an argument, and an argument as a course of reasoning which firmly establishes a matter about which there is some doubt.'[16] A classic example of a *topos* is *comparatio*.[17]

The second key notion, *thesis* (Latin: *propositum*), originated in Greek philosophy and was used in contradistinction to *hypothesis* (Latin: *causa*): the *hypothesis* referred to special questions that were related to a specific person, place, or time, whereas the *thesis* referred to general questions detached from any specific context.[18] This distinction was also used in rhetoric, within the

13 Frost (2005) 4 and 27–39; Rubinelli (2009) 12–21 and 84–85. The word 'place' is connected with the art of memory: Yates (1966) 46 referring to Aristotle, *Topike* 163b 24–30 argues that 'it is indeed probable that the very word "topics" as used in dialectics arose through the places of mnemonics.'

14 Aristotle, *Rhetorike* B II 26.1. For comments, see Rubinelli (2009) 12.

15 Abbreviated in the sense that the major premise – which is plausible if not necessarily true – is omitted.

16 Cicero, *Topica* 8. Unless otherwise stated, we quote Hubbell's translation (1949) throughout.

17 Other *topoi* Cicero discusses include definition, similarity, difference, cause, and consequents. For an overview, see *Topica* 9–11.

18 Cicero, *Topica* 79. See also *De oratore* 3.109, where Cicero adds an example of a *hypothesis* – 'Would it be a good decision to recover our prisoners of war from the Carthaginians by returning theirs?' – and of a *thesis* – 'What should be our general judgment and position regarding prisoners of war?' Translation May and Wisse (2001).

framework of *inventio* and *elocutio*: an argument could be found for the particular case, but it would become more persuasive if it was stripped of its particular elements and formulated in general terms. Paradoxically, once such a generalised statement had been used in a particular case, it could seldom be used again in another case. An example of a *thesis* based on the *topos comparatio* is 'He who is entitled to more must also be entitled to less.'[19]

The role of the *topos* and the *thesis* evolved and one event that helped shape that role occurred when, in the second century BC, Hermagoras of Temnos added a new element to rhetoric: the *status* theory. This theory has not been preserved in Hermagoras' own work (none of his actual writings have survived), but it has been reconstructed fairly well on the basis of later works, such as the *Rhetorica ad Herennium* and Cicero's *De inventione* (both dated to around 85 BC).[20] Hermagoras introduced his *status* theory at a time when Roman law was in full swing, developing not through legislation but in legal practice, through the law of procedure. The *status* theory amplified and became entrenched in this development: in later Greek and Latin rhetoric, it was the standard theory of *inventio*.

Under this theory, the *status* (Greek: *stasis*) refers to the main issue in a controversy and Hermagoras' procedure would help an orator who had to support a central proposition to decide how he would do so and which arguments he would use. To determine the nature of the issue, the orator could choose one of three questions: whether something is (*sit ne*), what it is (*quid sit*), and how it is (*quale sit*). The corresponding *status* would be *coniectura, definitio,* and *qualitas* respectively, and every *status* had its own particular *topoi*. As to the *thesis*, although Hermagoras recognised the *thesis-hypothesis* polarity, he used the *status* only to discuss the special questions, because in his view the general questions were the province of the philosophers.

Cicero initially followed suit. In describing Hermagoras' *status* theory in *De inventione* he restricted the *status* to the special questions, but he later changed his mind: in *De oratore* (55 BC), Cicero stressed repeatedly that any dispute can be reduced to a general question, both for finding the central proposition and for wording the arguments. Such a general question, the *thesis*, he himself, and his teacher Philo of Larissa before him, would have mined from the works of the philosophers.[21] He carried this view forward in *Orator* (46 BC) and even though this work is mainly about style, Cicero did insert a summary

19 D. 50.17.21. See Chapter 9, Section 2.

20 *Rhetorica ad Herennium* 1.18–25; Cicero, *De inv.* 1. 10–16.

21 Cicero, *De oratore* 2.133–134, 3.109–110. For comments, see Brittain (2001) 298–312 and Reinhardt (2003) 9–17.

about *inventio* advising the 'perfect orator' to move discussions away from the special case to general issues.[22] It was clearly a subject that interested him and he returned to it in *Topica*.

2 Cicero's *Topica*

Cicero wrote this short monograph *On Invention* in 44 BC, one year before his death, and the key to a proper understanding of its nature and purpose can be found in its introduction. In it, Cicero addresses the jurist Trebatius, a friend of his, and recalls how they had been sitting in Cicero's library in Tusculum when Trebatius had come across some scrolls that had puzzled him: these concerned 'certain Topics of Aristotle, which were expounded by him in several books.' Cicero then says:

> Qua inscriptione commotus continuo a me librorum eorum sententiam requisisti; 2. quam cum tibi exposuissum, disciplinam inveniendorum argumentorum, ut sine ullo errore ad ea ratione et via perveniremus, ab Aristotele inventam illis libiris contineri, verecunde tu quidem ut omnia, sed tamen facile ut cernerem te ardere studio, mecum ut tibi illa traderem egisti. Cum autem ego te non tam vitandi laboris mei causa quam quia tua id interesse arbitrarer, vel uteos per te ipse legeres vel ut totam rationem a doctissimo quodam rhetore acciperes, hortatus essem, utrumque, ut ex te audiebam, es expertus. 3. Sed a libris te obscuritas reiecit; rhetor autem ille magnus haec, ut opinor, Aristotelia se ignorare respondit. Quod quidem minime sum admiratus eum philosophum rhetori non esse cognitum, qui ab ipsis philosophis praeter admodum paucos ignoretur[.]
>
> Excited by the title, you immediately asked me what the subject of the work was. 2. And when I had made clear to you that these books contained a system developed by Aristotle for inventing arguments so that we might come upon them by a rational system without wandering about, you begged me to teach you the subject. Your request was made with the modesty which you show in everything, yet I could easily see that you were aflame with eagerness. Not so much to avoid labour as because I thought it would be for your good, I urged you to read the book by yourself, or acquire the whole system from a very learned teacher of oratory whom I named. You had tried both, as you told me. 3. But you

22 *Orator* 45–47. See Reinhardt (2003) 3–7.

> were repelled from reading the books by their obscurity; and that great teacher replied that he was not acquainted with these works which are, as I think, by Aristotle. I am not indeed astonished in the slightest degree that the philosopher was unknown to the teacher of oratory, for he is ignored by all except a few of the professed philosophers.

Cicero realised he ought to have helped Trebatius, but he had not got round to it. It was only when political problems – it was the summer after Julius Caesar had been murdered – forced Cicero to go to Greece and he visited Trebatius' country seat on the way that he remembered his promise, and on board a ship, without books, he wrote down what he could recollect and sent the resulting treatise to Trebatius.[23]

Cicero's introduction, from which the above excerpt is quoted, leaves some room for confusion: Cicero seems to suggest he wrote *Topica* for the express purpose of explaining Aristotle's work of the same name to Trebatius, but in terms of its content Cicero's *Topica* bears little to no resemblance to Aristotle's. Among Classicists, this dissimilarity has stirred up a discussion: was the version of Aristotle's *Topike* Cicero had access to the same as Aristotle's *Topike* that is known today?[24] Among Romanists, on the other hand, the outcome of such a discussion is a foregone conclusion: they commonly regard Cicero's *Topica* as a 'historical derivate' of Aristotle's *Topike*.[25] We believe this may be cutting corners a bit. Cicero himself does not explicitly say that he is presenting a condensed version of Aristotle's *Topike* – neither in *Topica* itself nor in his covering letter to Trebatius: *Itaque, ut primum Velia navigare coepi, institui Topica Aristotelea conscribere*. Glynn Williams translated this sentence as: 'So as soon as I began my voyage from Velia, I set about writing a summary on the Topics of Aristotle.'[26] However, the verb *conscribere* does not mean 'to write a summary', 'to translate', or *bearbeiten* (as we found in other translations) but 'to enroll', 'to write on', or 'to compose'.[27] Moreover, modern-day editions of Cicero's letter

---

23 According to Fuhrmann (2000) 55–56, Cicero's remark that he had written everything by heart must not be taken literally. He contends that, already before his journey, Cicero had made summaries of legal collections from which he could draw the examples, but that there had not been enough: until section 46, the examples are new, in sections 50–60 they are repetitions, and from section 86 onwards they are altogether absent.

24 On this discussion, see Reinhardt (2003) 177–180.

25 E.g., Horak (1969) 63 and, more recently, Babusiaux (2011) 65.

26 Cicero, *Ad fam.* 7.19, dated 28 July 44 BC. Glynn Williams (1983).

27 Shuckburgh (1912) has 'to translate' and Kasten (1989) 'zu bearbeiten'. However, De Guerle (1874) has 'composer' and Bayer (1993) 'nieder zu schreiben'. Similarly, Georges and Georges (1913) *ad locum*, Lewis and Short (1879) *ad locum*, and Glare (1969) *ad locum*.

to Trebatius and of *Topica* 1 habitually render *topica* with an upper-case initial letter ('T'), effectively pre-empting any other reading but a reference to Aristotle's *Topike* and obscuring a widespread capitalisation convention in older Latin manuscripts of using capital initials only at the beginning of a page or a paragraph.[28] In other words, both in his letter to Trebatius and in *Topica* 1 Cicero may well have referred to Aristotelian topics in general. In the light of these considerations and in view of the difference in content, it is reasonable to ask whether Cicero's *Topica* has anything to do with Aristotle's *Topike*.[29] As a preliminary step to addressing this question, we first outline the structure of Cicero's *Topica*.

This treatise is structured along the lines of Cicero's discussion of *topoi*. After setting the scene in the introduction, Cicero begins the discussion proper by stating that to trace a certain argument, its place must be known. In section 8, he defines a *topos* as the *sedes argumenti*, 'the location [literally 'seat', TC&T] of an argument', and an argument he defines as a *ratio quae rei dubiae faciat fidem*, 'a reasoning that lends belief to a doubtful issue'. These *topoi*, Cicero explains, are of two kinds: those that are connected to the case in question (*alii in eo ipso de quo agitur*) and those that are applied from without (*alii assumuntur extrinsecus*). Cicero then proceeds to discuss the individual *topoi*, at three levels: simple (sections 9–23), detailed (sections 24–78), and meta-theoretical (sections 79–100). It is these three levels that make up the three main parts of the work.

In the first part, Cicero presents an overview of seventeen *topoi*, along with, for each of them, a brief example of a legal problem and an applied argument.[30] In the second part, he discusses the same *topoi* in more detail, again providing examples from legal practice. In the third part, the *topoi* are combined with rhetorical theory and it is here that Cicero introduces the concepts of *thesis* and *hypothesis*.

In this third part, Cicero claims that while there is no discussion in which none of these *topoi* can be used, at the same time not all *topoi* apply to every question and for certain questions certain *topoi* are more suitable than others. He distinguishes between general and particular questions 'which the Greeks call *thesis* and *hypothesis* respectively, and we *propositum* and *causa*' (section 79). Cicero then examines the various modes of invention and formulates the general questions pertaining to them. Beginning with the *status* theory,

28 Nelson (1981) 25 on the manuscript of Gaius' Institutes.

29 In the introduction to *Topica*, Hubbell (1949) 377 also concludes that Cicero's *Topica* 'bears little resemblance to Aristotle's *Topica*'. Similarly, Reinhardt (2003) 177.

30 Cicero may well have intended this part as an aide-memoire.

he writes that *coniectura* is divided into four parts: whether something exists, whence it arose, what brought it about, and to which changes it is liable. He then gives examples of the questions that can be asked, for instance for existence: 'Do the honourable and the fair really exist, or are they all just a matter of opinion?' (section 82). After having dealt with all *status* and their questions, he describes the *topoi* that are suitable; for *coniectura*, for instance, they are the *topoi ex causis, ex effectis*, and *ex coniunctis* (section 87). Finally (section 91), Cicero turns to the particular questions (*hypotheseis*), combining them with the three types of cases (judicial, deliberative, and laudatory) and the parts of a speech (*exordium, narratio, argumentatio*, and *peroratio*). To discuss these particular questions, the various *status* may be used, and for suitable *topoi*, Cicero refers to what he said before about the *status* and to rhetorical handbooks.

Mystifying though the third part of *Topica* may be to some Classicists,[31] in the final section Cicero explains why he added it: he states that he wanted to make sure he did not give too little and that he had therefore given something extra, just like generous sellers do (section 100). It seems that Cicero thought a jurist could strengthen a legal argument by formulating the problem or, for that matter, his opinion about it in general terms, as a *thesis*.

3 Cicero's *Topica* and Aristotle's *Topike* and *Rhetorike*

In the previous section, we raised the question whether Cicero's *Topica* is in some way connected to Aristotle's *Topike* despite the contents of both books being so very different. In Romanist literature, it is taken for granted that Cicero was inspired by Aristotle's work, but opinions differ on the relationship between the two books and on the extent of their impact. We briefly discuss three such opinions: those of Viehweg, Horak, and Babusiaux.

In the middle of the twentieth century, Viehweg caused a minor sensation when his *Topik und Jurisprudenz* appeared in print. In it, he argued that law is not founded on a system but is characterised by a problem-oriented way of working inherited from classical rhetoric.[32] According to Viehweg, Cicero's *Topica* was a summary of Aristotle's *Topike*, but of inferior quality: it lacked the philosophical

31 Several Classicists have wondered whether this last part really belongs to *Topica*. E.g., Fuhrmann (2000) 53 writes that it seems Cicero forgot that he wanted to write a book about legal argumentation: he no longer thinks of Trebatius and no longer includes legal problems. We find the explanatory value of this reasoning slight.

32 See our summary of his argument in Tellegen-Couperus and Tellegen (2016) 34–36.

context and, much like a recipe book, merely contained a catalogue of *topoi*. Still, he regarded Cicero's *Topica* as historically more significant because of the influence it had had on Roman law. It would have been very attractive to jurists because it had been requested by, written for, and addressed to a jurist, and for his sake it shone with an abundance of legal knowledge. Viehweg did not, however, consider whether Trebatius ever used *Topica*. And although he did mention some *responsa* by other jurists containing topical arguments and suggested that the last section of the Digest, D. 50.17, was another catalogue of *topoi*,[33] he left unanswered the obvious and relevant question what reason(s) Justinian's compilers could have had for making such a catalogue.

Horak, too, believed that Cicero's *Topica* was an inferior variant of Aristotle's *Topike*, stating as his reason that Cicero did not regard topics as a method. This would appear from the fact that Cicero conflated the four Aristotelian types of interdisciplinary sources of problems (definition, genus, property, and accident) with the four Aristotelian *organa* and turned them into an arsenal of find-spots (*loci*) that lacked a logical construction. Horak even somewhat flippantly called Cicero's treatise a 'rhapsodische Aufzählung'.[34] Later jurists enthusiastically used whatever Cicero's *Topica* offered in argumentation theory – a practice that continues to this day – but to Trebatius and the Roman jurists in general it was too unusual to allow them to integrate it into their science, Horak contends.[35]

Babusiaux, finally, does not deliberate the relationship between both works, choosing instead to follow Aristotle's *Topike* in that she regards topics as a part of dialectics.[36] Unlike Horak, Babusiaux thinks that topics as an argumentation theory was useful to the Roman jurists: Cicero addressed his *Topica* to a jurist and he included many examples of how *topoi* can also coin or enrich legal argumentation. However, in her analyses of the texts in Papinian's *Quaestiones* she emphasises the dialectical element and it is only in passing that she compares the arguments used by Papinian or other jurists with *topoi* from Cicero's *Topica*.

Like so many Romanists, then, and irrespective of their views on the relative weight of Cicero's *Topica*, these authors assert or assume that Cicero's treatise essentially does no more than follow the tone set by Aristotle's *Topike*. In our view, it makes little sense to see Aristotle's *Topike* as the mould in which

33 Viehweg (1974) 56.

34 Horak (1969) 47.

35 Horak (1969) 48.

36 Babusiaux (2011) 64–66 with literature. She ignores the fact that Cicero distinguished between dialectics as *ars iudicandi* and topics as *ars inveniendi* (*Topica* 6).

Cicero's *Topica* was cast. Aristotle's treatise was a philosophical work and was not meant, either exclusively or expressly, for legal practice.[37] Moreover, it was written 300 years before Cicero drafted his pamphlet en route from Velia and rhetoric had by that time charted a course of its own, away from philosophy, a development spurred in no small part by Hermagoras' *status* theory (see Section 2). This change in direction and Cicero's obvious intention that *Topica* be used in legal practice explain why its content differs so markedly from that of its alleged prototype.[38]

We think it is not this work that inspired Cicero, but Aristotle's *Rhetorike*, and particularly Book 2, Chapter 23 (B II 23 for short), which contains a list of 29 *topoi*.[39] Earlier in this chapter (Section 2), we quoted Aristotle's definition of the *topos* as '[a heading] under which many enthymemes fall.' In *Rhetorike*, the enthymeme plays a fundamental role, but Aristotle does not deal with it consistently: he usually refers to the enthymeme as resting on a syllogistic structure, but in B II 23 he seems to refer to it more generally as an argument scheme. In 1929, Solmsen suggested that B II 23 originated in an older layer of *Rhetorike* and dated from the time of *Topike*, whereas the younger layers were conceived after Aristotle had developed the syllogism in *Analytica Priora*.[40] This theory has been generally accepted in modern literature, but the relationship between the older and the younger parts of *Rhetorike*, particularly that between the different descriptions of the enthymeme, remains controversial.[41]

For our purposes, this controversy is not relevant, but the discrepancy between the use of the term *topos* in B II 23 and in the other chapters of *Rhetorike* is: the *topoi* Cicero describes in *Topica* resemble the *topoi* mentioned in B II 23 in that they cannot always be reduced to rhetorical syllogisms either.[42] When Cicero applies a reasoning based on logic, he does so in accordance with the propositional logic developed by the Stoa.[43] Moreover, there

---

37 Similarly, Bayer (1993) 94.

38 Cicero does not explicitly say that this work is meant to be used in legal practice, but he suggests as much in that, in the first two parts, he constantly uses examples from legal practice and in that, in the second part, he refers several times to the usefulness of certain *topoi* for the jurists, e.g., in sections 44–45, 56, and 65–66.

39 References to Aristotle's *Rhetorike* take a variety of forms; we follow Rubinelli's documentation (2009).

40 Solmsen (1929) 31.

41 For an overview, see Rubinelli (2009) 72–90.

42 Similarly, Leeman and Braet (1987) 74 and, in more detail, Braet (1997) 106–108.

43 E.g., regarding the *topoi e consequentibus* (53–54), *ex contrariis* (55–57), and *causa* (58–59). For comments on sections 53–57 and 58–59, see Reinhardt (2003) 305–316 and 320–323 respectively.

is a striking resemblance of content between Cicero's *Topica* and Aristotle's *Rhetorike* B II 23: not only do the seventeen *topoi* Cicero discusses appear in Aristotle's list of 29 *topoi*, but the descriptions and examples Aristotle gives are also often related to legal practice.[44] These facts lend support to our supposition that when Cicero wrote his *Topica* he was inspired by Aristotle's *Rhetorike* B II 23 rather than by his *Topike*.[45]

Additional support can be found in Cicero's letter to Trebatius, where he states that he has written 'on Aristotelian topics'. Not only does our proposition chime in with this reference, it also meshes with the introduction of *Topica*, where Cicero describes how Trebatius came across 'certain topics of Aristotle, which were expounded by him in *several* books' (our emphasis). These book scrolls may well have included or contained parts of Aristotle's *Rhetorike*, amongst which B II 23. When Trebatius struggled to understand Aristotle's discussion of *topoi*, Cicero at his request wrote a book on the subject that was inspired by how Aristotle had described *topoi* in this part of *Rhetorike*. This to us indicates that 'Aristotelian topics' in Cicero's letter to Trebatius should not be taken to refer to Aristotle's *book* by that name but rather to topics as a *subject* he addresses in several works – and it is the *subject* Trebatius expressed an interest in to Cicero, not the *book*.

Finally, would Cicero's *Topica* be at risk of suffering the same fate of scholarly undervaluation when compared with Aristotle's *Rhetorike* B II 23 as when compared with Aristotle's *Topike*? We think not. The text of *Rhetorike* B II 23 lacks structure: the *topoi* are included in a haphazard way, making it a more likely contender for Horak's qualification of a 'rhapsodische Aufzählung' than Cicero's *Topica*. Perhaps they are only lecture notes, as has been suggested.[46] Moreover, Aristotle's *topoi* are not exclusively explained in a legal context but also in a political setting. Cicero's *Topica*, on the other hand, is well structured and the examples provided in the first two parts of the treatise all refer to legal practice. So when appraising the two works in terms of their usefulness to jurists, Cicero's *Topica* is hands down the better of the two. Having said that, we are aware that this reappraisal may not satisfy Romanists who are critical

---

44 Similarly, Hubbell (1949) 377 and Bayer (1993) 95–96.

45 Reinhardt (2003) 28–29 approaches the problem in a more differentiated way, stating that 'some of the *topoi* discussed by Cicero come from Aristotle's *Topica* rather than from his *Rhetorica*, or even from Stoic logic. [...] [W]e may assume that Cicero's *loci* reflect a post-Aristotelian tradition of rhetorical *topoi* which have been rearranged and supplemented with the help of *Topica* and other sources.'

46 E.g., Leeman and Braet (1987) 10.

of the legal and rhetorical quality of Cicero's *Topica* and in the next section we consider that point of criticism.

4 Cicero's *Topica* and Roman Law

In *Topica*, Cicero often refers to Roman law. This makes sense, because he wrote the book at the request of his friend, the jurist Trebatius Testa. However, some Romanists doubt whether these references are correct – both legally and rhetorically. Schmidlin and Watson, for instance, independently of each other interpreted the same section of Cicero's *Topica* and both found it, and the work as a whole, wanting. We now assess to what extent this critical evaluation itself stands up to criticism. The section at issue is section 21, in the first part of *Topica*. It runs as follows:

> A repugnantibus: Si paterfamilias uxori ancillarum usum fructum legavit a filio neque a secundo herede legavit, mortuo filio mulier usum fructum non amittet. Quod enim semel testamento alicui datum est, id ab eo invito cui datum est auferri non potest. Repugnat enim recte accipere et invitum reddere.
>
> From contradictions: If a *pater familias* has bequeathed to his wife the usufruct of maid-servants by his son and not by the substitute heir, on the death of the son the woman will not lose her usufruct. For what has once been given to someone by will cannot be taken from him to whom it has been given without his consent. For 'receiving legally' and 'surrendering unwillingly' are contradictory.

Cicero presents the following case. In his will, a testator had instituted as heir his underage son and he had appointed a substitute heir in case of his son dying before having reached adulthood.[47] In a *legatum per damnationem* he had obliged his son to grant to his wife the right of usufruct over some slave women. However, he had not also imposed this obligation on the substitute heir. The testator died and his young son became his heir. Observing his father's will, the son vested a right of usufruct in favour of the testator's widow,

47 The substitution must be a pupillary one, because it became effective through the son's death after he had become heir. The words *secundo herede* support this assumption. In case of a so-termed vulgar substitution, the instituted heir would have predeceased the testator and so would not have become heir at all.

probably by means of an *in iure cessio*, his guardian authorising the act. The son died before he reached adulthood. The substitute heir claimed the slave women from the testator's widow, but she refused to surrender them. Cicero then formulates an argument supporting the widow which he draws from the *topos* of contradictions, namely, a bequest cannot be taken from its recipient without their consent.

Schmidlin discusses this text in the last section of his book on Roman legal rules, where he takes the measure of Cicero's *Topica*.[48] He claims that Cicero only aims to show how topical arguments could work, not that they could be useful in legal practice. The examples Cicero chose, so Schmidlin argues, were basic and did not hold the slightest interest for jurists. As soon as the chosen example led to more complicated legal questions, the limits of the topical-rhetorical argumentation became visible and it is particularly in *Topica* 21 that this weakness became clear. The reasoning in the first sentence does not meet with any objection: the testator's wife will not lose the usufruct bequeathed to her. Schmidlin wonders why she would be at risk of losing the usufruct in the first place. If it had been granted to her by way of *in iure cessio*, it would have been superfluous for the substitute heir to grant it to her again, because *in iure cessio* vested a 'dingliche Berechtigung'.

According to Schmidlin, Cicero took a different approach: he applied the general premise *Quod enim semel testamento alicui datum est, id ab eo invito cui datum est auferri non potest*. This statement, he argues, would undeniably come close to the rule *Hereditas adimi non potest* (the inheritance cannot be taken away), a rule that was particularly used in the context of substitution. It referred to the situation when the *familiae emptor* had acquired an estate by means of the *mancipatio* and, after the death of the testator, had turned it over to the heir: the inheritance could not be claimed back from the heir in order to give it to a third party. This scenario, Schmidlin observes, had nothing to do with the case in question: there is a wide gap between not being able to take away an inheritance acquired by *mancipatio* and not being able to take away a usufruct established by means of *in iure cessio*. Cicero realised this and he therefore added the phrase *ab eo invito* [*cui*] *datum est* in an effort to mould the rule to fit his argumentation. In this way, the rule that rests on the *mancipatio familiae* transforms into quasi-logical evidence ('quasi-logische Evidenz') that fits the *topos a repugnantibus*. Schmidlin concludes that while the *topos* itself may retain its validity, it has no bearing on the actual legal question of the case. The topical-rhetorical argumentation slips away from the legal problem involved, a danger to which he contends *topoi* are inherently vulnerable.

48 Schmidlin (1970) 199–200.

Watson, too, is critical of how Cicero handles the case. In his book on the Roman law of succession in the later Republic, he deals with *Topica* 21 in the chapter on the institution of the heir, disinherison, and substitution.[49] Watson contends that while the individual decision itself may appear to be sufficiently accurate, Cicero's proposition that a bequest cannot be taken from its recipient without their consent is much too wide. Moreover, he argues that as an example the case was ill-chosen, because the argument from contradictions would not be valid here. In support of his statement that Cicero's proposition was far too wide, Watson refers to two texts dating from the Empire that supposedly show 'that then a provision from the *substitutus* in the will which was in conflict with a legacy granted from the *institutus* could deprive the earlier legatee of his bequest.' In the first of these two texts, D. 28.6.16 pr., Pomponius says that if a slave who is left as a legacy from a *pupillus institutus* is freed from the *substitutus*, the slave will become free (if the *pupillus* dies), *quasi legato adempto*. And the second text, D. 30.34.10 (Ulpian, 21 ad Sab.), records that 'if the same thing is left as a legacy to different people from the *pupillus institutus* and the *substitutus*, Julian held that both had *concursu partes* and that, therefore, in the meantime the legatee from the *institutus* will have his share.'[50] Watson concedes that Cicero's proposition may have been accurate in his day, but he maintains that it is more likely 'that Cicero, knowing the legal decision for the individual situation, deduced from it a proposition which was far too wide.'[51]

In our view, the interpretations ventured by Schmidlin and Watson are unconvincing. Schmidlin's conclusion that the *topos* does not suit the legal problem at issue is precarious, because it is actually the link he himself establishes between the premise 'a bequest cannot be taken from its recipient against their will' and the rule that 'an inheritance cannot be taken away' that does not suit the context: the issue at the heart of this case does not concern an *inheritance*, but a *legacy*, and the *topos* used refers to the contrast between *recte accipere* and *invitum reddere* of this legacy – as Cicero clearly states. Turning to Watson's view that Cicero's proposition was far too wide, we are not convinced by that either, for two reasons. First, we believe the comparison with the texts by Pomponius and Ulpian does not hold. Watson's paraphrase of Pomponius' text is not entirely accurate in that the jurist does not use the term *pupillus* but

49 Watson (1971) 57–58.

50 Watson (1971) 57.

51 In his commentary on *Topica* 21, Reinhardt (2003) 240 follows Watson's reasoning and concludes that 'Cicero, keen to expose the *a repugnantibus* structure of the example, inferred too general a rule from the case envisaged.'

filius; this could well imply that Pomponius refers to a case about an adult son for whom the testator had included a *substitutio vulgaris* in his will; the son died before the testator did, so the son never became heir, the legacy was not paid out, and nothing was taken away from anyone. That is why Pomponius says '*quasi* legato adempto' (our emphasis). Ulpian's case is about two contradictory legacies and about the reasonable solution offered: it is not about taking away a legacy. Second, Cicero's proposition is not 'far too wide', because it is a rhetorical argument formulated in general terms but meant to be used in one case only: it was neither 'much too wide' nor 'too wide', just 'wide' – as it should be. Finally, both Schmidlin and Watson assume that in *Topica* 21 Cicero presents a decision or a statement about the law. He does not: he presents an argument supporting the legatee. This argument is an excellent example of the *topos a repugnantibus* as we now attempt to demonstrate.

Of Cicero's intention there can be little doubt: he aims to give an example of a case in which the *topos a repugnantibus* can be applied. From the words *amittet* and *auferri* we deduce that in this case the question is whether the substitute can claim the slaves, or, conversely, whether the usufruct is legally valid. To assess whether Cicero handles the case in a legally and rhetorically plausible manner the next step is to reconstruct the likely reasoning of both the substitute and the legatee.

The substitute will have argued that he is entitled to the slave women, reasoning as follows. Complying with the legacy, the *pupillus* had created the usufruct by means of *in iure cessio* in favour of the testator's wife. Because the *pupillus* died before he reached adulthood, he ultimately did not become heir. Consequently, the usufruct had effectively not been created by the heir and the wife had therefore not become usufructuary. The substitute is the heir of the testator, so not only does the substitute inherit the slaves free from usufruct, he is also not obliged to create the usufruct in favour of the testator's wife, because he is not charged by legacy to do so.

The legatee, the testator's widow, will have argued that she had lawfully acquired the usufruct by virtue of the legacy: the *in iure cessio* had been validly performed in both form and content. The substitute was the heir of the *pupillus* and the slave women he had inherited were property encumbered by a previously and properly created right of usufruct for the benefit of the legatee. Consequently, the substitute cannot claim them from her without her consent. Cicero articulates the *topos a repugnantibus* in the phrase *Quod enim semel testamento alicui datum est, id ab eo invito cui datum est auferri non potest*, and pithily expresses it as a *thesis* in the phrase *Repugnat enim recte accipere et invitum reddere*.[52]

These summations, we believe, are a conceivable and tenable representation of the two parties' argumentation. Of course, we cannot be absolutely sure of the finer points of their reasoning, nor of the outcome had the substitute and the legatee been pitted against each other in a legal action. What is perfectly obvious, however, is that the parties' interests are as clear as they are diametrically opposed, and these interests reveal the underlying question in this case, namely whether the substitute was heir to the testator or to the *pupillus*. The jurists did not agree on this: while the *wording* of the substitution points to the testator (*heres mihi esto*), its *object* points to the *pupillus*, since the substitute acquired the testator's estate plus what the *pupillus* might have acquired after the testator's death.[53] In his handbook on the Roman law of succession, Voci amply discusses the 'duplicità' of the pupillary substitution: there is one testator and one will, but there are two successions, of the testator and of the *pupillus*.[54] Of course, this duality led to all sorts of complications that were not always easy to resolve. The case Cicero describes in *Topica* 21 is no exception: repetition of the legacy from the substitute would not settle the problem either.[55] In other words, there is no easy, predictable way out. To us, then, the legal intricacies of this case and the palpable uncertainty over its outcome suggest that it served Cicero beautifully: it allowed him to work the *topos a repugnantibus* to the greatest possible effect, in yet another demonstration of his enduring theme that rhetorical 'weapons' expertly wielded can help secure legal victory.

This familiar theme of Cicero's speaks to our view on the symbiosis of law and rhetoric and in this section we have aimed to show that Cicero's argument that what had been given to someone could not be taken away from him without his consent is sound – legally as well as rhetorically. Before moving to the final section of this chapter, there is one more point to make about

---

52 Note that in this phrase Cicero applies the propositional logic developed by the Stoa. For further comment, see Reinhardt (2003) 237.

53 Cicero, *De inv.* 2.122 and Jul. D. 37.11.8.1 (*testator*), Gaius, *Inst.* 2.182 and Ulp. D. 28.6.10.5 (*pupillus*) respectively. For more texts and a commentary, see Voci (1963) 171–173 and Watson (1971) 59–60.

54 Voci (1963) 174–184.

55 So, e.g., Jul. D. 30.81.7 (summarised): if the testator in his will charges his *pupillus* with a legacy and charges the substitute with the same bequest, and if the *pupillus* dies before reaching adulthood, then the repetition is irrelevant, because on the basis of the will the legacy is owed only once. In other words, such a repetition was not at all necessary and even superfluous.

the rhetorical dimension of Cicero's argument. While others have noted that Cicero worded his argument *Quod ... potest* in general terms, it has not generally been recognised or typified as a *thesis*.[56] The reason may be that this *thesis* is not formulated as a question, like the examples Cicero gives in the third part of *Topica*, but as a statement, because it forms part of his argument. On this note we return to the question raised in the introduction to this chapter – whether Cicero's *Topica* is likely to have inspired Trebatius to use *topoi* and *theseis* in his *responsa*.

5 Cicero's *Topica* and Trebatius Testa

So was Cicero's *Topica* a useful resource for Trebatius? Some Romanists (for example, Horak, Schmidlin, Nörr, and Wieacker) presume it was not, others (like Watson and Reinhardt) do not pronounce on the matter.[57] It is impossible to determine indisputably that Trebatius used Cicero's *Topica*; there are no sources to say he did. However, what is possible is to find out whether in his *responsa* Trebatius used *topoi* and *theseis*. If he did, that could be taken as a clue that Trebatius at the very least drew inspiration from *Topica*. A considerable number of Trebatius' *responsa* have been preserved (through having been quoted by later jurists) in Justinian's Digest and eleven of these *responsa* contain an argument. A few years ago, Leesen, together with one of us, showed that in at least three of these eleven *responsa* Trebatius used *topoi*.[58] Now we can add that in the first of these *responsa* Trebatius also used a *thesis* together with the *topos* in question. We here take a closer look at this *responsum*.

It appears in a text by Ulpian, D. 2.14.10.2, which deals with the situation that a debtor's procurator had made a *pactum de non petendo* with the creditor and the creditor contrary to this *pactum* sued the debtor. Not being a party to the *pactum*, the debtor could of course not rely on the *exceptio pacti*, so the legal question was whether he was entitled to the defence of the *exceptio doli*. According to Ulpian, he was, and he refers to other jurists who held the same opinion. He specifically quotes Trebatius and the argument he had added.

> D. 2.14.10.2 Ulpianus 4 ad ed. Plerumque solemus dicere doli exceptionem subsidium esse pacti exceptionis: quosdam denique, qui exceptione pacti

56 Remarkably, even Reinhardt (2003) 71 and 240 appears to not have done so.

57 Horak (1969) 48, Schmidlin (1970) 198, Nörr (1977) 48, Wieacker (1988) 613.

58 Tellegen and Leesen (2016) 113–129. These *topoi* are *e contrario* in Ulp. D.2.14.10.2, *ambiguitas* in Iav. D. 35.1.40.4, and *definitio* in Ulp. D. 43.20.1.18.

> uti non possunt, doli exceptione usuros et Iulianus scribit et alii plerique consentiunt. ut puta si procurator meus paciscatur, exceptio doli mihi proderit, ut Trebatio videtur, qui putat, sicuti pactum procuratoris mihi nocet, ita et prodesse.
>
> Generally, we are accustomed to say that the defense of fraud supplements the defense of pact: that is to say that some people who cannot use the defense of pact will be able to use the defense of fraud as Julian writes and most others agree. For example, if my procurator makes a pact, the defense of fraud will benefit me, as Trebatius held, asserting that just as a pact made by my procurator will prejudice me so it will also benefit me.[59]

In modern Romanist literature, this passage has been the subject of lively discourse and for our purposes it is particularly interesting to see how Trebatius' argument has been interpreted. We briefly discuss two different opinions, offered by Horak and MacCormack respectively.

In his acclaimed monograph on *rationes decidendi* in Roman law, Horak discusses D. 2.14.10.2 in the context of arguments based on analogy.[60] In his view, this text is hardly relevant, because it is only about deducing a positive legal effect from the negative legal effect of a procurator's *pactum*. The analogy would rest on the unity of the procurator's function whose legal acts may not produce the effect of direct representation but which come close to that effect by the praetor's granting an exception. This reasoning may seem plausible, but it is not, because Trebatius does not use it. An argument based on analogy presumes similarity, and what Trebatius does is accentuate a dissimilarity: he contrasts loss and benefit.[61]

MacCormack's interpretation, while perfectly sound in its own right, to us appears to overlook something. In his paper '*Dolus* in Republican Law' he discusses the *exceptio doli* and in that context he refers to D. 2.14.10.2: 'There is an obvious discrepancy between the pretence of abandoning the claim disclosed in the *pactum de non petendo* and the real intention evidenced by the bringing of the action on the original claim. Trebatius would have had little difficulty in inferring from the beginning of the action an antecedent to deceive. Since the intention became manifest in the action one has a case of *dolus praesens*

59 Translation by G. MacCormack in Watson (1985).

60 Horak (1969) 256.

61 In *Topica* 42, Cicero describes analogy in the *topos similitudo*. Somewhat confusingly, Horak (1969) 82 mentions the argument *e contrario* as an example of reasoning by analogy.

falling under the *neque fiat* clause.'[62] According to MacCormack, Trebatius could have used the argument that claiming the debt was in itself a case of *dolus*, but to us the important point is that Trebatius did not.

The argument we believe Trebatius used in support of his view that the debtor could defend himself by means of an *exceptio doli* is another one: '[J]ust as a pact made by my procurator will prejudice me so it will also benefit me.' We read this as a rhetorical argument based on the *topos e contrario*. Trebatius may well have found it in *Topica* 47, where Cicero explains that there are several types of opposites, one of these consisting of 'things which, while falling under the same *genus*, are as different as possible from each other, e.g. wisdom and stupidity.' On this view, Trebatius formulated his argument in general terms, as a *thesis*. It seems that Ulpian had no objections against this rhetorical argument. The opposite may, in fact, be true: he quotes Trebatius' *responsum* approvingly.

In conclusion, we are confident that our observations in this section, resting on the foundations laid in the preceding sections, make a plausible case that for Trebatius, and possibly also for other Roman jurists of his and later times, Cicero's *Topica* could well have been a particularly useful source of inspiration. In the next chapter we show that earlier jurists, too, used rhetorical arguments.

62 MacCormack (1985) 37. Similarly, Ter Beek (1999) 784. The *neque fiat* clause forms part of the wording of the *exceptio doli* as described in Gaius, *Inst.* 4.119: *si in ea re nihil dolo malo auli agerii factum sit neque fiat*.

CHAPTER 3

Quintus Mucius Scaevola *pontifex*: Jurist and Orator

In the previous chapter we argued that Trebatius, likely drawing inspiration from Cicero's *Topica*, used *topoi* and *theseis* in his *responsa* to substantiate his opinion on a legal problem. A logical and equally intriguing next question is whether other, earlier jurists did so too. The first one to come to our mind is Quintus Mucius Scaevola: not only is he one of the earliest jurists of whom *responsa* have been preserved (a neat 50), he is often also viewed as the archetypal jurist, one who would simply not use such rhetorical means as *topoi* and *theseis,* relying instead on his legal experience. In Roman times, Scaevola's fame rested in part on his having acted as advocate in the *causa Curiana* (92 BC). Today, his advocacy in this trial is generally viewed as proper for a professional Roman jurist. We, however, are not so sure. In this chapter, we first aim to show that construing Scaevola's trial performance as that of a professional jurist is too limited a view, because his fame in the *causa Curiana* was based first and foremost on his use of rhetoric, including *topoi* and *theseis*. Next, we demonstrate that he also used a *topos* and a *thesis* in a *responsum* of his that was preserved in D. 32.29.1. The real surprise is that this same *topos* (*in maiore minus inest*) also features in D. 50.17,[1] where it was used by other Roman jurists alongside other *topoi.* In a way, that discovery, our eureka moment, was the launch pad for this book.

1 Scaevola's Advocacy in the *causa Curiana*

The celebrated *causa Curiana* is known mainly through Cicero's work.[2] The facts of the case are as follows. An unnamed testator made a will in which he instituted his son, were he to have one, as his heir, and in which he named M. Curius as his substitute heir if the instituted heir should die before reaching adulthood.[3] The testator died without male issue and the inheritance then went to Curius, because it was assumed that the condition relating to

1 Repeatedly, in fact. See the concluding paragraph of this chapter.

2 *De oratore* 1.180 and 242–244; 2.24; 2.140–1; 2.220–222. *Brutus* 144–5, 194–8 and 256. *Topica* 44; *Pro Caecina* 53, 67, 69. *De inv.* 2.122.

3 The precise wording of the will is not known, but the institution and the substitution can be reconstructed on the basis of *De inv.* 2.122 and *De oratore* 2.141.

 | DOI:10.1163/9789004711020_004

the substitution – no son born to the testator had come of age – had been fulfilled. But then the heir *ab intestato*, called Coponius, intervened. Believing that the condition for the substitution had *not* been fulfilled and that it was he who was entitled to the inheritance, he summoned Curius to appear before the *centumviri* court and claimed the inheritance through the *hereditatis petitio*. Coponius, the plaintiff, was represented by Scaevola, while L. Licinius Crassus represented the defendant, Curius.[4] The *centumviri* court found for Curius, winning Crassus the case.

For close to a century now, this *cause célèbre* has invited numerous interpretations, and almost without exception these were prompted by an article published in 1926 (and republished in 1949) by the German philologist Stroux.[5] In it, Stroux stated that in the late Roman Republic the rhetoric that had originated in Greece, and in particular the *status* theory as formulated by Hermagoras of Temnos, gave to the archaic and formalistic Roman law a much needed interpretation method that chimed in with the ideas of the time, one crucial new addition being the concept of *aequitas*. Stroux posited that law and rhetoric were not separate but complementary disciplines practised by the same group of people, and he referred to the *causa Curiana* and Cicero's speech *pro Caecina* as classic examples of how the new method of legal interpretation was applied.

Amidst a host of responses Stroux' interpretation drew among Romanists, the prevailing view was that as disciplines Roman law and rhetoric were poles apart.[6] It was Schulz who in his account of the development of Roman legal science laid the foundation for the modern interpretations of the *causa Curiana*.[7] He saw this case as a dispute between two advocates, one a jurist arguing for a literal interpretation of the will and the other an orator appealing to the testator's intention, with their speeches reflecting their respective professions. Later authors such as Wieacker modified this interpretation somewhat in that they no longer regarded Crassus' speech as being pre-eminently rhetorical.[8] Only Vaughn did not toe the line, insisting instead that Scaevola and Crassus did not have radically different roles (those of jurist, or 'jurisprudens' in Vaughn's

4 L. Licinius Crassus and Q. Mucius Scaevola were actually good friends, sharing most positions in the *cursus honorum*, including the consulship. *De oratore* 2.221 records that in his *causa Curiana* speech Crassus spared his opponent's dignity, by extension preserving his own. On Scaevola and Crassus, see Kunkel (1967) 18 and Bauman (1983) 340–351.

5 Stroux (1926) 9–66, on the *causa Curiana*, 42–48.

6 For an overview, see Voci (1963) 1006–1016.

7 Schulz (1946) 79–80.

8 Wieacker (1967) 151–164; Manthe (1997) 74–84.

paper, and orator respectively) and postulating that 'each man argued as an orator on behalf of his client's interests'.[9] In a paper on the *causa Curiana* which we wrote some twenty years ago we discussed many of these modern interpretations in detail, concluding that the speeches of Scaevola and Crassus had both rhetorical and juridical characteristics.[10] Here, we consider the question whether Scaevola pleading on behalf of Coponius used rhetoric, and more especially *topoi* and *theseis*. Contrary to the prevailing view, and tying in more naturally with Vaughn's reading, we think he did. As we explain below, these opposing views of the two advocates' roles rest on different constructions of the legal question at the heart of the *causa Curiana*.

Schulz asserted, and many assented, that the central legal question concerned the pupillary substitution, more especially whether this substitution included a vulgar one. This legal issue is generally explained as follows.[11] In making his will, the testator could make allowance for the eventuality that his designated heir did not inherit by appointing a second heir, the substitute heir. To that end, the testator could add a so-termed *substitutio vulgaris*:

> Titius mihi heres esto. Si Titius mihi heres non erit, tunc Seius heres mihi esto.
>
> Titius must be my heir. If Titius will not be my heir, then Seius must be my heir.[12]

Now suppose the testator wanted to institute as heir his underage son. At the testator's death, the son would become his heir, but if the son were to die before reaching adulthood and so before being able to make a will himself, the inheritance would pass to the intestate heirs. To block that particular scenario, the testator could include a modified substitution in his will, the *substitutio pupillaris*:

> Titius filius meus mihi heres esto. Si Titius filius meus ante moriatur quam in suam tutelam venerit, Seius heres mihi esto.
>
> My son Titius must be my heir. If my son Titius dies before reaching adulthood, Seius must be my heir.

---

9 Vaughn (1985) 222.

10 Tellegen and Tellegen-Couperus (2000) 171–202. Vaughn's article was, regrettably, not known to us at the time.

11 Cf., e.g., Voci (1963) 215–216; Wieacker (1967) 153–154; Kaser (1971) 690; Wieling (1972) 9–11; Vaughn (1985) 210–211; Manthe (1997) 76–77; Liebs (2012) 46–49.

12 Our own translation, of both substitutions.

This substitution concerned the situation of the son the testator had instituted as his heir being alive at the time of the testator's death; it did not pertain to the testator hoping, assuming, or believing he would have a son by the time he died. Romanists generally assume that to cover the eventuality of dying without male progeny the testator could combine a pupillary substitution with a vulgar one to ensure the substitute heir inherited if the named first heir, for whatever reason, did not inherit. In the *causa Curiana*, the testator had included only a pupillary substitution, and the matter to be decided therefore would have been whether Curius could become substitute heir even though his institution had been conditional on a son having been born to the testator and having died while still a minor. In other words, the legal question in the *causa Curiana* would have been whether the *substitutio pupillaris* included a *substitutio vulgaris*.[13]

In our view, this reconstruction of the legal question is fragile, because it is not supported by the sources: neither party to the lawsuit claimed or denied that the testator could or should have added a vulgar substitution.[14] We can only infer that the legal question at issue is likely to have been a different one. Cicero recounts, both Scaevola and Crassus interpreted the wording of the pupillary substitution, with Scaevola maintaining that the condition relating to the substitution had not been fulfilled and Crassus arguing that it had.[15] It is quite possible, then, that the legal question was not whether the *substitutio pupillaris* included the *substitutio vulgaris* but whether the condition of the *substitutio pupillaris* had been fulfilled. Looking at the case from this angle, we can try to answer the question whether Scaevola pleading on behalf of Coponius used rhetorical means, and more especially *topoi* and *theseis*.

Scaevola stated that, read literally, the condition had not been fulfilled, because no son had been born to the testator and someone who had not been born could not die. He based his argument on the special nature of the law of succession and on old formulations, and explained how the will should have been formulated if the testator had also wanted Curius to be his heir if no son had been born.[16] 'What a snare was set for plain people if the exact wording of a will were ignored and if intentions were to be determined by guess-work, and if the written words of simple-minded people were to be perverted by the interpretation of clever lawyers.'[17] Scaevola also invoked the authority of his

13 Voci (1963) 215–216 calls this a 'sostituzione volgare tacite'.

14 But it is doubtful whether that would have solved the problem, because a vulgar substitution takes effect only when there is an heir who can be replaced.

15 Cicero, *De oratore* I 180.

16 Cicero, *Brutus* 195.

17 Cicero, *Brutus* 196.

father, who had always upheld the doctrine of strict interpretation, and the observance of the civil law.[18]

Scaevola's use of rhetoric becomes clear when his argumentation is measured against the textbooks on rhetoric of the time. In *De inventione* Cicero fully explains which *topoi* are suited to a literal interpretation, to the *verba*. One of them is that the advocate may say: 'It is not right for us to argue about the intent of one who left us a clear indication of his intent in order that we may not dispute it.'[19] And that is what Scaevola does when he explains how the will should have been formulated if the testator had also wanted Curius to be his heir if no son had been born.[20] Scaevola's last two arguments (his father's authority and the importance of the *ius civile*) are also to be found in the textbooks on rhetoric, particularly in the section on general *topoi* (*loci communes*).[21] Yet the most distinctive rhetorical element of all (arguably all the more so because it is the one Crassus took care to 'burn' right at the start of his speech) may well be the logical reasoning on which Scaevola based his main proposition: someone who is not born cannot die; in this case no son has been born, so he did not die either. In *Topica*, Cicero describes this kind of reasoning when dealing with the *topos a consequentibus*: 'For whatever follows something is inevitably connected with it.'[22] He then describes three types of argument the dialecticians distinguish, the second one of which runs as follows: 'When you deny that which is attached, so that that to which it is attached is to be denied, this is called the second type of argument.'[23] Scaevola's argument 'Someone who is not born cannot die' is a textbook example of this second type. Not only did Scaevola use the *topos e consequentibus*, he also formulated the argument in general terms, as a *thesis*. In sum, then, we believe that comparing Scaevola's speech with contemporary textbooks on rhetoric justifies the conclusion that when he acted as an advocate in the *causa Curiana* the jurist Scaevola used rhetorical means. A relevant follow-up question is whether Scaevola's use of rhetoric in this speech is an isolated incident. We believe it is not.

18 Cicero, *Brutus* 197.

19 Cicero, *De inv.* 2 125–128, with the quotation in 2 128.

20 Cicero does not report the correct formulation, maybe because it was impossible to formulate such a will. Wieacker (1967) 159 erroneously assumed that Scaevola refers to the vulgar substitution.

21 The reference to *auctoritas* in *Topica* 73; the importance of the *ius civile* in *De inv.* 2 143.

22 *Topica* 53: ... *Quidquid enim sequitur quamque rem, id cohaeret cum re necessario.*

23 *Topica* 54: ... *cum id quod annexum est negaris, ut id quoque cui fuerit annexum negandum sit, secundus is appellatur concludendi modus.* ... Later, this came to be called the *modus tollendo tollens.* Cf. the comment by Hubbell (1949) 422 note a.

2 The *topos in maiore minus inest* in D. 32.29.1

It appears that in at least one *responsum* Scaevola used a *topos* and a *thesis*. It is the *topos in maiore minus inest* (*immi*), 'The smaller is contained in the greater', and it is classical in every sense of the word: Aristotle already mentions it, calling it the *topos ek tou mallon kai ètton* (of more and less).[24] In *Topica*, Cicero deals with the *topos a maiore ad minus* in the context of the *topos comparatio*.[25] Scaevola's *responsum* is included in D. 32.29.1: it has been preserved in a text by Labeo as summarised by Iavolenus.[26] It runs as follows:

> Labeo libro secundo posteriorum a Iavoleno epitomatorum. Cum ita legatum esset, ut Titia uxor mea tantandem partem habeat quantulam unus heres, si non aequales partes essent heredum, Quintus Mucius et Gallus putabant maximam partem legatam esse, quia in maiore minor quoque inesset, Servius Ofilius minimam, quia cum heres dare damnatus esset, in potestate eius esset, quam partem daret. Labeo hoc probat idque verum est.
>
> Labeo, Posthumous Works, Epitomized by Javolenus, book 2. A legacy was left in these terms: 'Titia my wife should have a share just as great as what little share has been left to one heir.' If the heirs do not have equal shares, Quintus Mucius and Gallus thought that the greatest share had been bequeathed, because the smaller is contained in the greater, and Servius and Ofilius the smallest, because since the heir was obliged to give, it would be in his power to decide what share to give. Labeo approved this last and that is correct.

A testator left to his wife a part of his estate by means of a legacy. It is generally assumed that the husband did not institute his wife as his heir, because he could not legally do so: belonging to the first *census* class, he was forbidden under the *lex Voconia* to institute a woman as heir.[27] Yet even as a legacy the testator's bequest was problematic, and it has been interpreted in different ways, both then and now. D. 32.29.1 is especially interesting, because it includes the arguments. We first discuss two modern readings of the text, and then give our own interpretation.

---

24 See *Rhetorike* B II 23.4.

25 Cicero, *Topica* 23. Quintilian, *Inst. Or.* 5.10.87.

26 Lenel (1889) I col. 302 no. 171.

27 Voci (1963) 343. Wieling (1972) 23, Backhaus (1983) 169, and Paulus (1992) 277 also mention this explanation. On the *lex Voconia*, see Voci (1967) 123–124, Van der Meer (1996), and Fumagalli (2008).

To our knowledge, it is Wieling and Backhaus who in previous decades discussed D. 32.29.1 most extensively. It is worth noting that their interpretations are based on an adaptation of the Latin text, and particularly of the legacy in question. Wieling's adaptation features in his monograph on the interpretation of wills in Roman law when he discusses interpretation based on wording and by means of *topoi*. He writes that Gallus and Scaevola stuck to the words *tantandem partem quantulam unus heres*, which they interpreted as *quantulam unusquisque*: the wife must receive as much as does *any* heir.[28] After all, if she were to receive as much as the smallest portion, she would not receive as much as the heir with the largest portion; but if she receives as much as the largest portion, then she will also have as much as the heir with the smallest portion, for the smaller portion is included in the larger one. That is why the wife's legacy must be calculated by the largest portion to comply with the words of the legacy. Labeo, Ofilius and Servius decided differently, but they did not base their decision on the testator's intention: in their view, the wife must receive as much as the smallest part, because the heir who is to pay out the legacy is entitled to decide what portion he will give. Wieling contends that a legal principle or *topos* is involved, because in the case submitted by Servius and Ofilius only one heir is involved, whereas in the original case there were more heirs. The *topos* would be that if the duty of the heir is unclear, he need pay out only the smallest portion (*favor heredis*).[29]

Backhaus deals with D. 32.29.1 in his paper on *immi*, as one of the dozen or so Digest texts that in modern literature are connected with this topic. Like Wieling, he adapts the legacy, but in a different way.[30] He claims that in the will *two* persons had been instituted as heirs, set to receive unequal portions, and that to the wife a legacy of a portion had been granted. Backhaus holds that the text of this legacy would have run as follows: *uxor mea tantandem partem quantam unus heres*. Iavolenus, he argues, would have changed the word *quantam* into *quantulam* in order to suggest that the testator had meant the smaller portion. It was probably by mistake that he had not indicated whether the size of the legacy should be calculated on the basis of the larger or the smaller portion. In a note, Backhaus explains that such a mistake was easily made: in his will, the testator may have included two equal portions, but

28 Wieling (1972) 22–23.

29 According to Wieling (1972) 22, a legal *topos* differs from a rhetorical *topos* in that it does not want to persuade but invites to be considered in the decision ('er fordert Beachtung bei der Entscheidung'). It is a point of view that jurists recognise as a legal value, Wieling contends.

30 Backhaus (1983) 169–172 with literature.

later, in a confirmed codicil, he may have changed these portions. Scaevola and Gallus affirm that the wife could claim the largest portion; Servius and Ofilius arrive at the smallest one, and their opinion would later have prevailed. In explaining Scaevola's use of *immi*, Backhaus follows Wieling: if the wife receives as much as the largest portion, she will also have as much as the heir with the smallest portion.[31]

Backhaus parts ways with Wieling once again in his comment on the argument used by Scaevola: he qualifies it as weak, not only logically but also legally, because *immi* can be used to motivate the opposite opinion as well. Being trained in Stoic philosophy, Scaevola must have known as much, yet that did not keep him from using it. Backhaus argues that Scaevola did so, because he saw *immi* as a rhetorical *topos* that could and should be used when a court consisting of lay judges had to be convinced by means of easily digestible arguments. But other jurists, Backhaus continues, did not agree with his point of view. Servius already found the decisive counterargument, not by generally referring to the *favor heredis*, as Wieling suggests, but by equating the legacy of a portion with the legacy *per damnationem*; the latter type gave the heir the right to choose what to pay out to the legatee if more than one object had been bequeathed and only one had to be chosen.[32] The case in question looked like that, and so Servius could justifiably argue that the heir was entitled to choose just like he could in case of a legacy *per damnationem*. Since the portions were not equal in size, the heir would probably choose the smaller one and so only the smaller portion could be regarded as owed, Backhaus concludes.

Although the interpretations put forward by Wieling and Backhaus do differ, they have two elements in common that in our view weaken either's analysis: one, both rely on a changed wording of the legacy, and, two, both appear to not take account of the fact that the jurists mentioned in D. 32.29.1 were not all close contemporaries. We believe this text can and should be interpreted in a way that does not require changing its wording and that reflects a more balanced chronology.

In our view, it is essential to a sustainable reconstruction of the legal issue in D. 32.29.1 to bear in mind the considerable lapse of time between Titia wondering how much she would receive and her husband's estate actually being divided. During that time, the situation changed several times, and consequently the *responsa* of the various jurists refer to different situations. There

31 Backhaus (1983) 170 with note 177, for a similar interpretation referring also to Horak (1969) 94–95, Watson (1971)132, Wieling (1972) 23, and Stein (1978) 179.

32 This happened when several things had been bequeathed at the heir's choice or when something had been bequeathed that was determined in kind. Backhaus (1983) 172.

are two reasons why we think so. First, while Scaevola, Gallus, and Servius certainly did not live eons apart, Scaevola firmly belonged to an earlier generation of jurists: he lived in the late second and the early first centuries BC, Gaius Aquilius Gallus and Servius Sulpicius Rufus both in the first half of the first century BC. The other three jurists mentioned in D. 32.29.1 did not have first-hand knowledge of the case, because they belonged to even later generations: Aulus Ofilius and Marcus Antistius Labeo lived in the second half of the first century BC and Lucius Iavolenus Priscus in the second half of the first century AD. Second, in his *responsum* Scaevola mentions several heirs (*heredum*), whereas Servius refers to one heir (*heres*). With these 'filters' in place, we reconstruct the case as follows.

Around 100 BC, a testator made a will in which he instituted several persons, possibly his children,[33] as his heirs, leaving to each the same modest portion. He also included a legacy in favour of his wife, Titia, with her share being equal in size to the portion left to one heir. The testator may have done so to evade the rule of the *lex Voconia*, which forbade (1) a testator with an estate worth more than 100,000 *sestertia* from instituting a woman as heir and (2) a beneficiary under a legacy or *donatio mortis causa* from receiving more than an heir. In this particular case, however, this legacy of part of the estate was tricky, because the portions left to the heirs necessarily made up the whole 12/12 of the estate, so that it was hard if not impossible to combine them with the legacy.[34] From the clause *si non aequales partes essent heredum* we deduce that sometime later, in a codicil, the testator changed his will in such a way that the portions left to the heirs were no longer equal.[35] It seems that Titia became aware of this change and that she made inquiries of Scaevola about the size of her legacy in the event of her husband's death. He answered that she would be entitled to a legacy as large as the largest portion, because the larger contains the smaller. He clearly derived that argument from the *topos comparatio* and formulated it in general terms, as a *thesis*.

33 Paulus (1992) 277 assumes that the testator had instituted as heirs his children as well as *extranei* and had also included substitutions with different shares. The text. however, does not contain such information.

34 This legacy resembles a *legatum partitionis*, in which the testator orders the heir to divide the estate between himself and the legatees. According to Voci (1963) 344, it was very difficult to implement such a legacy. In the case under discussion this was even worse. Suppose there were six heirs who each were given a 2/12th share of the estate. If Titia were to receive 2/12ths as well, that would be equally deducted from the six heirs' shares with the result that they would each receive less than 2/12ths.

35 Similarly, Backhaus (1983) 170 note 173, see above.

By the time the testator died, the situation must have changed drastically: to us the words *cum heres dare damnatus esset* suggest that all save one of the persons who originally had been instituted as heirs had died. Through accretion the deceased heirs' shares now fell to the surviving heir. How should Titia's legacy now be interpreted? Remembering Scaevola's *responsum* and backed by Gallus' view, Titia claimed that she was entitled to the largest portion mentioned in the will. The heir disagreed and asked Servius for advice. He replied that the smallest portion mentioned in the will was owed, because only one heir was left now and he was entitled to decide on the portion he would pay out to the legatee.[36] Servius, too, then, uses the *topos comparatio*, but the outcome is the opposite of Scaevola's conclusion, and it was Servius' reply that Ofilius, Labeo, and Iavolenus later approved of.

While Scaevola and Servius used the same *topos*, their *responsa* addressed different situations. In fact, Scaevola's *responsum* was irrelevant, because the testator was still alive at the time; this may also explain why he chose to take the largest portion as the benchmark for the size of the legacy.[37] This presumably went down well with Titia and it allowed Scaevola to skirt a question that was delicate and indelicate at the same time.[38] Servius faced a different situation: the testator had died and only one of the instituted heirs had survived him. How to interpret Titia's legacy? It would be unreasonable for her to receive the largest portion. Servius answered that it would be enough for the heir to pay out the smallest portion mentioned in the will.

In the light of this reconstruction, we do not subscribe to Backhaus' qualification of Scaevola's argument as logically and legally weak, because that view rather suggests that it would have been possible to find a legally strong solution. And that, we believe, was not the case. As we explained above, the legacy intended for Titia was debatable from the very start. Moreover, the testator had complicated matters by changing the portions left to the heirs. It strikes us as curious that none of the jurists explicitly qualified the legacy as invalid and that their interpretations all appear to assume it could somehow be carried out. So perhaps Scaevola, whether instinctively or intentionally, did not go out

36 Backhaus' assumption that Servius is reasoning here by analogy of a legacy of choice is not based on the text.

37 In this way, Scaevola remained within the limits of the *lex Voconia*, because Titia would not receive more than the share one heir stood to inherit.

38 It was a delicate question because – as we mentioned above and in note 34 – it was difficult to calculate how much his wife would receive, and the question was indelicate because the husband was still alive at the time of his wife's asking. Although the text does not say so, Titia might have been the testator's second and younger wife, and as such she would have had to share the estate with her husband's children from his first marriage.

of his way to argue the legal merits of a case for which there was no viable legal solution, seeking instead to underpin his advice with a rhetorical argument, the same one Servius used to support the opposite conclusion.

Our final observation relates to the subtitle of Backhaus' paper: 'Eine justinianische *regula iuris* in den klassischen Rechtsquellen – Herkunft, Anwendungsbereich und Funktion'. In the introduction to his paper, Backhaus explains this subtitle as follows: *immi* appeared so often in the sources of classical Roman law that Justinian viewed it as 'a succinct statement having a broad general application'[39] and consequently felt compelled to include it in his catalogue of *diversae regulae iuris antiqui* (D. 50.17). And in a footnote to this explanation, Backhaus mentions as many as seven texts in D. 50.17 that feature *immi*.[40] That being so, and given what we have argued in this chapter and the previous one, it is conceivable that D. 50.17 also contains other topical arguments worded as *theseis*. In the following chapters we aim to find out.

---

39 Backhaus (1983) 136 note 2, quoting Stein (1966) 115.

40 Even if, for reasons best known to himself, in his paper he only deals with the one in D. 50.17.110 pr.; Backhaus (1983) 136 note 3, referring to Schmidlin (1970) 203. The latter did not deal with these texts either.

CHAPTER 4

D. 50.17 *De diversis regulis iuris antiqui*

We concluded the previous chapter by expressing our intention to find out whether D. 50.17 contains topical arguments, *topoi*, worded as *theseis*, and in the following chapters we will do just that. This chapter sets the scene for that expedition by introducing the concept of *regula*, by presenting our selection of twenty *regulae*, and by outlining our exegetical method. These preparations are in order, because title D. 50.17 is a puzzling one. In the *Constitutio Tanta*, the elaborate preface to the Digest, it is mentioned only once, namely where the content of Book 50 is summarised, and its last title (17) is referred to as *quaeque regulariter definita*, 'and those things that were drawn up as rules'.[1] In the opening text of D. 50.17, the compilers do define the word *regula*, but this definition has exercised the minds of modern scholars.

Around 1970, two of these, Stein and Schmidlin, published monographs on the *regulae*, with Stein describing the history of the concept of *regula* from the time of early Rome to sixteenth century Western Europe, and Schmidlin discussing the *regula* in the legal sources of Roman antiquity.[2] Their work attests not only that in the course of Roman history the term *regula* had different meanings, such as definition, principle, and legal rule, it also shows that in modern literature this word has been explained in different ways. Schmidlin discusses whether the *regula* was a binding legal rule, which kinds of *regula* can be distinguished, and how these relate to doctrine; he does not, however, address the *regulae* of D. 50.17. Stein does.

According to Stein, the *regulae* of D. 50.17 are succinct statements having a broad general application: maxims.[3] Some had already been developed in classical law, but most were originally 'explanations by the classical jurists of

1 *Constitutio Tanta* 8c, *in fine*. Translation Scott (1932). In Watson (1985) these words are not translated. Stein (1966) has 'whatever is expressed in the form of a *regula*'.

2 Stein (1966) and, more broadly, Stein (1999). Schmidlin (1970); on this book, see Nörr (1972) 18–93 and in response Schmidlin (1976) 91–109. In more recent times, the *regulae* have made something of a comeback: they were the theme of the 2014 SIHDA conference in Naples (papers were published that year, in *RIDA* 61), and in 2022 the Ghent Legal History Institute organised a workshop on '*Regulae iuris* and maxims of law in the legal historical perspective' (papers expected to be published in 2024). We note that renewed interest in the *regulae iuris* concerns the *regula* concept as it evolved from the eleventh century. For an overview of modern literature on that concept, see Kotlyar (2021).

3 Stein (1966) 114–123, particularly 115.

 | DOI:10.1163/9789004711020_005

decisions which they had already stated.'[4] By isolating them from their original context and by generalising their wording, Stein proposes, the compilers had turned them into maxims as well. However, the original context of the *regulae* rather suggests that it was the classical jurists themselves who had formulated their arguments in general terms for a specific case to make them more convincing. Stein failed to recognise this stratagem as a rhetorical element of the *regulae*.[5]

Earlier, in the 1950s, Viehweg had introduced a completely different view on D. 50.17. In his famous treatise *Topik und Jurisprudenz*, he argued that the Roman *ius civile* was based on problem-oriented thinking and, just like *topoi*, aimed at collecting points of view and summarising them in catalogues.[6] D. 50.17 on this view would be a good example of such a catalogue of *topoi*, and Viehweg illustrated it by referring to five *topoi*, one of them being *in maiore minus inest* (*immi*) in D. 50.17.110 (which we discussed in Chapter 3). This, however, poses a problem, because *immi* was not always qualified as a *topos*: Aristotle marked it as one, but Cicero regarded it as a *thesis* based on the *topos comparatio*. Also, if Viehweg is right, D. 50.17 would be a rather clumsy catalogue of *topoi* for it lacks structure, and thinking of *regulae* as points of view is too broad a definition to be helpful.

We submit that the *regulae* in title D. 50.17 are topical arguments formulated in general terms for one particular case. This view can be tested only in texts which have come down as *leges geminatae*, that is, texts whose original *responsa* have been preserved elsewhere in the Digest. It is only in these texts that we can assess whether the *regula* functioned as an argument in the *responsum* in question. Lenel's reconstruction of the works of the classical jurists in his *Palingenesia Iuris Civilis* has enabled us to find such texts.[7]

We have identified twenty *regulae* in D. 50.17 that can be connected to a *lex geminata*. For seven *regulae*, this is certainly the case because the *regula*

4 Stein (1966) 118.

5 Nor does he clarify whether the *regulae* of D. 50.17 could function as a premise in a logical reasoning, a syllogism. Earlier in his book (p. 95) when discussing the classical ideas of *regulae iuris*, he states that 'once a proposition is recognized to be a *regula*, consequences may be deduced from it', and then refers to p. 34ff where he explains how Aristotle introduced the syllogism as a tool for deducing conclusions from propositions and how the Roman jurists applied this and other related techniques to develop the science of Roman law. In his review of Stein's book, Wieacker (1967) 436–437 is rather critical of this 'scientific revolution'. Our exegesis of the twenty selected *regulae* confirms this criticism, because not in a single one of them was the *regula* used as a premise of a syllogistic reasoning.

6 Viehweg (1974) 55–56. We discussed his view in our paper (2013) 34–36.

7 Lenel (1889).

concerned is also included in the text in question: 4, 31, 88, 156.1, 180, 192.1, and 195. Twelve other *regulae* Lenel confidently linked to a particular text of the same jurist because of their content: 7, 9, 10, 13, 20, 21, 29, 35, 64, 74, 75, and 113. For the twentieth *regula* (167.1), Lenel referred to a *responsum* whose content is a fit, but which was given by a different jurist. Among the remaining *regulae* in D. 50.17, we noticed a group of 24 we qualify as *dubia*, because they are *theseis* but for various reasons their link to a *lex geminata* is weak.[8] Moreover, 30 *regulae* turned out to be not *theseis* but comments on legal texts like the praetorian edict.[9] The remaining 137 *regulae* could very well be *theseis* but for lack of a *lex geminata* they cannot be qualified as topical arguments.

As we stated at the outset of this chapter, in the chapters to follow, we present our exegesis of the twenty *regulae* that can be connected to a *lex geminata*. We do not arrange them by the nature of the legal issue, because that angle is not relevant to our research, and for the same reason we do not present these twenty *regulae* in the order of title D. 50.17 either.[10] Rather, we cluster those *regulae* which refer to the same topical argument and – more or less like Cicero does in the third part of his *Topica* – we arrange them in the order of the *status* or types of question they suit.

For the types of question that turn on facts (*Is it, What is it,* and *How is it?*), Cicero describes which *topoi* had best be used, starting with *coniectura*: in section 87, he states that to the first type of question (*Is it?*) are best fitted the *topoi* which can be drawn from causes, effects, and conjuncts. In our list of *regulae*, the latter two *topoi* do not occur, but five *regulae* refer to *causa*.[11] They form the first part of our exegesis (Chapter 5). Then comes *definitio*, turning on the second type of question (*What is it?*). Cicero argues that 'the knowledge and science of defining is important for definition. Closely allied to this is what I said was called sameness and difference, this being a kind of definition.' Here, he seems to refer back to section 47 where he discussed the *topoi*

8 The *dubia* are D. 50.17.6, 8, 11, 12, 24, 26, 28, 30, 38, 44, 52, 103, 119, 123 pr., 128 pr.-1, 132, 146, 157 pr., 160.2, 172 pr.-1, 183, and 210.

9 The relevant *regulae* are D. 50.17.2, 5, 17, 18, 19 pr., 22.1, 23, 27, 34, 42, 43 pr.-1, 60, 65, 68, 77, 78, 84 pr., 87, 101, 104, 124 pr., 153, 154, 161, 165, 173 pr., 176 pr., 189, 191, and 205.

10 According to Bluhme (1820), the compilers divided the works of the classical jurists into three categories, or masses as he called them: Sabinian, Edictal, and Papinian. He also identified an Appendix category and contended that every Digest title consists of texts from these categories in that order. In D. 50.17, however, the order is slightly different: Sabinian (2–40), Edictal (41–57), Papinian (58–95), Edictal (102–167), and Appendix (168–211). For Bluhme's theory and later discussions on this topic, see du Plessis (2010) 59–60 and Stagl (2023).

11 D. 50.17.13, 31, 35, 167.1, and 180.

of *similitudo, differentia*, and *e contrario*. In section 88, Cicero also mentions the *topoi* of *consequentia, antecedentia*, and *repugnantia* as being suitable for a question of *definitio*. In our list of *regulae*, four are related to the *topos* of *e contrario*: one refers to the *topos consequentia*, none to *antecedentia*, and three refer to *repugnantia*.[12] These eight *regulae* form the second part of our exegesis (Chapters 6–8). Next up is *qualitas*. In section 89, Cicero states that in dealing with the third type of question (*How is it?*), 'those points are useful for comparison which were enumerated shortly before under the *topos comparatio*.' In our list of *regulae*, four refer to this *topos* and they form the third part of our exegesis (Chapter 9).[13] Further on, in sections 95–96, Cicero discusses another type of question, one that turns on the interpretation of a written document (for example, a law or a will). He does not mention the relevant *topoi*, describing instead what kind of disputes or quasi *status* may arise: *ambiguitas, verba voluntas*, and *leges contrariae*. For their treatment, Cicero refers to other works.[14] In our list of *regulae*, three refer to the *'status' ambiguitas*, and these form the fourth and last part of our exegesis (Chapter 10).[15]

In analysing our selection of twenty *regulae* we follow much the same pattern. We begin by explaining the context Lenel established or suggested for a *regula* and present its text and that of the relevant *lex geminata* in Latin and in translation. Next, we try to ascertain the legal problem involved. As most of the selected *regulae* (and often their contexts, too) have been discussed in Romanist literature, we present some interpretations from this literature as well as our comments. We then try to reconstruct both the case and the opinion and argumentation of the jurist concerned. For each of the twenty cases under scrutiny it is our proposition that the jurist used a topical argument and that he formulated it in general terms, as a *thesis*, even though it served to apply to the case at hand only.

12 D. 50.17.7, 10, 29, and 195 (*e contrario*); D. 50.17.88 (*e consequentibus*); D. 50.17.4, 74, and 75 (*a repugnantibus*).

13 D. 50.17.9, 21, 113, and 156.1.

14 For instance, in *De inv.* 2 116–121, Cicero describes in detail the arguments that can be used in case of *ambiguitas*.

15 D. 50.17.20, 64, and 192.1.

CHAPTER 5

The *status coniectura*: The *topos causa*

1 Ulpianus D. 50.17.13

Non videtur cepisse, qui per exceptionem a petitione removetur.

D. 50.17.13 stems from Book 19 of Ulpian's commentary *ad Sabinum*. Lenel inserted it as the second of a series of eleven texts, after D. 30.28 pr.[1] We ascertain whether this *regula* forms part of the case dealt with in D. 30.28 pr. and, if so, how it may be explained in that context. The two fragments run as follows:

> D. 30.28.pr. Ulpianus 19 ad Sab. Si creditori meo, tutus adversus eum exceptione, id quod ei debeo legem, utile legatum est, quia remissa exceptio videtur, sicut Aristo ait id quod honoraria actione mihi debetur si legetur mihi, legatum valere, quia civilis mihi datur actio pro honoraria.
>
> D. 50.17.13 Ulpianus 19 ad Sab. Non videtur cepisse, qui per exceptionem a petitione removetur.

> If I, being protected against my creditor by a defense, bequeath to him what I owe him, it is a valid legacy, because the defense is held to have been withdrawn. Similarly, Aristo says that a bequest to me of what is due to me by a praetorian action is a valid bequest, because a civil action is thereby granted me instead of a praetorian.
>
> Someone whose claim has been barred by a defense is not regarded as having received something.

Lenel states that Book 19 of Ulpian's commentary *ad Sabinum* was titled *De legatis* and carried the subtitle *De dote relegata*. In it, Ulpian combines *responsa* on the legacy of a dowry, which a husband could include in his will in favour of his wife, with opinions on the legacy of a debt. Both legacies concern an existing debt. The legacy of a dowry was valid only if it offered an extra benefit to the wife,[2] and a similar rule applied to the legacy of a debt. In the eleven

1 Lenel (1889) II col. 1076, no. 2597.

2 In note 7 to no. 2597, Lenel refers to D. 33.4.1.2 Ulp 19 *ad Sabinum*, where Ulpian compares the legacy of a dowry to the *actio rei uxoriae* and remarks that the legacy can be claimed immediately, whereas the *actio rei uxoriae* can only be brought after a year.

 | DOI:10.1163/9789004711020_006

texts, Ulpian deals with all sorts of problems that could arise around such a legacy, and this makes for a natural fit with the main subject of Book 30 of the Digest: legacies in general.

We first try to reconstruct the legal problem that is at the heart of the first fragment, D. 30.28 pr., and discuss how Ulpian solves it. We then compare this fragment with the second one of this series, D. 50.17.13, and consider whether the *regula* may have been used as an argument in it.

Using the clues offered by the text of D. 30.28 pr., we reconstruct the underlying conflict as follows. Someone promises (presumably by means of a *stipulatio*) to pay a certain amount of money to another person, but for unspecified reasons he does not keep his promise. The creditor is unable to claim the money, probably because he and the debtor have concluded a *pactum de non petendo*, a standstill agreement: an agreement that the debt will not be claimed. As a result, the debt has effectively been remitted. Later, the debtor makes a will in which he bequeaths to his creditor the money he formally still owes him, probably in a *legatum per damnationem*.[3] After the debtor's death and the opening of his will the creditor claims this legacy, but the heir for unknown reasons refuses to pay over the money. What is clear is the legal question: is the legacy of the debt valid?

Ulpian contends it is, because it improves the creditor's position: the standstill agreement was considered to have been set aside by the legacy.[4] Ulpian refers to Aristo, who was of the opinion that something that can be claimed with a praetorian action can be validly bequeathed because on the basis of the legacy it can now be claimed with a civil action. Ulpian's *responsum* follows a familiar course: a legacy of a debt is valid only if it implies a benefit to the creditor, such as the removal of a condition or a deadline. It is in this sense that D. 30.28 pr. has been discussed in Romanist literature.[5]

We now turn to the *regula* of D. 50.17.13. In itself, that *regula* makes little sense, because at first glance 'receiving something' has nothing to do with a 'claim that has been barred'. Yet Lenel suggests there is a connection between this *regula* and D. 30.28 pr., so we now try to explain D. 50.17.13 by comparing it with D. 30.28 pr.[6] Both texts share an essential element: a creditor who cannot claim the money owed to him because his debtor has an exception, a defence.

3 The assumption that it was a *legatum per damnationem* is based on the fact that a sum of money was bequeathed. Similarly, Voci (1963) 324 with note 288.

4 Perhaps, in this way, he aims to refute the heir's argument that this defence also applies to the legacy of the debt.

5 See, e.g., Palazzolo (1968) 105, Bernasconi (1976) 32, and Quadrato (1983) 17.

6 In Romanist literature, these texts have not been connected.

D. 30.28 pr. contains another essential element, namely, the debtor bequeathing to his creditor the money he still owes him. This element is lacking in D. 50.17.13, but Lenel's palingenetic reconstruction suggests that the debtor in D. 50.17.13, too, bequeaths to his creditor the money he formally still owes him. As legatee, the creditor tries to claim the legacy using the *actio ex testamento*, but the heir refuses to pay. We now reconstruct the arguments of these two parties in the light of D. 50.17.13.

The creditor states that he never received the money because the debtor had recourse to an *exceptio* for fending off his claim. It seems that, in this way, the creditor aims to refute the heir's argument that he is looking to collect the same sum twice, as creditor and as legatee.

The *topos* the creditor (or rather Ulpian) uses is *causa*: the debtor's *exceptio* is the cause of the creditor's inability to collect the debt. In *Topica*, Cicero distinguishes two kinds of *causa*: one that has the quality of producing an effect and one without which the effect cannot be produced.[7] In our view, Ulpian uses the first kind of *causa* here: the *exceptio* had a direct effect, making it impossible for the creditor to claim the money owed.[8]

Ulpian phrases the creditor's argument in general terms, as a *thesis*: someone whose claim has been barred by a defence is not regarded as having received something. The general terms were meant to reinforce the argument in this specific case only. On its own, the proposition cuts no ice, but it is its quality of being articulated in general terms that made the compilers include it in D. 50.17.

2 Ulpianus D. 50.17.31

> Verum est neque pacta neque stipulationes factum posse tollere: quod enim impossibile est, neque pacto neque stipulatione potest comprehendi, ut utilem actionem aut factum efficere possit.

D. 50.17.31 derives from Book 42 of Ulpian's commentary *ad Sabinum*. Lenel included it as the third in a series of five texts.[9] The second and the fourth texts

---

7 Cicero, *Topica* 58: *Causarum enim duo genera sunt; unum quod vi sua id quod sub eam vim subiectum est certe efficit, ut: Ignis accendit; alterum, quod naturam efficiendi non habet sed sine quo effici non possit, ut si quis aes statuae causam velit dicere, quod sine eo non possit effici.*

8 Ulpian uses the same *topos* when arguing in D. 30.28 pr. that the legacy enabled the creditor to collect the debt.

9 Lenel (1889) II col. 1170, no. 2886.

make up D. 21.2.31. We appraise how D. 50.17.31 relates to these two texts. In reconstruction, the three texts run as follows.

> D. 21.2.31 Ulpianus 42 ad Sab. Si ita quis stipulanti spondeat 'sanum esse, furem non esse, vispellionem non esse' et cetera, inutilis stipulatio quibusdam videtur, quia si quis est in hac causa, impossibile est quod promittitur, si non est, frustra est.
>
> D. 50.17.31 Ulpianus 42 ad Sab. Verum est neque pacta neque stipulationes factum posse tollere: quod enim impossibile est, neque pacto neque stipulatione potest comprehendi, ut utilem actionem aut factum efficere possit.
>
> D. 21.2.31 Ulpianus 42 ad Sab. Sed ego puto verius hanc stipulationem 'furem non esse, vispellionem non esse, sanum esse' utilem esse: hoc enim continere, quod interest horum quid esse vel horum quid non esse. Sed et si cui horum fuerit adiectum 'praestari', multo magis valere stipulationem: alioquin stipulatio quae ab aedilibus proponitur inutilis erit, quod utique nemo sanus probabit.

> If, when the question is put, someone promises that 'the slave is sound, is not a thief, is not a corpse bearer'[10] and the like, there are some who think that such stipulation is useless, because if the slave is of such character[11] the promise is impossible, and if he is not it is without effect.
>
> It is true that neither agreements nor stipulations can do away with a fact; this is impossible and cannot be included in an agreement or a stipulation so that it would establish a valid action or a fact.

10 According to Wesel (1963), 392–394 a *vispellio* or corpse bearer belonged to the *turpes personae* and that could be a reason for a buyer to not want such a slave. In the Middle Ages, this would no longer be understood, and so the word *vispellio* would have been interpreted as corpse robber. That meaning recurs in the two English translations of the Digest: Scott (1932) has 'violator of graves' and Watson (1985) 'corpse robber'. The other translations have an equivalent of or a variation on 'corpse bearer': Otto, Schilling, and Sintenis (1832) 'Todtengräber'; d'Ors (1972) 'sepulturero' and 'enterrador'; Spruit (1996) 'doodgraver', and Behrends and Knütel (2005) 'Leichenträger'.

11 I.e., if he is sound, if he is neither a thief nor a corpse bearer. The fact that the stipulation includes a positive (*esse*) and a negative (*non esse*) element leads to confusion in translating the words *in hac causa*. For instance, Watson (1985) has 'otherwise', which in our view is not correct. Behrends and Knütel (2005) have 'wenn nämlich der Sklave die Eigenschaft hat [deren Abwesenheit versprochen wird]', covering only the negative element. Better: Otto, Schilling, and Sintenis (1832): 'in einem solchen Zustand'.

> However, my view is that a promise that 'the slave is not a thief, is not a corpse bearer, is sound' has substance; for its essence is the buyer's interest in his being or not being so. But also if a guarantee were added to any of these statements, the stipulation would be the more valid. Otherwise the stipulation introduced by the *aediles* will be useless, and certainly no rational person would approve that.

Book 42 of Ulpian's commentary *ad Sabinum* carries the title *De furtis*. Our text fits in here as it deals with the guarantee that a particular slave who is being sold is not a thief. In the Digest, the context is very different: D. 21.2 has as its title *De evictionibus et duplae stipulatione.* The connection between the text and the title is probably the edict of the *aediles* containing the wording of a *stipulatio duplae* to be used in case of eviction and in addition a stipulation guaranteeing against hidden defects.[12]

In D. 21.2.31, Ulpian describes a discussion on the validity of a stipulation in which the seller of a slave promises that he has certain qualities. Some say it is not valid because such a promise is either impossible or pointless; Ulpian himself thinks that such a stipulation is valid when it is regarded as a guarantee. In D. 50.17.31 he states that an agreement cannot remove a fact. What does this discussion mean and how do D. 21.2.31 and D. 50.17.31 connect?

While rarely linked in Romanist literature, D. 21.2.31 and D. 50.17.31 have attracted much attention,[13] and two phrases in particular: the meaning of the words *quod interest* in the second part of D. 21.2.31, and the stipulations guaranteeing against hidden defects that are quoted in the first and second parts of this text. We first briefly discuss modern Romanist literature and present our comments; then we argue that D. 21.2.31 can be better understood if D. 50.17.31 is read as an argument to the first part of Ulpian's text.

In the 1960s, there was much discussion about the interpretation of the words *id quod interest* in the *formula* of the *iudicia bonae fidei*. It started with the monograph published by Medicus in 1962.[14] At that time, in German private law, damages were regarded as a compensation of the interest, and this was assumed to have been the case in Roman law as well. Medicus disagreed with this assumption; he argued that the Roman jurists used the clause *id quod interest* to indicate the difference between the value of the thing sold as it should have been and as it actually was. One of the texts he referred to is D. 21.2.31 and particularly the phrase *quod interest horum quid esse vel horum quid non esse.*

---

12 For an example, see Lenel (1927) 567–568.

13 In *Fiuris*, D. 21.2.31 and D. 50.17.31 have 30 and 11 hits respectively, sharing five.

14 Medicus (1962), 110–111 with older literature.

Several years later, in a paper on the function of *Leistungsunmöglichkeit* (obligations to do what is impossible), Medicus returned to this text, this time also referring to Ulp. D.50.17.31.[15] On the basis of Lenel's reconstruction he summarised the case as follows: Ulpian first stated that according to *quidam* an obligation to do what is impossible was invalid, but he disagreed with them and contested their opinion with various arguments. According to Medicus, the strongest argument was the distinction Ulpian drew between *factum tollere* (D. 50.17.31) and *praestari*, in the sense of the obligation to pay the difference in value (D. 21.2.31, second part). By doing so, Ulpian not only recognised the special function of the guarantee, but also described its concept. Legal certainty is given to the creditor enabling him to serve his interest in shifting the damage irrespective of the primary obligation being performed.

While several Romanists (for example, Sanguinetti and Schieder) have endorsed Medicus' view on *id quod interest*, Honsell has refuted it, arguing that the phrase *quod interest horum quid esse vel horum quid non esse* only indicates that the buyer has an interest in the slave being free of defects.[16] A positive (*quid esse*) and a negative (*quid non esse*) clause being combined follows from the quality of being free of defects being expressed in positive and negative terms in the opening lines of D. 21.2.31. Ulpian's recommendation to add the verb *praestari* has made Honsell conclude that the *actio ex stipulatu* aimed at damages, and this could go beyond compensation for the lesser value of the object sold. Honsell's opinion has become generally accepted,[17] and we concur. As far as we know, the contrast Medicus posited between *factum tollere* in D. 50.17.31 and *praestari* in the second part of D. 21.2.31 has not elicited any response.[18] In fact, we believe it is inconceivable that Ulpian contrasted these two completely different concepts; we submit he only contrasted his opinion that the stipulation was valid with the opinion of *quidam* that the stipulation was invalid.

15 Medicus (1969), 94–95.

16 Sanguinetti (1999) 174 note 45 and Schieder (2011) 105–107. Honsell (1969), 63–66.

17 E.g., by Kaser (1973) 216 and Zimmermann (1996) 310. Tafaro (1971) 364–365 is critical in his review of Honsell's book.

18 Jakab (1997) 242 agrees with Medicus' interpretation of D. 21.2.31 in conjunction with D. 50.17. 31 but argues that it only holds for the first part of D. 21.2.31, i.e., until the ultimate sentence beginning with the words *Sed et si*. In her view, Roman law had two different stipulations for giving a guarantee for hidden defects: one that was developed in the practice of contracts, and one that was proposed in the aedilician edict. In D. 21.2.31, Ulpian describes both: the one from practice in the first part until *Sed et si*, followed by the one from the edict. We think this is an overly dogmatic and unnecessary distinction: the idea of a model is that people can adapt it to their own particular situation.

The other discussion about D. 21.2.31 concerns the stipulation in which the seller guaranteed that the slave he was selling was healthy and was neither a thief nor a corpse bearer. Roughly a quarter of a century ago, Cardilli addressed this topic in a monograph he wrote on the obligation of *praestare* and contractual liability in Roman law from the second century BC to the second century AD.[19] He discusses the question whether *praestare* had an independent meaning as an object of an obligation apart from *dare* and *facere*. To him, D. 21.2.31 is important in the context of the early history of *praestare*. The guarantee stipulation as quoted by Ulpian was first used in the second century BC by M. Manilius.[20] According to Cardilli, the *quidam* who criticised this stipulation as being pointless were jurists who post-dated Manilius but predated Sabinus (first century AD). Sabinus would have quoted them in his *Iuris civilis libri tres*, the book on which Ulpian commented in D. 21.2.31. Their argument has been preserved in D. 50.17.31: it is impossible to change a certain situation by means of a stipulation. This argument would resonate in a time when it became popular to render the debtor's obligation in the *formula* of an action from contract with the words *dare facere*. Ulpian was to have refuted the *quidam*'s criticism by regarding the presence or absence of certain qualities as the object of the stipulation and by recommending that the term *praestari* be used, for that word was also used in the edict of the *aediles* in the sense of *stare praes*, to guarantee. We agree with Cardilli's interpretation except for his assumption that the *quidam* were jurists antedating Sabinus: Sabinus himself and later jurists may also have rejected this kind of stipulation.[21]

We now take a closer look at D. 21.2.31 in conjunction with D. 50.17.31. Ulpian raises the question whether a stipulation in which a seller promises that a slave is healthy and is neither a thief nor a corpse bearer is valid. Some jurists think it is not, because such a stipulation is impossible or pointless, and they explain why. In general terms, they state that a *pactum* or *stipulatio* cannot change an actual situation, nor can it bring about a valid action or a fact (D. 50.17.31).[22] So they use the topical argument of the *causa*, and particularly the *causa* which 'by its own force surely produces that effect which depends on this force.'[23] The promise that a certain slave is healthy, et cetera, cannot bring about that if that

19 Cardilli (1995) 135–140. See also the detailed review by Capogrossi Colognesi (1998) 527–538.

20 Cf Varro, *De re rustica* 2.3.5.

21 Similarly, Arangio Ruiz (1954) 357 and, in his detailed review of Cardilli's book, Capogrossi Colognesi (1998) 529.

22 According to Arangio Ruiz (1954) 357 note 1, this statement is a postclassical annotation.

23 Cicero, *Topica* 58.

slave is ill, he becomes healthy. This argument in its general wording is quite convincing and forces Ulpian to come up with some good counterarguments.

First, Ulpian states that the stipulation can be regarded as valid, because the buyer of a slave can have an interest in the slave having or not having certain qualities. Second, the stipulation gains power if the word *praestari* is added to that quality: it then becomes clear that the buyer aims at acquiring a guarantee for that quality.[24] Ulpian's third and decisive argument is that if such a stipulation were regarded as invalid, the aedilician stipulation would also be invalid and no sane person would want that. This is a textbook example of an *argumentum ad absurdum*.

We propose that D. 21.2.31 and D. 50.17.31 make sense only when read together. The three fragments form one *responsum* consisting of a case, an argument, and a counterargument. The question is whether a particular guarantee stipulation is valid. Some jurists think it is not, and they support their opinion with the topical argument of the *causa*. This argument smacks of uncompromising dogmatism. Ulpian also uses a topical argument to support his opinion, an *argumentum ad absurdum*. His opinion is far from dogmatic, he was just solving a practical problem.

We conclude that the argument in D. 50.17.31 is formulated in general terms; in other words, it is a *thesis*. That is why the compilers moved it from its original context to D. 50.17.[25] And for that reason, this text should not be regarded as a dogmatic rule which was generally accepted. It was an argument that was only meant to support the opinion of *quidam*, some jurists, in one specific case only.

3 Ulpianus D. 50.17.35

> Nihil tam naturale est quam eo genere quidque dissolvere, quo colligatum est. Ideo verborum obligatio verbis tollitur: nudi consensus obligatio contrario consensu dissolvitur.

D. 50.17.35 derives from Book 48 of Ulpian's commentary *ad Sabinum*. Lenel included it as the second text in a group of four.[26] The first of these texts, D. 46.4.8.3, as well as the *regula*, is about *acceptilatio*, the formal release of a

24 That this word was used in practice is shown by a document of the sale of a slave dating from the year 142 AD, quoted by Lenel (1927) 568.

25 We consequently disagree with Wollschläger (1970) 15, who argues that D. 50.17.31 acquired a general purport because the compilers moved this text from its original context.

26 Lenel (1889) II col. 1188, no. 2955.

debt. The third fragment, D. 46.2.2, is about *novatio*, which is indirectly related to that topic.[27] We believe that originally these three texts belonged to the same case, and we attempt to show how they are connected.

> D. 46.4.8.3 Ulpianus 48 ad Sab. Acceptum fieri non potest, nisi quod verbis colligatum est: acceptilatio enim verborum obligationem tollit, quia et ipsa verbis fit: neque enim potest verbis tolli, quod non verbis contractum est.
>
> D. 50.17.35 Ulpianus 48 ad Sab. Nihil tam naturale est quam eo genere quidque dissolvere, quo colligatum est. Ideo verborum obligatio verbis tollitur: nudi consensus obligatio contrario consensu dissolvitur.
>
> D. 46.2.2 Ulpianus 48 ad Sab. Omnes res transire in novationem possunt: quodcumque enim sive verbis contractum est sive non verbis, novari potest et transire in verborum obligationem ex quacumque obligatio, dummodo sciamus novationem ita demum fieri, si hoc agatur, ut novetur obligatio: ceterum si non hoc agatur, duae erunt obligationes.

> There can be no formal release of a debt except when it has been put together by formal words; for the release discharges an obligation made by formal words, being itself made by formal words; for nothing can be discharged by formal words what was not contracted by formal words.[28]
>
> Nothing is so natural as to dissolve something in the same way as that it is put together. So a verbal obligation is verbally dissolved. The obligation of bare consent is dissolved by contrary consent.
>
> All matters can be brought to novation; for anything, whether or not contracted verbally, can be novated and, from any obligation, be converted into a verbal obligation, provided that we appreciate that novation will occur only if the intention is that the obligation be novated; if that is not the case, there will be two obligations.

The title of Book 48 of Ulpian's commentary *ad Sabinum* is *De verborum obligatione*, and according to Lenel the last part of that book is about the *acceptilatio*. In the Digest, title D. 46.4 also pertains to the *acceptilatio*, and title D. 46.2 to *novatio* and *delegatio*.

---

27 Lenel may have included D. 36.3.8 as a fourth text in this group because just as the last sentence of D. 46.2.2 it refers to a second obligation being created. In footnotes to D. 46.2.2, D. 46.4.8.3 and D. 50.17.35, Mommsen indicated that they were connected, but he did not include D. 36.3.8.

28 Our translation.

In classical Roman law, the *acceptilatio* was the most important mode to release a debtor from his debt.[29] It is closely connected to the *stipulatio*, a promise to give or do something which was made by a formal question and answer. The *acceptilatio* was developed as a way to dissolve a *stipulatio* after the debtor had done what he had promised. In the third century BC, it also came to be used if the creditor wanted to remit a debt. Like the *stipulatio*, the *acceptilatio* was made by a formal question and answer. In his Institutes, Gaius provides the following example: *Quod ego tibi promisi, habesne acceptum? Habeo.* 'What I promised you, have you received? Yes, I have.'[30] He explains that this mode of release can be used for verbal contracts only, 'for it has been held appropriate that an obligation created by words should be discharged by other words. However,' he adds, 'what is due on some other ground can be thrown into a stipulation and then be discharged by *acceptilatio*.'[31] Here, Gaius refers to *novatio*, the conversion of any obligation into an obligation from *stipulatio*. In this way, the *acceptilatio* became 'a fairly convenient and universally applicable form of release.'[32]

In his commentary *ad Sabinum*, Ulpian introduces the *acceptilatio* much in the same way as Gaius does.[33] His opening statement (in D. 46.4.8.3) is that an *acceptilatio* can only dissolve a debt based on a *stipulatio*. Then (in D. 50.17.35), he explains that it is only natural to dissolve something in the same way as it was put together, for instance, a *contractus verbis* by words and a *contractus consensu* by dissent. Also just like Gaius, Ulpian concludes (in D. 46.2.2) that by means of *novatio* every debt can be converted into an obligation from *stipulatio*, but unlike Gaius he adds that the parties' true intention is to renew the obligation.

Of these three texts, it is D. 50.17.35 that has attracted most attention in modern Romanist literature. Since the early twentieth century, one or more phrases of this text have been considered interpolations.[34] In 1959, Daube even argued that the whole text of D. 50.17.35 stems from the compilers: by generalising D. 46.4.8.3 and particularly the second sentence they created an *umfassendes Prinzip* and proclaimed the idea of the *actus contrarius* as a *regula*.[35] According

29 Cf. Zimmermann (1996) 754–756. See also Mollá Nebot (1993) and Ankum (1998) 267–285.
30 Gaius, *Inst.* 3.169. Unless stated otherwise, we use De Zulueta's 1946 translation.
31 Gaius, *Inst.* 3.170.
32 Zimmermann (1996) 757.
33 Similarly, Stoll (1924) 9.
34 Cf. *Index Interpolationum* (1935) 593.
35 Daube (1959) 244–245.

to Daube, the beginnings of this idea can be found in the works of the classical jurists. Daube's theory provoked much discussion.

In his monograph on the dissolution of consensual contracts, Knütel followed Daube's theory. He begins by stating that the idea of the *actus contrarius* is of old, sacral origin.[36] By way of example, he mentions the *diffarreatio* as a 'symmetrische Aufhebungsakt' of the *confarreatio*.[37] The *pontifices* would have used this principle for legal purposes, having stripped it of its supernatural connotation. Knütel asserts that the 'Symmetrieprinzip' was applied particularly to the law of obligations, as would appear from the *acceptilatio* versus the *stipulatio*. The classical jurists would not have used this principle for all *contractus consensu*: they did so for sale and hire, but not for *societas* and *mandatum*. It is in this context that Knütel also discusses D. 50.17.35, particularly the last phrase: *nudi consensus obligatio contrario consensu dissolvitur*. In his view, this phrase could not have been written by Ulpian, not only because it was superfluous between D. 46.4.8.3 and D. 46.2.2, but also for linguistic reasons: the words *nudi consensus obligatio* would be a *novum* and the text would be grammatically weak. That is why, like Daube, Knütel believes the compilers formulated the general principle of the *actus contrarius* on the basis of D. 46.4.8.3, introducing it with the 'rhetorische Pseudobegründung' *Nihil tam naturale est*.[38]

Schmidlin and Liebs crossed swords with Daube, both contending that D. 50.17.35 originates with Ulpian – but for different reasons. Ancient Roman law, Schmidlin asserts, had a principle of formal symmetry, but it lost much of its vigour as ancient formalism dwindled and informal consensual contracts gained prominence.[39] Even so, the classical jurists would have tried to hold on to the symmetry principle, as, for instance, Ulpian did in D. 50.17.35.[40] The compilers did not know how to explain it and so, by way of introduction, they allowed themselves a little rhetorical flourish ('Floskel'): *Nihil tam naturale est*.

Liebs, on the other hand, insists that there was no principle of formal symmetry in ancient Roman law but that the Roman jurists did occasionally use the *actus contrarius*.[41] Scaevola is known to have done so, as did Pomponius

36 Knütel (1968) 15–17 with literature. Also in Knütel (1971) 98.

37 *Confarreatio* is a formal marriage as described by Gaius in *Inst.* 1.112; *diffarreatio* is the formal divorce.

38 Mollá Nebot (1993) 121–123 broadly follows Daube's and Knütel's interpretations.

39 Schmidlin (1970) 74–79, particularly 77.

40 Schmidlin (1970) 74–75 also mentions Pomp. D. 46.3.80, Gai. D. 50.17.100, and Paul. D. 50.17.153.

41 Liebs (1970) 149–153. Similarly, Kaser (1971) 40 and 230, and Nörr (1972) 59–60.

and Gaius in their commentaries on Scaevola. Later, Liebs argues, Ulpian used the idea of the *actus contrarius* to limit the *acceptilatio* to *contractus verbis*, whereas Papinian and Paul discovered that it also fitted the law of property. Liebs believes that, except for some editorial changes, D. 46.4.8.3 and D. 50.17.35 are classical, including the words *contrario consensu* in the latter text.[42] Three times, the compilers placed the *actus contrarius* in the spotlight of a general *regula iuris*: in D. 50.17. 35, 100 and 153 – not as positive law but as a 'Kernstelle' from the abundance of literature that had been preserved.[43]

As the discussion sparked by Daube's theory shows, the two most hotly debated issues are that of a symmetry principle and that of D. 50.17.35 belonging to classical Roman law. As to the so-termed symmetry principle, we side with Liebs in maintaining that there was no such principle in Roman law; it is not found in the sources and any symmetry that may be seen in an *actus contrarius* is the result rather than the cause of a legal act. We also concur with Liebs's view that D. 50.17.35 essentially belongs to classical Roman law. We find Knütel's assumption that the compilers must have written it because it is grammatically weak unconvincing. It makes more sense to suppose that as the compilers were native speakers of Greek and had learned Latin at school, they were keen to stick to the rules of grammar.[44]

Also, Knütel's assumption that D. 50.17.35 was superfluous between D. 46.4.8.3 and D. 46.2.2 is unfounded, because the three texts each have their own tenor and complement each other. That alone makes it implausible that the compilers themselves made up the middle one. Moreover, if they had, the inscription of D. 50.17 – *De regulis iuris antiqui* – would be off the mark, and it would be hard to explain why the compilers formulated the same *regula* in D. 50.17.35, 100, and 153 in three different ways.[45] Finally, Knütel's as well as Schmidlin's assumption that the introductory words *Nihil tam naturale est* were merely a rhetorical embellishment also lacks conviction: the Digest contains a wide variety of appeals to nature – in Ulpian's texts, too – and they have nothing to do with rhetoric, but rather with law.[46]

In our view, D. 46.4.8.3, D. 50.17.35, and D. 46.2.2 closely cohere. In the first of these three texts, Ulpian states that, just like the *stipulatio*, the *acceptilatio*

---

42 Liebs (1970) 152 note 167.

43 Liebs (1970) 152–153 with note 169.

44 According to Nelson (1981) 261, the compilers had an excellent knowledge of Latin.

45 E.g., using *solvere* (35), *pereunt* (100), and *liberamur* (153) for 'to dissolve'.

46 In Heumann and Seckel (1907) 359–36 the lemma *natura* takes more than four columns. Ulpian was the jurist who formulated the famous definition of *ius naturale* (in D. 1.1.1.3): *Ius naturale est quod natura omnia animalia docuit.*

must be performed by pronouncing certain words: what is contracted by formal words is also dissolved by formal words. The words are the *causa* of the contract as well as of its dissolution. In the second text, D. 50.17.35, he explains this statement in general terms, namely, that nothing is so natural as to un-bind something in the same way as it had been bound. Not content with giving one example (the *contractus verbis*), Ulpian also mentions the *contractus consensu*. In doing so, he clears the way for the third text, D. 46.2.2, about *novatio*, which is often used to convert a *contractus re, litteris,* or *consensu* into a *stipulatio* and thus make it fit for *acceptilatio*.[47] Apparently, this mode of dissolution offered more certainty to parties than an informal dissent. The structure of these three texts suggests that they refer to the same legal problem, a problem that was lost over the course of more than 300 years before the texts were included in the Digest. This problem may have concerned the dissolution of a *contractus consensu*, because that was most likely to lead to disagreement.

Returning to our central hypothesis about the jurists wording topical arguments in general terms, in D. 50.17.35, Ulpian introduces his explanation with a *thesis*, namely, with the general proposition that 'Nothing is so natural as to dissolve something in the same way as that it is put together.' The two concrete examples he then gives show that he used the *topos causa*: '[A] verbal obligation is verbally dissolved. The obligation of bare consent is dissolved by contrary consent.' The *verba* and the *consensus* are both a *causa* 'which has the quality of producing an effect.'[48] Since the argument of D. 50.17.35 suits a classical jurist schooled in rhetorical argumentation, as Ulpian was, to a T, it defies probability to assume the compilers of the Digest crafted it.

4 Paulus D. 50.17.167.1

> Qui iussu iudicis aliquid facit, non videtur dolo malo facere, qui parere necesse habet.

D. 50.17.167.1 was taken from Book 49 of Paul's commentary *ad edictum*; Lenel inserted it at the very end of that book.[49] In a footnote, he refers to D. 39.3.4 pr.,

47 Apathy (1975) 98 assumes that when the compilers drafted D. 46.2 and moved this text by Ulpian from its original context they eliminated the *acceptilatio* and limited Ulpian's remarks to the *novatio*. Lambrini (2006) 35–36 thoroughly discusses D. 46.2.2 but does not connect it with D. 46.4.8.3 and D. 50.17.35.

48 Cicero, *Topica* 58; see Chapter 5, Section 1 *in fine*.

49 Lenel (1889) I col. 1060, no. 636.

which comes from Book 53 of Ulpian's commentary *ad edictum* and is about the *actio aquae pluviae arcendae*. Lenel had apparently noticed some resemblance between the two texts and had inferred that D. 50.17.167.1 also bears on the *actio aquae pluviae arcendae*. Although the texts are ascribed to different jurists, we think that a comparison of the two may help explain the meaning of the *regula*.[50]

> D. 50.17.167.1 Paulus 49 ad ed. Qui iussu iudicis aliquid facit, non videtur dolo malo facere, qui parere necesse habet.
>
> Someone who does something at the order of a judge is not regarded as acting with evil intent, because he acts out of necessity.[51]
>
> D. 39.3.4 pr.: Ulpianus 53 ad ed. Quamquam autem cum domino operis tantum aquae pluviae arcendae sit, tamen Labeo scribit, si quis sepulchrum aedificaverit, ex quo aqua noceat, etiamsi operis dominus esse desierit loco facto religioso, attamen magis probandum est, inquit, aquae pluviae eum teneri: fuitenim dominus, cum opus faceret: et si iussu iudicis compulsus opus restituerit, non esse sepulchri violati actionem.
>
> Labeo writes that although an action to ward off rainwater only lies against the owner of a piece of work, nonetheless, if someone has built a tomb and water from it causes damage, despite the fact that the builder has ceased to be the owner because the site has become religious, the view is still to be approved that he is liable to an action toward off rainwater, since he was the owner at the time the work was carried out, and that if, on a judge's instructions, he restores the site to its previous condition, no action for the violation of a tomb lies.

The last sentence in Ulpian's text bears a striking resemblance to Paul's *regula*: both jurists mention a *iussum iudicis* and its consequences. Could they conceivably be referring to the same or a similar case? And what does that mean for the interpretation of D. 50.17.167.1?

50 In Chapter 4, we qualified such a *regula* as a *dubium*.

51 In a footnote to the word *qui* in *qui parere necesse habet*, Mommsen remarks that some editions have *quia*. Watson's translation has 'as being someone who', but most translations read *qui* as *quia*. This reading makes sense, because the phrase is clearly meant as an argument.

In D. 39.3.4 pr., Ulpian quotes Labeo commenting on a case about damage caused by water. The main rule is that if someone makes rainwater cause damage to somebody else, usually a neighbour, by a construction on his land, he as owner of the land is liable to the *actio aquae pluviae arcendae*.[52] In this case, the following problem arose. Somebody had built a funerary monument on his land. Later, a body was buried there so that the monument turned into a *res religiosa*.[53] From that moment on, the builder was no longer the owner. It then became evident that it had been the building of the monument that had caused water damage to someone else's land. But since the builder was no longer the owner, he was not liable to an *actio aquae pluviae arcendae*. Labeo, however, thinks the builder of the monument remains liable because he was the owner when it was built.[54]

Labeo's view creates another problem: if in the context of the *actio aquae pluviae arcendae* the judge orders the defendant to remove the monument or change it in some other way (*restituere*), the defendant might have to move or remove the body and that might expose him to an accusation of violating a tomb. Labeo opines that the defendant will not face such a charge, because he has acted on a court order.

In D. 50.17.167.1, Paul states that someone acting on a court order is not considered to act with evil intent as he is obliged to obey. As we observed, this *regula* links up with Ulpian's last sentence (quoting Labeo) in that they both refer to the *iussum iudicis*. Like Ulpian, Paul may have quoted Labeo's comment on this or a similar case; in Book 49, in which he deals with the *actio aquae pluviae arcendae*, he often refers to Labeo.[55] For that reason, and on the basis of Lenel's palingenesis, we believe it is safe to assume that in both cases the judicial order was given in the context of a trial based on the *actio aquae pluviae arcendae*.

Even so, the texts are different in two ways. First, Ulpian-quoting-Labeo refers to a particular remedy, the action for violating a tomb, as being unavailable, whereas Paul does not refer to a particular remedy but states generally that the owner is not considered to have acted with evil intent. Second, Ulpian does not explain his opinion, whereas Paul proffers the argument that the owner had to comply with the court order.[56]

52 Cf. Iav. D. 39.3.18 pr.; Pomp. D. 39.3.22.2; Ulp. D. 39.3.4. pr. and 2. On this topic, see Sitzia (1977) 174–179. It is remarkable that in D. 39.3.4 pr. the liability is twice ascribed to the *dominus operis*.

53 Cf. Gaius, *Inst.* 2.6.

54 With Horak (1969) 191, we think that this solution may be practical and just, but that it is also somewhat arbitrary because normally the former owner is not liable.

55 In D. 39.3.2.1,2, 5, 6, 7, 8, 9, and 10, and in D. 39.3.5.

56 See note 51.

While these differences do make it plausible that the two texts served different purposes, that in no way disqualifies them from referring to the same or at least a similar case. The action for violating a tomb only lies against someone who has acted with evil intent,[57] and Paul's text may for that reason also have referred to a case of tomb violation.[58] The absence of an argument in D. 39.3.4 pr. does not conclusively show that Labeo/Ulpian did not substantiate his opinion: his argument(s) may have got lost before or in Justinian's time. The compilers included Labeo's quotation in D. 39.3 from Ulpian's commentary on the edict only but preserved Paul's argument formulated as a *thesis* in D. 50.17.167.1.

Because the *regula* was formulated in general terms, it could also be used in other cases. It is impossible to verify whether at the time this was actually done. In the twentieth century, Romanists used D. 50.17.167.1 in a very different context. Nörr, for instance, mentioned this text as proof 'für das *ius imperandi* der Provinzstatthalter, das den Täter entschuldigt', and Mayer Maly regarded it as an example of the 'Exkusationseffekt' of the *parendi necessitas* of a *filius familias*.[59] It would seem that they considered D. 50.17.167.1 to be a legal rule, although it originally was not.

Our conclusion is that D. 50.17.167.1 may have belonged to a text of Paul's discussing Labeo's comment on a case in which someone was ordered by a judge to remove a tomb. His argument that this person was not liable is based on the *topos causa*: the order of the judge is the cause of the challenged act, and that is why in this case there was no evil intent. As we had occasion to observe,[60] Cicero in his *Topica* distinguishes two types of *causa*. We think the second type was applied here: the one without which the effect cannot be produced.[61]

---

57 Cf. Ulp. D. 47.12.3 pr., quoting the words of the edict.

58 Rodger (1984) 84–85 thinks that D. 50.17.167.1 deals with a completely different case. Referring to the footnote where Lenel mentions D. 39.3.4 pr., he assumes that Paul's text 'concerned a situation which may arise where the defendant in an *a.a.p.a.* has been forced by the *judex* to remove some *opus*, say an irrigation channel. If he had previously promised the land, including the irrigation channel, under a stipulation, for instance, he would normally be open to an action for *dolus* if he deliberately removed the channel prior to delivery. But where the promisor is ordered by the *judex* to remove the *opus*, the text tells us that there is no *dolus* because he has no choice but to obey.' Neither D. 39.3.4 pr. nor D. 50.17.167.1 is about irrigation channels. It is not clear to us what could have made Rodger assume they are.

59 Nörr (1965) 95 note 147; Mayer-Maly (1966) 63 note 56, referring to Nörr and to D. 50.17.169 pr.

60 In Chapter 5, note 7.

61 Cicero, *Topica* 58.

Without the court order, which had to be obeyed, the removal of the tomb would have been regarded as an act of violation.

5 Paulus D. 50.17.180

> Quod iussu alterius solvitur, pro eo est, quasi ipsi solutum esset.

In his palingenesis of Paul's work *ad Plautium*, Lenel inserted this *regula* as the penultimate sentence in a *responsum* listed as D. 12.4.9,[62] apparently believing that the two texts are closely connected. We consider whether they are and how such a connection might inform the interpretation of D. 50.17.180.

> D. 12.4.9.pr. -1 Paulus 17 ad Plaut. Si donaturus mulieri iussu eius sponso numeravi nec nuptiae secutae sunt, mulier condicet. Sed si ego contraxi cum sponso et pecuniam in hoc dedi, ut, si nuptiae secutae essent, mulieri dos adquireretur, si non essent secutae, mihi redderetur, quasi ob rem datur et re non secuta ego a sponso condicam. 1.Si quis indebitam pecuniam per errorem iussu mulieris sponso eius promisisset et nuptiae secutae fuissent, exceptione doli mali uti non potest: maritus enim suum negotium gerit et nihil dolo facit nec decipiendus est: quod fit, si cogatur indotatam uxorem habere. Itaque adversus mulierem condictio ei competit, ut aut repetat ab ea quod marito dedit aut ut liberetur, si nondum solverit.
>
> D.50.17.180 Paulus 17 ad Plaut. Quod iussu alterius solvitur, pro eo est, quasi ipsi solutum esset.
>
> D. 12.4.9 (1) Sed si soluto matrimonio maritus peteret, in eo dumtaxat exceptionem obstare debere, quod mulier receptura esset.

> I am minded to make a gift to a woman. At her request I pay her fiancé. If no marriage follows, the woman will have the *condictio*. But suppose I make a contract with the fiancé and give him money on the understanding that if the marriage follows the woman shall have it as her dowry. If no marriage happens, it must be given back to me, and I shall have my *condictio* against the fiancé as for something given for a purpose never materializing. 1. Suppose that, on the authority of a woman, someone promises her fiancé money mistakenly supposed to be owed, and the

62 Lenel (1889) I col. 1175–1176, no. 1237.

> marriage does follow. He cannot use the defense of fraud, for the husband is only looking to his own interest and is not perpetrating any fraud, nor ought he to be deceived, which he would be if forced to take an undowered wife. So the *condictio* must go against the woman either to get back from her the payment to the husband or, if nothing has yet been paid, to effect a discharge.
>
> Anything which is paid at the order of another is in the same position as something which is paid to the person himself.
>
> However, if the husband sues after the marriage has been dissolved, he ought to encounter a defense only in respect of the proportion which the woman would have taken from him.

Paul's Book 17 *ad Plautium* deals with two topics, the second one being the *condictio*, and it is under this heading that Lenel inserted the *responsum* known as D. 12.4.9. The compilers included it in book D. 12.4 (*De condictione causa data causa non secuta*), except for the penultimate sentence: that was moved to D. 50.17.

In D. 12.4.9, four cases are discussed whose common denominator is that they are about an outsider securing a dowry for a woman to bring to her future marriage. In the first two cases, described in the *principium*, the outsider provides the dowry to make a gift to the woman, but the intended marriage does not take place.[63] The other two cases are found in D. 12.4.9.1; in both, the outsider promises the dowry to pay a debt to the woman, the marriage is concluded, but the debt turns out to be non-existent. The second case additionally reports that the marriage was later dissolved. Lenel inserted the *regula* of D. 50.17.180 in D. 12.4.9.1, between these two cases. This insertion can be taken to imply that Lenel regarded the *regula* as forming part of the first case in D. 12.4.9.1. Is there a connection between the *regula* and this case?

The first case in D. 12.4.9.1 is about someone who thinks he owes money to a woman and who at her order (*iussum*) promises in a stipulation to her fiancé to pay him this money by way of dowry. The marriage is concluded and the husband claims payment of the promised sum, probably using the *condictio*. By then, however, the outsider has discovered that he does not in fact owe the woman money. The question is whether he has to pay the money regardless, and if he has already done so, how he can get it back. According to Paul, the praetor will not grant the outsider an *exceptio doli* against the husband's

63 In the second case, the outsider can recover the money with the *condictio causa data causa non secuta*, and that is why the compilers included the text in D. 12.4.

condictio, because the husband is only looking to his own interest, has not committed any fraud, and should not be deceived either.[64] In other words, the outsider must pay. Paul does add, however, that he can bring the *condictio* against the wife to claim from her the money he paid to her husband or, if he has not paid yet, to obtain a discharge.

In D. 50.17.180, Paul states that anything paid at the order of another is in the same position as something paid to the person himself. In other words, he is referring to the effect of *delegatio*: the payment by the debtor to a third party at the order of the creditor ranks as payment to the creditor himself.

We think there is a connection between the *regula* and the first case of D. 12.4.9.1. First, the *regula* contains two elements that are also essential to the case of D. 12.4.9.1: the order of the creditor to the debtor and the payment by that debtor to a third party. Second, in the *regula* and in the first case of D. 12.4.9.1 the legal question turns on the relationship between the original creditor and the debtor. In her monograph on the *delegatio* in Roman law (1971), Sacconi raised doubts about the two texts being connected. We now discuss her view.

Sacconi assumes that Roman law made a dogmatic distinction between *delegatio dandi* or *solvendi* (belonging to the law of property) and the *delegatio promittendi* (belonging to the law of obligations) that was developed in the second century AD. In either scenario, the creditor (*delegans*) issues a *iussum* to the debtor (*delegatus*), but in the first scenario the *iussum* is followed by a *datio* or *traditio* of the *delegatus* to the third party (*delegataris*), whereas in the second scenario the *iussum* is followed by a *promissio* of the *delegatus* to the *delegataris*. For both types of *delegatio* it was assumed that payment and promise, respectively, led to liberation of the *delegatus* (from his obligation to the *delegans*), but in the second century this was limited to the *stipulatio* and finally abolished, Sacconi contends. For her, both D. 50.17.180 and D. 12.4.9.1 are important, but for different reasons, and they therefore figure in her book in different places.

Sacconi avers that Paul. D. 50.17.180 concerns the *delegatio dandi*, the subject of the first chapter in her book. This text and two other texts by Paul, Sacconi argues, demonstrate that payment by the *delegatus* to the *delegatarius* is considered to have been done by the *delegatus* to the *delegans*.[65] The *iussum* of the *delegans* would have been the crucial element in this construction. In a

64 Not bringing a dowry was regarded as dishonourable, for both the husband and the wife. Cf. Tellegen and Leesen (2016) 123–124.

65 Sacconi (1971) 6: '[O]pera sul presupposto di una finzione di pagamento (…) del delegato al delegante e del delegante al delegatario.' The other two texts are D. 46.3.56 and D. 46.3.64.

footnote to D. 50.17.180 Sacconi discusses the possible connection between this text and D. 12.4.9.1.[66] Before dealing with this footnote, we briefly outline her interpretation of D. 12.4.9.1.

Sacconi treats D. 12.4.9.1 in the second chapter of her book, which is about the *delegatio promittendi*,[67] paying particular attention to the phrase in which Paul states that the supposed debtor has a *condictio* against the wife either to claim from her the money he paid to her husband or, if he did not pay yet, to effect a discharge. Sacconi infers from this phrase that the *stipulatio* by the *delegatus* to the *delegataris* did not lead to a discharge between the *delegatus* and the *delegans*. Only the actual payment to make good the *promissio* made by the *delegatus* to the *delegataris* is considered to effect a shift of property between the *delegatus* and the *delegans*.

Rather than consider the merits of Sacconi's interpretation of the two texts[68] we return to the footnote in which she comments on the potential connection between D. 50.17.180 and D. 12.4.9.1. She claims that Lenel inserted D. 50.17.180 after the first full sentence in D. 12.4.9.1, where Paul states that if the *delegatus* promised money to the fiancé and the marriage follows, he cannot use an *exceptio doli* against the *condictio* of the husband (*Si quis … indotatam uxorem habere*). Sacconi doubts whether D. 50.17.180 fits in as a justification, because in D. 12.4.9.1 the obligation to pay was based on the *promissio* of the *delegatus* to the husband. However, this promise was in its turn based on the woman's *iussum promittendi*, whereas in D. 50.17.180 the right of the *delegatus* to reclaim the money from the woman (*delegans*) would be based on a *iussum solvendi*. Sacconi concludes that Lenel should not have inserted D. 50.17.180 in D. 12.4.9.1. Thirty years later, Alonso endorsed this view in his monograph on the *delegatio*.[69]

The devil is in the details, for Sacconi may be in error: Lenel inserted D. 50.17.180 not after the *first* but after the *second* full sentence in D. 12.4.9.1, that is to say, after Paul's remark that the *delegatus* has the *condictio* against the woman either to recover what he had unduly paid to the husband or to effect a discharge. And here, D. 50.17.180 does seem to fit. The words *Quod iussu*

66 Sacconi (1971) 4 note 11.

67 Sacconi (1971) 81–84.

68 See the rather critical reviews by Sturm (1971) 260–269 and Wagner (1974) 452–465.

69 Alonso (2001) 189 note 10. Zandrino (2010) 59 note 128 does mention both texts but only with reference to the terms *iussum solvendi* (D. 50.17.180) and *iussum promittendi* (D. 12.4.9.1). Stagl (2009) 173–174 refers to Lenel's *Palingenesia* in his discussion of D.12.4.9.1 but he ignores the *regula* Lenel inserted in this text. Giomari and Beccari (2022) 501–502 rule out that the *regula* formed part of D. 12.4.9.

alterius solvitur in D. 50.17.180 do not exclude that this payment is based on a *iussum promittendi*, because the *promissio* meant that the *delegatus* would pay a certain sum of money to the *delegataris* to settle a debt he owed the *delegans*. We believe it is entirely possible that D. 12.4.9.1 and D. 50.17.180 referred to the same case of *delegatio* based on a *iussum promittendi*. How would such a case have unfolded?

After the debtor had promised, in a *stipulatio* to the fiancé, that he would pay him a sum of money he thought he owed the woman, and after the marriage had taken place, he discovered that he in actual fact did not owe her anything. Yet the husband could now claim the money on the basis of the *stipulatio*. According to Paul, while the debtor could not rely on an *exceptio* and would therefore have to pay, he could in his turn claim the money from the woman. Naturally, he could not do so if he himself had not yet paid the money to the husband, in which case, Paul stated, he could demand a discharge from her.

The *regula* of D. 50.17.180 only refers to the scenario where the husband had succeeded in making the debtor pay. The fact that the debtor then had recourse to the *condictio* against the wife can only be logically explained if what he had paid to the husband is considered to have been paid to the wife. This is exactly Paul's argument in D. 50.17.180, and we believe Lenel was right to have inserted it here.

The argument formulated in D. 50.17.180 makes perfect sense in the context of D. 12.4.9.1. It is a rhetorical argument that brings to mind one of the two types of the *topos ex causa*: the creditor's *iussum* was the cause of the debtor's promise by *stipulatio* to the creditor's fiancé.[70] But it appeared that the *iussum* was based on a mistake, namely a spurious claim. Consequently, what was paid to the husband after the marriage had been concluded on the basis of the *iussum* could be considered unduly paid to the creditor and could be reclaimed with a *condictio*. And as the argument is formulated as a *thesis*, the compilers included it in D. 50.17.

70 Cicero, *Topica* 58.

CHAPTER 6

The *status definitio*: The *topos e contrario*

1 Pomponius D. 50.17.7

> Ius nostrum non patitur eundem in paganis et testato et intestato decessisse: earumque rerum naturaliter inter se pugna est 'testatus' et 'intestatus'.

This *regula* stems from the third book of Pomponius' commentary *ad Sabinum* titled *De testamentis*.[1] In a footnote to this text, Lenel suggests a connection between it and the next one.[2] This other text, D. 28.5.19, comes from Ulpian's commentary on Sabinus, with Ulpian quoting several jurists, including Pomponius. The jurists in D. 28.5.19 discuss a problem concerning the division of shares of an inheritance.[3] If Lenel is right, then it is conceivable that the two texts originally concerned the same case. To find out, we discuss both texts. They read as follows.

> D. 50.17.7 Pomponius 3 ad Sabinum. Ius nostrum non patitur eundem in paganis et testato et intestato decessisse: earumque rerum naturaliter inter se pugna est 'testatus' et 'intestatus'.
>
> D. 28.5.19 Ulpianus 7 ad Sabinum. Ex facto etiam agitatum Pomponius et Arrianus deferunt, si quis vacua parte relicta ita instituerit: 'si mihi Seius heres non erit', quem non instituerat, 'Sempronius heres esto', an hic occupare possit vacantem portionem. Et Pegasus quidem existimat ad eam partem admitti: Aristo contra putat, quia huic pars esset data, quae nulla esset: quam sententiam et Iavolenus probat et Pomponius et Arrianus et hoc iure utimur.

---

1 Lenel (1889) II col. 90, no. 410.

2 Note 6: *Ad fr.* 410.411 cf. *Ulp.* 7 *ad Sab. sub rubr.* '*de portionum distributione*'. In note 7, at the end of this text, Lenel refers to Ulp. D. 28.5.13.2, which deals with the division of the inheritance in a case where the testator left a quarter of the inheritance to each of the two heirs: the part that was not divided should go to the two heirs as well.

3 In the *praefatio* to the first part of his *Palingenesia*, under V, Lenel explains his inserting this kind of indirect *responsa*. He included D. 28.5.19 in *Pal.* II col. 1036–1037, under no. 2489.

 | DOI:10.1163/9789004711020_007

> Our law does not allow the same person among civilians to die both testate and intestate; for there is a natural conflict between the states of 'testate' and 'intestate'.
>
> Pomponius and Arrianus relate a case which occurred and is also discussed: If someone, leaving one share unfulfilled, made an institution as follows, 'if Seius,' whom he had not instituted, 'shall not be heir to me, let Sempronius be heir,' can the latter claim the vacant share of the inheritance? And Pegasus, in fact, considers that he can be admitted to that share; Aristo thinks the opposite, because he had been given a share which did not exist; and Javolenus approves this view, as do Pomponius and Arrianus, and this is the law we apply.

De testamentis, the third book of Pomponius' commentary *ad Sabinum*, carries the subtitle *De adquirenda vel omittenda hereditate*, 'On acquiring and waiving an inheritance'. Book 7 of Ulpian's commentary *ad Sabinum* is also titled *De testamentis* and consists of two parts, the first one dealing with acquiring and waiving an inheritance and the second one with the division of shares of an inheritance. It is at the end of this second part that Lenel included D. 28.5.19. In the Digest, Ulpian's fragment has been included in Book 28.5 *De heredibus instituendis*, 'On instituting heirs'.

The Romanist literature we consulted does not explicitly connect D. 50.17.7 to D. 28.5.19, but both texts have been studied separately. We first summarise and discuss some modern commentaries and then ascertain whether a combined reading of the two texts advances understanding of the *regula* of D. 50.17.7.

D. 50.17.7 is one of the sources underpinning the rule *Nemo pro parte testatus pro parte intestatus decedere potest* as formulated in Romanist literature, and several authors regard it as a fundamental principle of the Roman law of succession.[4] The other sources are Cicero's *De inventione*, a text in the Digest, and a text in Justinian's Institutes.[5] The essence of the principle is that if a testator did not dispose of his entire estate or if an instituted heir refused the inheritance or was disqualified from inheriting, then what is left does not accrue to

4 Voci (1967) 496 and Kaser (1971) 677, both with sources and literature. See also Pérez Simeón (2001) 363.

5 Specifically, Cicero, *De inv.* 2.63 (on pupillary substitution), Ulp. D. 29.1.6 (on a soldier's will), and *Inst.* 2.14.5 (on dividing shares of an inheritance).

the intestate heirs but to the other testamentary heirs in proportion to their share. Soldiers' wills are excepted; to these, the principle does not apply.[6]

Scholarly discussion of D. 50.17.7 has mainly turned on the origin of the rule, which in recent times has been sought in the *mancipatio familiae:* the whole property was mancipated to the *familiae emptor*, who, according to Gaius, was *heredis loco*.[7] This leads Voci to conclude that the second half of D. 50.17.7 must have been interpolated: the compilers could not base their argument on a legal institution like the *mancipatio*, because it had long gone out of use, and they therefore introduced a distinction, between *testatus* and *intestatus*, which in itself carries no significance.[8]

Voci's conclusion is not shared by Pérez Simeón in his monograph on the rule *Nemo pro parte testatus pro parte intestatus decedere potest*.[9] In his view, Pomponius may describe a principle dating back to the third or second century BC but explains it using a terminological rather than a historical argument. The words *testatus* and *intestatus* exclude each other: they specify that *naturaliter* there is a conflict between the terms, not between the legal institutions of intestate succession and succession by will. Furthermore, Pérez Simeón explicitly endorses Lenel's suggestion that D. 50.17.7 may refer to the missing out on a share, but he does not mention D. 28.5.19, not even in his Chapter on the 'vacancia de una cuota hereditaria'; instead, he summarily points to the diversity of topics in the third book of Pomponius' commentary on Sabinus and merely urges caution.[10]

We now turn to D. 28.5.19, which Talamanca extensively discusses in a long article on the division of the shares of an inheritance.[11] In his view, this text is about the question of whether the *condicio institutionis* must be identified with the *condicio substitutionis*. The *prudentes* disagreed with each other. Pegasus considered substitution to be a normal conditional institution of an heir; the

---

6 That is why in this text Pomponius used the words *in paganis* in the sense of 'among civilians, non-military persons'. For other exceptions, cf. Voci (1967) 497- 498 and Pérez Simeón (2001) 384.

7 Gaius, *Inst.* 2.103 and 105. For a summary of the discussion, see Schmidlin (1970) 62–66.

8 Voci (1967) 499–500.

9 Pérez Simeón (2001) 382 note 41.

10 Pérez Simeón (2001) 366–379 does deal with Cicero, *De inv.* 2.62–64. He concludes that as an orator Cicero applied the *Nemo pro parte* principle in a different way than the jurists did: he used it from the heirs' perspective, whereas the jurists did so from the testator's perspective. And while Cicero's purpose was to convince his audience, the jurists' goal was to explain the only correct solution, Pérez Simeón contends. For the record, in D. 28.5.19 the jurists take on the problem raised there from the *heirs'* perspective and reach a *majority* solution.

11 Talamanca (1995–1996) 620–630.

condition was fulfilled and so the substitution came into operation.[12] Aristo differed, arguing that the substitution was invalid, not because the relevant institution of the heir was missing, but because he regarded Sempronius as having been instituted heir of a *pars nulla*, a non-existing share.[13] Talamanca expresses surprise that neither jurist referred to the testator's intention, and he rejects the notion of Seius, who had not been instituted as heir, being an heir upon intestacy, because the *responsum* does not say so.

In our view, the interpretations of D. 50.17.7 and D. 28.5.19 presented above are inconclusive. As to D. 50.17.7, if the *Nemo pro parte* rule had truly been a fundamental principle of Roman law, it would not merely have featured in a supporting role in a discussion about a soldier's will,[14] nor would it have been casually mentioned in the description of the number of shares into which an inheritance was usually divided.[15] Moreover, it is by no means inevitable that the second half of this text is an interpolation, as Voci concludes. Quite the contrary. The phrase *naturaliter inter se pugna est* is a stylish metaphor that works well in an argument. As for Pérez Simeón's interpretation of D. 50.17.7, it, too, and for three reasons, lacks conviction. First, the incompatibility of the two modes of succession cannot properly be said to be a consequence of the contrast between the terms *testatus* and *intestatus*; these are merely terms conceived and used to express an inherent incompatibility. Second, Simeón does not examine a potential connection between D. 50.17.7 and D. 28.5.19. And third, he completely ignores the latter text in his monograph.

Talamanca's interpretation of D. 28.5.19 also fails to sway us. To begin with, his reconstruction of Pegasus' argument impresses us as arbitrary: it may be right, but it may also be wrong. Originally, the text may have contained his argument, but later it may have been left out since Pegasus' opinion was not generally accepted. There is simply no way of knowing for sure. Furthermore, Talamanca's explanation of Aristo's argument seems strained. The only established fact is that Aristo rejected Sempronius' claim because it concerned a non-existing share. Also, we think that Talamanca has little cause for surprise that the *voluntas testatoris* is ignored: not only is the testator's intention far from clear, intention did not have the argumentative force modern Romanists tend to think it had.[16] But by far the most pressing objection to Talamanca's interpretation is that it bypasses the essence of the legal problem, namely that

12 Talamanca (1995–1996) 624.
13 Talamanca (1995–1996) 628.
14 D. 29.1.6. See our observation about one of the exceptions to the principle in note 6.
15 Just. *Inst.* 2.14.5.
16 See Tellegen-Couperus and Tellegen (2016) 35–46.

Seius, who had not been an instituted heir in the will, must have been an heir upon intestacy. How else can it be explained that the testator thought Seius stood to inherit in any case and that it was not necessary to explicitly appoint him as heir in his will? The actual problem is that the testator did not dispose of his entire estate in his will, and that the question now is to whom the non-allotted share accrues: to the intestate heir and through him to the substitute, or to the other testamentary heirs? In other words, the real problem concerns the division of the shares.

A more plausible interpretation, we believe, requires reading D. 28.5.19 together with D. 50.17.7. D. 28.5.19 points to a dispute between Pomponius and his otherwise unknown contemporary Arrianus[17] over a problem concerning the law of succession which earlier (late first to early second century AD) had also caused two other jurists, Pegasus and Aristo, to disagree. The problem concerned a testator who appointed several persons as heirs whose combined shares did not make up the full 12/12ths of his estate and who included a substitution for a person whom he had not explicitly instituted as heir: 'If Seius shall not be heir to me, let Sempronius be heir.'[18] It is more than likely that Seius was an intestate heir and that the testator mistakenly thought that Seius therefore did not have to be appointed heir in the will. By the time the will was opened Seius had died, and the testamentary heirs and the substitute heir Sempronius found themselves at loggerheads over the non-allotted share.

The testamentary heirs will most likely have argued that the non-allotted share accrues to them by virtue of the *ius accrescendi*, while Sempronius will doubtlessly have claimed it under the testamentary substitution. Pegasus represented Sempronius and Aristo assisted the testamentary heirs. Perhaps their respective schools, the *Proculiani* and *Sabiniani*, were also involved, for Pegasus was the leader of the *Proculiani* and Aristo, as a student of their leader Cassius Longinus, probably belonged to the *Sabiniani*. Moreover, Iavolenus Priscus, who later became the leader of the *Sabiniani*, agreed with Aristo.[19] Later, when Pomponius and Arrianus and later again Ulpian seconded Aristo's

17 On Arrianus, see Kunkel (1967) 243.

18 Ulpian's use of the word *instituerit* is confusing because it refers to the institution of an heir whereas in this case it actually refers to a substitute.

19 In this way, the conflict turned into a school controversy. This frequently happened when the leaders of the two schools, who had the *ius respondendi*, entertained contradictory opinions about a legal problem. See Tellegen (1988) and Leesen (2010) 21–27. According to Kunkel (1967) 141, Aristo was not a leader of a school but together with Iavolenus and Neratius he numbered among the most prominent jurists of his day. On Aristo and the *ius respondendi*, see Kunkel (1967) 318–320.

point of view, the schools had lost their relevance. By then, Aristo's view had prevailed.

Of the arguments brought forward by the contending parties only the one Aristo offered has been retained in D. 28.5.19: Sempronius could not inherit, because as a substitute he had been allotted a share that did not exist, that is to say, a share for which no heir had been instituted in the will. This argument is aimed at the case in question in rhetorical terms; it is formulated as a *hypothesis*.

It is conceivable that the text known as D. 50.17.7 also served as an argument in this conflict. Pomponius may have argued that Sempronius could not claim the share left to him by means of substitution, because that would imply that the estate would accrue partly to the testamentary heirs and partly to an intestate heir. More in general, he observed that Roman law does not allow that someone dies both with and without a will. Because this argument was formulated in general terms, as a *thesis*, it was included by the compilers as a *regula iuris* in title D. 50.17. By juxtaposing testate and intestate succession, Pomponius applied the *topos e contrario* of the kind Cicero called *privantia*:[20]

> [48] Sunt enim alia contraria, quae privantia licet appellemus Latine, Graeci appellant *sterètiká*. Praeposito enim 'in' privatur verbum ea vi quam haberet si 'in' praepositum non fuisset, dignitas indignitas, humanitas inhumanitas, et cetera generis eiusdem, quorum tractactio est eadem quae superiorum quae adversa dixi.
>
> For there are other contraries which we may call *privantia* (privatives) in Latin; the Greeks call them *steretika*. For if 'in' is prefixed, a word loses the force which it would have if 'in' were not prefixed, such as dignity and indignity, humanity and inhumanity and others of this sort; these are handled in the same way as the former class which I called 'opposites.'

Our conclusion is that a combined reading of the two texts admits of an interpretation that is more straightforward and more secure than can be achieved by attempting to understand them in isolation. If Voci and Pérez Simeón had connected D. 50.17.7 with D. 28.5.19, they might well have realised that the *regula* was in fact a rhetorical argument, not a fundamental legal principle. If Talamanca had similarly connected the two texts, he might likely have recognised that the legal problem in D. 28.5.19 turned on the division of the shares of an inheritance and that the *regula* in D. 50.17.7 offers a precise argumentative

20 Cicero, *Topica* 48.

fit. In sum, there is a great deal of merit to Lenel's suggestion that the two texts belong together.

2 Paulus D. 50.17.10

> Secundum naturam est commoda cuiusque rei eum sequi, quem sequentur incommoda.

Originating from the third book of Paul's commentary *ad Sabinum*, this text was included by Lenel as the last one of a group of four texts.[21] We explore whether there is a connection between D. 50.17.10 and the penultimate text, D.36.1.20, and particularly with its last *lex*, D. 36.1.20.2.

> D. 36.1.20.2 Paulus 3 ad Sab. Qui in distrahendis conservandisve rebus hereditariis sumptus factus est, imputari heredi debet.
>
> D. 50.17.10 Paulus 3 ad Sab. Secundum naturam est commoda cuiusque rei eum sequi, quem sequentur incommoda.

> The expense which is incurred in disposing of or in preserving the goods which form part of the inheritance should be charged on the heir.
>
> It is according to nature for the advantages of anything to attach to the person to whom the disadvantages attach.

Lenel noted that the third book of Paul's commentary *ad Sabinum* is about legacies, and in a footnote at the beginning of D. 50.17.10, he stated that *haec* ('these fragments') also seem to refer to the *legatum partitionis*, the legacy of a portion of a testator's estate.[22] We take this observation to mean that this legal concept is the topic of both D. 50.17.10 and D. 36.1.20.2, and their content appears to link up with the first two texts of this group, D. 30.15 and 23, which explicitly deal with the legacy of a portion of a testator's estate.

D. 36.1 is titled *Ad Senatus Consultum Trebellianum.* This senatorial decision dating from the time of the Emperor Nero pertains to the *fideicommissum* of a portion of an estate, regulating the relationship between the heir and the

21 Lenel (1889) I col. 1256, no. 1638.

22 *Haec quoque spectare videntur ad partitionem legatam.* The term *partitio legata*, commonly used in Romanist literature, does not appear in the sources. We follow Voci (1963) 343 and use the term *legatum partitionis*.

beneficiary of the bequest. The compilers included D. 36.1.20 here because its first two *leges* deal with this topic.

D. 36.1.20.2 answers the question who must meet the costs of selling or preserving assets of an estate: only the heir or someone else, too? Given that the context is the *legatum partitionis* or the *fideicommissum universale*, this other person may have been the beneficiary to whom a portion of the estate has been left by legacy or *fideicommissum*. For a proper understanding of D. 36.1.20.2 it is necessary to first explain the two legal concepts involved, the *legatum partitionis* and the *fideicommissum universale*.

A testator could order his testamentary heir to share the inheritance with a legatee by including a *legatum partitionis* in his will. This type of legacy was probably introduced to mitigate the effects of the *lex Voconia* of 169 BC; this law forbade wealthy Romans from instituting women as their heirs and limited the size of legacies that could be left to women.[23] As was usual, the ability of the legatee to collect on his claim depended on the heir accepting the inheritance: if a testator disposed of his entire estate by means of legacies, the heir would have no reason to accept the inheritance and the legacies would consequently lapse. In an attempt to moderate this effect, in 40 BC the *lex Falcidia* was introduced, ordaining that a testator could not bequeath more than three quarters of his estate in the form of legacies.[24] This law also applied to the *legatum partitionis*. Because only the heir was able to collect what was owed to the estate and only the heir could be sued for what the estate owed to others, it was customary for the heir and the legatee to promise to each other by means of stipulations to share the payments and the claims (*stipulationes partis et pro parte*).

In the early Empire, a testator could also use the less formal *fideicommissum* to divide his estate between his heir(s) and a third party, the *fideicommissarius*.[25] Initially, the heir(s) and the *fideicommissarius* had to guarantee to each other by means of stipulations that they would share the receipts and expenditure for the estate. In the middle of the first century AD, the *Senatus Consultum Trebellianum* ensured that this effect could be achieved with one legal act. If all of the estate were transferred, under the *ius honorarium*, the *fideicommissarius* would be *heredis loco*; if a portion was transferred, the heir would be entitled to

23 On the *legatum partitionis*, see Van der Meer (1996) 99–101 with sources and literature. See also Voci (1963) 343–344.

24 On the *lex Falcidia*, see Voci (1963) 755–789.

25 The *fideicommissum* was already used in the late Republic but it was the Emperor Augustus who made it enforceable at law. On the *fideicommissum* of part of an estate, see Voci (1963) 344–368.

the remainder of the estate. The *Senatus Consultum Pegasianum*, dating from the time of the Emperor Vespasian, offered protection to the heir in much the same way the *lex Falcidia* did: the testator could not bequeath more than three quarters of his estate through *fideicommissa*.

In the early Empire, the two forms of bequeathing a portion of an estate existed side by side, but because the relevant rules were rather complicated there was often confusion about the rights and duties of the parties.[26] That may have been the case in D. 36.1.20.2 as well. We now aim to reconstruct the case, assuming that it turned on a *legatum partitionis*.[27]

A testator instituted one person as his heir and in his will included a legacy ordering his heir to share a portion of the estate with another person. The testator died, and the testamentary heir accepted his inheritance. Consequently, he had to wind up the estate and pay over the legacy. This may have been a complicated business that took some time. In that time, the heir had to spend money to sell assets belonging to the estate (for instance, valuation costs) and to preserve the assets belonging to the estate (for instance, the cost of living for the slaves). It appears that the heir then tried to charge these expenses to the legacy. But the legatee, supported by Paul, objected to this tactic, insisting that the heir alone must meet these costs.

D. 50.17.10 could have served as an argument: it is only natural for the advantages of anything to attach to the person to whom the disadvantages attach. Could this argument have worked in the case at issue in D. 36.1.20.2? There the starting point is the expense, the disadvantage, whereas the argument in D. 50.17.10 is premised on the advantage. In Romanist literature, there is a long record of the two texts having met with some confusion, both separately and together.[28]

From as early as the sixteenth century, scholars have doubted whether Paul really took the view that the heir should bear the costs of selling and maintaining assets of the estate. Gothofredus, for instance, construed the word *heredi* in D. 36.1.20.2 to mean *fideicommissarius*, and a certain Jensius was in favour of either inserting *non* before *heredi* or taking the dative as an ablative (*ab*

26 Kaser (1971) 745 claims that the *legatum partitionis* was later superseded ('verdrängt') by the *fideicommissum hereditatis*. We are unsure what he means. The late classical jurist Paul discussed both types of bequest in his commentary on Sabinus.

27 As Lenel believed, see above at note 2. Voci (1963) 364, however, refers to D. 36.1.20.2 in the context of the *fideicommissum hereditatis*.

28 Stagl (2007) 687 mentions D. 50.17.10 in his article 'Die Ausgleichung von Vorteil und Nachteil als Inhalt klassischer "aequitas"' but he ignores the content of this text and its possible connection with D. 36.1.20.2. The same holds for Harke (2014) 88 note 180 who suggests that originally D. 50.17.10 may have referred to a contract of sale.

herede impetrari debet), implying in either case that those costs should not be charged *to* but *by* the heir.[29] In his *editio maior* of the Digest, Mommsen suggested that the word *heredi* be read as *hereditati*, but he added a question mark; in the *editio stereotypa*, Krüger repeated this emendation in a footnote, without the question mark.[30] Of the modern translators, d'Ors and Spruit included the emendation *hereditati* in their translations and so essentially changed the purport of D. 36.1.20.2.[31]

The reason why in this case Paul's opinion has caused confusion is to be found in one of the next texts in this title, D. 36.1.23.3, where Ulpian states that the heir who has incurred expenses for the benefit of the estate may deduct them.[32] Other jurists, like Julian and Modestinus, also held this opinion, and in itself it does seem a reasonable enough view.[33]

Still, we prefer to read Paul's *responsum* as it has been preserved in the *Florentina* manuscript and to assume that Paul meant to express the view that the heir had to pay the costs of selling and maintaining assets of the estate. For one thing, the circumstances of the case may have prompted Paul to take this view: the text as it has been preserved in the Digest, for instance, contains no information on the shares of the heir and the legatee. Moreover, there is reason to assume Paul did not inevitably regard Ulpian's view as being conclusive in all matters. In another case concerning a *legatum partitionis*, Paul states that the late Emperor Hadrian had laid down in a rescript that neither the value of the slaves that had been freed in the will nor the costs of the burial should be charged to the legacy.[34] It would certainly appear that in D. 36.1.20.2 Paul essentially applied Hadrian's rescript.

Apart from the confusion about the interpretation of D. 36.1.20.2, there is also confusion about the question of whether the *regula* of D. 50.17.10 may have served as an argument for this case. The problem is that D. 36.1.20.2 turns on the question of who had to bear certain costs for the benefit of the estate, or in other words, who was to have the disadvantage, whereas D. 50.17.10 (the advantage attaches to the person who has the disadvantage) seems to answer

---

29 The reference to Gothofredus and Jensius can be found in Otto, Schilling, and Sintenis (1831) 730 note 28.

30 Mommsen and Krüger (1870) 235 note 7; Mommsen and Krüger (1872) 566 note 32 referring to Mommsen. It is impossible to check when this subtle change was made.

31 d'Ors (1972) 692 has 'debe imputarse a <la herencia>'; Spruit (2000) 145 has 'aan de nalatenschap worden doorberekend', adding a footnote about the change.

32 Ulp. D. 36.1.23.3 *Sed et ipse si quem sumptum fecit in res hereditarias, detrahet.* Voci (1963) 364 note 104 mistakenly also mentions D. 36.1.20.2 here.

33 E.g., Jul. D. 30.104.7 (dowry); Mod. D. 31.9 (dowry and manumissions).

34 Paul. D. 31.8.5.

the question of who is to have the advantage. In modern literature, various conclusions have been drawn. Van den Bergh, for instance, thinks D. 50.17.10 is too pompous to have served as an 'argument explicatif' in a simple case like D. 36.1.20.2.[35] Moreover, he contends, the two texts contradict each other, the one saying that he who has the advantage should also have the disadvantage, the other saying exactly the reverse. With Lenel, Van den Bergh agrees that D. 50.17.10 may have dealt with the *legatum partitionis*, but in his view D. 50.17.10 and D. 36.1.20.2 are completely unconnected.

Harder, on the other hand, thinks they are connected because they both refer to the *legatum partitionis*.[36] Moreover, he compares D. 36.1.20.2 with a remark by Gaius in *Inst.* 2.254 about the *pro rato* division of gain and loss between heir and legatee, and then concludes that Paul's argument in D. 50.17.10 complements the idea of a fair division between heir and legatee in a natural and consistent way.

We agree with neither scholar. Unlike Van den Bergh, we think that D. 36.1.20.2 does not contradict D. 50.17.10 per se. The former text contains Paul's opinion on a particular legal question, whereas D.50.17.10 is formulated *in abstracto* and as such could be an argument for this opinion. And as an argument, we want to stress, D. 50.17.10 is hardly pompous; it is merely formulated in general terms. Harder's comment offers little to further our understanding: he is right in pointing out the common topic of D. 36.1.20.2, D. 50.17.10, and Gaius' *Inst.* 2.254, but he fails to explain how D. 50.17.10 can relate to D. 36.1.20.2.

We conclude this section by addressing that issue. How could the *regula* of D. 50.17.10 have served as an argument for the case described in D. 36.1.20.2? Again, we run up against the problem that this text of Paul contains very little information on the case. We reconstruct the respective arguments of the heir and the legatee as follows. The heir would have stated that the legatee must share in the costs of maintaining and selling assets of the estate, because they have expressly agreed to do so by means of *stipulationes partis et pro parte*. To which the legatee could have replied that these stipulations do not refer to new debts but to the assets and liabilities of the estate existing at the time when the heir accepted the inheritance. In other words, the legatee could have used a strictly legal argument. Instead, he opted for the rhetorical argument that once the heir had accepted the inheritance, he had acquired the estate's assets and that it consequently fell to him to meet the costs of maintaining and selling the

35 Van den Bergh (1971) 37–38.

36 Harder (1976) 364, though in a completely different context, namely, that of the *actio furti* as a replacing *commodum* in a contract of sale. In his view, D. 36.1.20.2 dealt with 'Surrogate von Erbschaftssachen'.

assets of the estate.[37] This rhetorical argument is then formulated in general terms, as a *thesis*: it is only natural for the advantages of anything to attach to the person to whom the disadvantages attach. By taking the heir's benefits as a starting point, the legatee strengthened his argument that the heir also had to bear the burdens. It is clear that he, or rather Paul, used the *topos e contrario* by contrasting advantage (*commoda*) and disadvantage (*incommoda*), more specifically opting for the variant of the *privantia* by using the prefix *in*.[38] In addition to his skillful and deliberate use of a *topos,* Paul gives the argument an elegant rhetorical nudge through the figure of speech of chiasmus: *commoda … sequi – sequentur incommoda.*

This reading helps us make sense of the argument's new surroundings. The compilers moved the argument as they found it to title D. 50.17. By simply pasting it into another context, they, probably inadvertently, created an uneasy fit. When the question is who has to suffer the disadvantages of something, one would expect the answer to be the person who benefits from its advantages. Instead, and possibly out of respect for their source, they kept it as they found it, supporting our hypothesis that the *regulae* in this title were not legal rules or principles but rhetorical arguments formulated in general terms for greater effect and intended to be used in one particular case only.

3 Paulus D. 50.17.29

> Quod initio vitiosum est, non potest tractu temporis convalescere.

D. 50.17.29 stems from Book 8 of Paul's commentary on Sabinus, and Lenel included this text after D. 26.8.3, under a separate number.[39] He did not suggest that the two texts are *leges geminatae* but in modern literature scholars have assumed that there is a connection between them. For that reason, we examine both texts and ascertain whether combining them can help clarify the meaning of D. 50.17.29.

37 This is not unique: in Ulp. D. 2.14.10.2, the jurist Trebatius ignores the legal argument he could use and instead uses a rhetorical argument to support his view. Cf. Tellegen and Leesen (2016) 114–120.

38 Cicero, *Topica* 48.

39 Lenel (1889) I col. 1276, nos. 1783 and 1784.

> D. 26.8.3 Paulus 8 ad Sab. Etiamsi non interrogatus tutor auctor fiat, valet auctoritas eius, cum se probare dicit id quod agitur: hoc est enim auctorem fieri.
>
> D.50.17.29 Paulus 8 ad Sab. Quod initio vitiosum est, non potest tractu temporis convalescere.
>
> Even if a tutor gives his authority without being questioned, his authorization is valid, since he says that he approves what is being done; for this is the meaning of authorization.
>
> Something which is defective at the outset cannot be validated with the passage of time.

Book 8 of Paul's commentary on Sabinus is titled *De tutelis*. In the Digest, title D. 26.8 carries the heading *De auctoritate et consensu tutorum et curatorum*. This suggests that both texts relate to guardianship and particularly to the granting of authority by the guardian for transactions carried out by his ward. In a footnote to D. 50.17.29, Lenel mentioned a text by Gaius which is also included in title D. 26.8 and which he thought might be comparable with Paul's *regula*.[40]

In Romanist literature, D. 50.17.29 is often referred to, but D. 26.8.3 is not. In discussions about the 'convalescence' of an invalid act, scholars often state that classical Roman law did not allow this kind of retroactive remedy and that D. 50.17.29 concisely expressed it so.[41] Moreover, they often regard this *regula* as a legal rule that the Roman jurists applied in all sorts of situations,[42] and it is a rare occasion that an attempt is made to explain D. 50.17.29 in its original context, guardianship. Two such attempts, relatively recent ones, are those by Schanbacher and Potjewijd.

40 He referred to D. 26.8.9.5, adding a question mark.

41 In a legal context, the verb *convalescere* means 'to become valid'. Heumann and Seckel (1907) 106 *ad locum* explain it as follows: 'besonders gebraucht, wenn in Frage kommt, ob anfänglich unwirksame Rechtsgeschäfte infolge späterer Ereignisse nachträglich wirksam warden.' As far as we know, the noun *convalescentia* is not used in Roman legal sources, but in Romanist literature it is common practice to use the word 'convalescence' in the sense indicated by Heumann and Seckel.

42 For instance, it was applied to the ban on donations between husband and wife (Schanbacher, 1992), to the SC *Macedonianum* (Wacke, 1995), and to *mancipatio* (Potjewijd, 1998). Often reference is also made to D. 50.17.210 but Pergami (2012) 47 rightly thinks that the two texts are too short and deal with cases that are too different to allow a general principle to be deduced.

We first discuss their interpretations of D. 50.17.29 in connection with D. 26.8.3. We subsequently present our view and argue that D. 50.17.29 is not a legal rule but a rhetorical argument which may have been used for the issue described in D. 26.8.3.

In the last chapter of his book, Schanbacher discusses D. 50.17.29 in the context of defectively created security rights becoming valid.[43] He notes that, since Julian, many sources refer to the convalescence of defective contracts of *pignus*, but that Paul in D. 50.17.29 rules out convalescence. In older literature, Paul's view has been explained as an exception to the rule but, Schanbacher postulates, these opinions concern two different kinds of problem: Paul refers to *contractus vitiosi*, contracts which as such are absolutely invalid, whereas Julian and other jurists write about *contractus inutiles*, contracts that are invalid due to circumstances unrelated to the transaction but that can become valid later.[44]

Schanbacher deals with D. 50.17.29 and D. 26.8.3 when discussing how Paul used such terms as *vitiare* and *vitiosum*.[45] He suggests that the two texts were once connected by a sentence like the one Gaius used in D. 26.8.9.5. It says that the guardian must give his authorisation *statim in ipso negotio*; authorisation given later in time or by letter is invalid.[46] From the fact that the guardian had to be present and sanction the transaction Schanbacher concludes that originally there had been a solemn ritual of question and answer. This ritual, Schanbacher believes, would still have had effect ('nachwirken') in D. 26.8.3. An *auctoritas tutoris* consisting solely of a simple agreement by the guardian without a personal declaration when the transaction was carried out fell short of this ritual and was invalid. The *regula* of D. 50.17.29 was probably a reaction to some such conclusion, where the *vitiosum* did not refer to the transaction by the pupil but to authorisation by the guardian: a defective *auctoritas tutoris* could not later become valid. Finally, Schanbacher thinks that D. 50.17.29 did not only refer to this particular authorisation but that, from the very start, it was applicable to all legal acts ('Rechtsakte überhaupt').

The other Romanist who fairly recently studied D. 50.17.29 in the context of guardianship is Potjewijd. He mentions this text when writing about the convalescence of a failed disposition.[47] In his view, Roman law did not allow

43 Schanbacher (1987) 190–200.

44 So Schanbacher (1987) 214 asserts in the summary of the final chapter of his book.

45 Schanbacher (1987) 197.

46 *Tutor statim in ipso negotio praesens debet auctor fieri, post tempus vero aut per epistulam interposita eius auctoritas nihil agit.*

47 Potjewijd (1998) 164. For a review, in German, see Ankum (2001) and, in French, Wubbe (2001). Unfortunately, neither Ankum nor Wubbe discuss the problem under scrutiny here.

any defective legal act to be cured and this is concisely expressed in D. 50.17.29. Referring to Lenel's *Palingenesia*, Potjewijd states that this text bears on the *auctoritas* of the *tutor*. In his view, the guardian had to give his authorisation at one specific moment, namely when the ward carried through his transaction. Consequently, the *tutor* could not make his authorisation dependent on a condition (Ulp. D. 26.8.8) and if authorisation was lacking at the moment when the ward carried out the transaction, the *tutor* could not correct this defect and authorise it after the fact (Gai. D. 26.8.9.5).

Potjewijd contends that the same rule applied to the transfer of *res mancipi*. If a person who transferred such property by *mancipatio* lacked the legal capacity to do so, he could not cure the failed transfer by later becoming capable of doing so.[48] In some cases an exception was made, for instance, in case of *usucapio*: when possession had been transferred by a non-owner, the transferee could yet acquire the invalidly transferred property by lapse of time.[49] But Potjewijd cautions that acquisition of property by means of *usucapio* should not be regarded as a way of curing a defective transfer, because *usucapio* and *traditio* were both legitimate, albeit very different, ways of acquiring property.

Schanbacher and Potjewijd are to be commended for being aware of the importance of the original context of D. 50.17.29, but in our view their interpretations of this text are unsatisfactory. Schanbacher's assumption that there had originally been a solemn ritual of question and answer for the granting of *auctoritas tutoris* is not confirmed in the sources he mentions: Gaius does not say so in D. 26.8.9.5[50] and the term *interrogatus* in D. 26.8.3, which may have inspired Schanbacher, does not really point to the aftereffect of a ritual.[51] To us, then, it is most improbable that the *regula* of D. 50.17.29 refers to the assistance of a guardian being legally ineffective because a ritual had not been performed, and if that is the case, Schanbacher's interpretation does not bring us closer to discerning a connection between D. 50.17.29 and D. 26.8.3.

Potjewijd does not offer a detailed interpretation of D. 50.17.29, but he does use this text and D. 26.8.9.5 to draw a parallel with *mancipatio* by a non-owner: in both cases, the transaction is invalid under the *ius civile* and cannot

---

48 Potjewijd (1998) 164–165.

49 Potjewijd (1998) 167–168. He does not, however, refer to the passing of time in D. 50.17.29.

50 Quite apart from the fact that there is no reason to assume that the two texts by Paul were connected by a sentence like the one in D. 26.8.9.5.

51 Similarly, Watson (1967) 132 note 2: 'The normal form of this even[t] in classical law is question and answer: D. 26.8.3 (Paul, 8 *ad Sab.*). But Buckland is right that there is no authority that this dialogue was ever ritual.' Schanbacher (1992) 197 note 1099 mistakenly mentions these authors among those who assume that the *auctoritas tutoris* originally did have to be given ritually.

be cured.[52] The comment that the *usucapio* is not an exception to this rule because it does not imply a transfer seems to be overly dogmatic. *Usucapio* was a prescriptive acquisition: a person became the owner of property by being in possession of it for the prescribed period of time.[53] During that time, the praetor would protect him from anyone claiming the property except from the person who was the rightful owner under the *ius civile*. This substantial praetorian protection indicates that a situation which was invalid at the outset was regarded as relatively valid, while after a certain period of time had lapsed it was regarded as absolutely valid. That being so, the comparison with D. 50.17.29 does not hold water and D. 50.17.29 itself remains unexplained.

Yet our main objection to the readings put forward by Schanbacher and Potjewijd is that they appear to misconstrue the text of D. 50.17.29. Their readings imply that the text says that if the *auctoritas tutoris* was invalid from the beginning, the transaction cannot be cured by an *auctoritas* given later. In fact, D. 50.17.29 only says that that which is defective at the outset cannot become valid by lapse of time itself; there is no mention at all of authorisation given later.[54]

Our interpretation of D. 50.17.29, on the other hand, does not rest on the premise that it is a legal rule but rather an argument. What could it have meant to say by way of argument that that which is defective at the outset cannot be validated by the passage of time? To answer that question, we return to D. 26.8.3, which Lenel inserted before D. 50.17.29. It concerns a case about someone making a deal with a ward in the presence of his guardian. Later, one of the two parties tried to negate the deal claiming that the guardian had

52 This also holds for D. 26.8.8: the conclusion that the guardian could not make his authorisation depend on a suspending condition seems to serve only the purpose of drawing a parallel with *mancipatio*, which in Potjewijd's view (p. 165) could not be made dependent on a suspending condition either. In D. 26.8.8, no connection is made with the requirement that the guardian gives his authorisation *statim in ipso negotio*, whereas in D. 26.8.9.5 no mention is made of a suspending condition.

53 According to Du Plessis (2010) 184.

54 Slightly different interpretations are offered by Wacke and Pergami. Wacke (2000) 1030 submits that both texts make it clear that a transaction involving a ward without the *auctoritas tutoris* does not become automatically valid when the ward reaches puberty. That, however, is not the conflict dealt with in D. 26.8.3. Pergami (2012) 79 concludes from D. 50.17.29 that if an action is *vitiosus* at the outset because, as in this case, the authorisation of the guardian is lacking, the defect of the action cannot be remedied simply by the passing of time but only by a later declaration of the guardian that he explicitly approves of the ward's conduct. This *a contrario* reasoning is not correct either, because D. 26.8.3 is not about a later declaration of the guardian but about his informal declaration at the time of the ward's carrying out his transaction.

not been specifically asked to authorise the transaction and that it was consequently invalid. Who can have said so? It is not likely that it was the guardian himself; why would he have been present if not to authorise it? The likelier scenario is that it was the other party who invoked the invalidity of the deal, whereas the guardian insisted the deal was valid. What arguments did they use?

Linking D. 26.8.3 to D. 50.17.29 merits the assumption that the other party argued that the guardian had not been specifically asked to authorise the transaction, although that was normal practice, and that therefore the transaction was invalid and could not become valid by the passing of time either. Contrasting the validity and the invalidity of the transaction points to the *topos e contrario*. Legally, this argument was weak, because *interrogatio* was in no way required for authorisation and because lapse of time was irrelevant in this context. Rhetorically, however, his argument was strong, suggesting as it does that the invalidity of the transaction cannot be doubted.

The guardian may have replied simply that his authorisation was valid, but that type of defence holds little appeal and little persuasive force. The guardian is more likely to also have used an *a contrario* argument: if the transaction had been invalid from the outset, it could not have become valid by the passing of time. In fact, the transaction was valid from the outset precisely because the guardian had been present to authorise it and its validity therefore did not rely on the passing of time, which would have been ineffective anyway.

In his explanation of the *topos e contrario*, Cicero mentions various kinds of contrasts. The first category consists of concepts that are of the same kind but are as different as possible from each other, like wisdom and stupidity.[55] Our reading suggests that in the case of D. 26.8.3 considered in connection with D. 50.17.29, the guardian (or rather Paul) used a contrast of this kind.

The *regula iuris* of D. 50.17.29 is formulated in general terms, as a *thesis*: if something is wrong from the outset, it cannot be put right by the passage of time. It is a rhetorical rule that can be used as argument in this specific case; it is not a legal rule that can be applied retrospectively to other cases. This becomes clear only by explaining the rule in its context, as we have done in this section by linking D. 50.17.29 to D. 28.6.3.

55 Cicero, *Topica* 47.

4 Modestinus D. 50.17.195

Expressa nocent, non expressa non nocent.

This *regula* is found in the Digest twice: in D. 50.17 and as the last sentence in D. 35.1.52. The latter text comes from Book 7 of Modestinus' *Differentiarum libri IX*,[56] and concerns the wording of a conditional legacy. We examine how the *regula* accords with its original context.

D. 35.1.52 Modestinus 7 Diff. Nonnumquam contingit, ut quaedam nominatim expressa officiant, quamvis omissa tacite intellegi potuissent nec essent offutura. Quod evenit, si alicui ita legatur: " Titio decem do lego, si Maevius Capitolium ascenderit". Nam quamvis in arbitrio Maevii sit, an Capitolium ascendat et velit efficere, ut Titio legatum debeatur, non tamen poterit aliis verbis utiliter legari: 'si Maevius voluerit, Titio decem do': nam in alienam voluntatem conferri legatum non potest. Inde dictum est: 'expressa nocent, non expressa non nocent'.

D. 50.17.195 Modestinus 7 Diff. Expressa nocent, non expressa non nocent.

It sometimes happens that things stated expressly constitute an obstacle, although when omitted they could be tacitly understood and would not be an obstacle. This occurs where a legacy is bequeathed to someone as follows: 'I give and bequeath ten to Titius, if Maevius goes up the Capitol.' For although it lies in Maevius' discretion whether he goes up the Capitol and wishes to make the legacy due to Titius, still, the legacy cannot be validly bequeathed in other terms, like, 'I give ten *aurei* to Titius if Maevius should consent', as a legacy cannot be made dependent upon the will of another. Hence it has been said that 'what is expressed in words damages, what is not expressed does not damage'.[57]

What is expressed in words damages, what is not expressed does not damage.

Book 7 of Modestinus' *Differentiae* contains six texts on different topics. Lenel included them in the order in which they appear in the Digest. To D. 35.1.52,

56 Lenel (1889) I, col. 705.

57 Our translation. Remarkably, of the translations we consulted, the one by d'Ors is the only one in which the last sentence of D. 35.1.52 and D. 50.17.52 are identical.

the penultimate one, he added the heading *De expressis et non expressis*. In the Digest, title D. 35.1 has the heading *De condicionibus et demonstrationibus et causis et modis eorum quae in testamento scribuntur*: 'On conditions, declarations, explanations for and modalities of provisions in wills'.[58]

Modern literature has paid decidedly underwhelming attention to D. 35.1.52 and D. 50.17.195. David Daube with Peter Stein in his wake concluded from the words *Inde dictum est*, which introduce the *regula* in D. 35.1.52, that it already existed as a maxim in classical law, and that the compilers gave it a much wider purport by isolating it in D. 50.17.[59] What they did not consider, however, is the content of the *regula*. Neither did Voci, although in his handbook he referred to D. 50.17.195 twice.[60]

To the casual eye, Modestinus does not deal with a particular legal problem in D. 35.1.52 but in general terms describes a problem that can occur when a testator is formulating a legacy. When he attaches to the legacy the condition that a third party do something ('[i]f Maevius goes up the Capitol'), then the legacy is valid, but if he makes the bequest on the condition that a third party agree with the legacy ('If Maevius wants it'), then the legacy is not valid.[61] And yet in both cases it is in the third party's power to decide whether the legacy will be due or not. Modestinus then states that what is expressed in words damages, but what is not expressed does not damage. This begs the question how this outlandish statement, so counter-intuitive to lawyers, is to be explained.

This is how we imagine a case in which this problem occurred might have unfolded. In his will, a testator includes a legacy imposing the condition 'If Maevius goes up the Capitol'. The heir refuses to pay over the legacy because it depends on the intention of a third person. Modestinus comes to the legatee's rescue with the argument that the condition may be read like this but that the legacy does not say so literally. To make his argument more compelling, he produces the *thesis* 'What is expressed in words damages, what is not expressed does not damage.' In doing so, he contrasts *expressa* and *non expressa*; in other words, he uses the topos *e contrario*.[62]

58 The term *demonstratio* is difficult to translate: Scott (1932) has 'designation', Watson (1985) has 'particularization'. We follow Lewis and Short (1879) 543.

59 Daube (1959) 234; Stein (1966) 118. Légier (1966) 23 and 30 mentions both texts in the context of the *tacita condicio*, a doctrine he contends was developed by the Byzantine jurists, and he concludes that both texts were interpolated.

60 Voci (1963) 615 note 116 and 881 note 13.

61 Daube (1959) 234 erred in assuming that Maevius was the heir.

62 Ulpian did not distinguish between these two types of condition, and in both cases he regarded the legacy as valid: D. 31.1 pr.

In this context, the *regula* is highly plausible: one should read what is written in the will. It is written that the legacy is owed if Maevius goes up the Capitol. If he does, then the condition is fulfilled and the legacy is owed; if he does not, then the legacy is not owed. The condition is purely factual and its fulfilment is an entirely factual matter. For instance, going up the Capitol could be risky: elsewhere in de Digest it is recorded that fatal accidents could occur, such as when donkeys had to pull a cart up the hill (D. 9.2.52.2). In short, Maevius' will is irrelevant here, so when the heir argues that the legacy depends on the legatee's will he is mistaken. In this way the *regula* functions as an argument.

And what about the scope of the *regula* as a *thesis*? We have argued that in the context of D. 35.1.52 *Expressa nocent, non expressa non nocent* makes eminent sense. Take away the context and the *regula* is literally out of place. Isolated, as it is in D. 50.17.195, it could easily be taken to suggest that it is preferable to *not* write down something explicitly – for instance, in a will – because writing it down can be detrimental. Few jurists or other legal experts would counsel such a course of action, because for legal texts clarity is a prime requirement. Unclear texts – and texts that leave things unsaid are the very definition of unclarity – all too easily invite misconstruction and provoke unwanted interpretations. Moreover, we have explained that a condition like *Si Maevius voluerit* would not generally have been regarded as invalid. To us, these considerations make it abundantly clear that this *regula* is not a maxim, let alone that it would have been so before Modestinus: as a *thesis* it only works in this particular context.

CHAPTER 7

The *status definitio*: The *topos e consequentibus*

1 Scaevola D. 50.17.88

Nulla intellegitur mora ibi fieri, ubi nulla petitio est.

This text of Quintus Cervidius Scaevola also forms part of Scaev. D. 45.1.127.[1]

> D. 45.1.127 Scaevola 5 Quaest. Si pupillus sine tutoris auctoritate Stichum promittat et fideiussorem dedit, servus autem post moram a pupillo factam decedat, nec fideiussor erit propter pupilli moram obligatus: nulla enim intellegitur mora ibi fieri, ubi nulla petitio est. Esse autem fideiussorem obligatum ad hoc, ut vivo homine conveniatur vel ex mora sua postea.
>
> D. 50.17.88 Scaevola 5 Quaest. Nulla intellegitur mora ibi fieri, ubi nulla petitio est.

> If a *pupillus* without his tutor's authority promises a slave Stichus and has given a surety, but the slave dies after the *pupillus* is guilty of delay, the surety will not be liable for the delay of the *pupillus* either: for it does not count as delay when no action lies. The point of the surety's obligation is that he can be sued during the slave's lifetime or, for delay on his own part, afterward.
>
> It does not count as delay when no action lies.

Book 5 of Scaevola's *Quaestiones* contains five texts, which refer to five different rubrics of the edict, and Lenel included D. 45.1.127 as the last one in it. Between this text and the penultimate one which, in his view, relates to the rubric of *Si quid in fraudem patroni*, he placed an asterisk (*) to indicate that the two texts appear to be entirely unconnected. In the Digest, title D. 45.1 carries the heading *De verborum obligationibus*, and contains *responsa* on the obligation created by *stipulatio*. That is also the topic of D. 45.1.127.

In that text, Scaevola deals with a case about *fideiussio*, one of the three forms of surety created by stipulation. In Romanist literature, D. 45.1.127 has

1 Lenel (1889) II col. 275–6, no. 156.

 | DOI:10.1163/9789004711020_008

primarily featured as part of a general discussion on suretyship. In the previous century, scholars (particularly German and Italian ones) contemplated how the two oldest forms of surety by stipulation (*sponsio* and *fidepromissio*) may have differed from the younger one (*fideiussio*).[2] It is hard to pin down such differences, because *sponsio* and *fidepromissio* had already disappeared as living institutions soon after the end of the classical period and the compilers of the Digest systematically replaced these terms by *fideiussio*.[3] Luckily, Gaius wrote about the three forms of surety in *Inst.* 3.115–119a.

He records that *sponsio* and *fidepromissio* differed considerably from *fideiussio* in two ways: the former two could only be used to guarantee that an *obligatio verborum* (*stipulatio*) would be performed, whereas *fideiussio* could also be used together with the other *obligationes ex contractu*. Moreover, the former two could only be added to an obligation that was valid in accordance with the *ius civile*, whereas *fideiussio* could also be added to a natural obligation, an obligation that was not legally enforceable. Romanists found a third difference, regarding accessoriness. This concept, a construct of modern law,[4] indicates the dependence of the surety's obligation on that of the principal debtor. That brings us back to D. 45.1.127, because it is on the basis of this text that Romanists have expressed different opinions on accessoriness in Roman law. We confine ourselves to those of Flume and Frezza.

Using Gaius' description, Flume asserted that *sponsio* and *fideipromissio* guaranteed any transaction structured as an *obligatio verborum* regardless of its validity, whereas *fideiussio* could guarantee any obligation however contracted, provided that it was valid; *fideiussio* was therefore fully accessory to the main obligation.[5] One of the texts Flume referred to is D. 45.1.127, which is about a *fideiussor*. Flume, however, assumed that the text had been interpolated and that it originally was about a *sponsor*. The debtor in this case was a *pupillus*, that is to say, a boy under the age of 12 who was *sui iuris* and had a guardian. The *pupillus'* obligation would have been invalid because the boy had acted without his guardian's seal of approval; only under post-classical or Justinian law would it be recognised as a natural obligation. Flume deduced from D. 45.1.127 that Scaevola believed that the *sponsor* was not liable for the delay (*mora*) of the *pupillus* but that he was for his own delay, and Flume concluded that the obligation created by *sponsio* did not depend on the pupil's

---

2 See Zimmermann (1996) 117–121 and Briguglio (1999) 11–28, both with literature.

3 Zimmermann (1996) 125.

4 But the term and the idea do go back to Roman law. Cf. Zimmermann (1996) 121–122, with literature.

5 Flume (1932), 118–119, and (1996) 106–109, with literature. Similarly, Briguglio (1999) 20–23.

debt. Although the *sponsor*'s liability for his own delay is mentioned in the last sentence, Flume did not rule out the possibility that this sentence was added in postclassical times or by Justinian.

Frezza thought that the three forms of surety did not really differ with regard to accessoriness, and that the *sponsor* and *fidepromittor* were essentially as dependent on the principal debt as the *fideiussor* was.[6] In his view, D. 45.1.127 was about *fideiussio* but it could also be about *sponsio* because the principal debt was created by stipulation. Following Scaevola, Frezza assumed that the *pupillus* was not bound by the stipulation so that he could not be in delay, and that the *fideiussor* was liable only for a delay on his own part. Although the latter phrase forms part of the last sentence, Frezza regarded this sentence as superfluous and he assumed it had been a gloss in the margin that had subsequently been included in the text.

Romanists have also mentioned D. 45.1.127 in the context of delay. In his handbook on the law of obligations, Zimmermann writes that in Roman law there was *mora* when there was a debt which was both actionable and due if the debtor had failed to perform at the proper time and if his failure to perform had been his fault. Zimmermann refers to D. 45.1.127 as a source for the debt having to be actionable.[7]

In our view, Scaevola's *responsum* has not been given its proper due. It makes little sense to draw conclusions from D. 45.1.127 about the accessoriness of surety by stipulation when as a dogmatic concept it was unknown to Roman law. This also renders the issue of the text having been interpolated irrelevant: Scaevola probably dealt with a case of *fideiussio*, which in his time was the common form of surety by stipulation and which could also be used for a natural obligation.[8] What is more, scholars have failed to identify the legal problem in D. 45.1.127 and as a result they have also failed to explain the second half of the *responsum*. It is there that Scaevola presents the arguments why in his view the *fideiussor* is not liable, yet these arguments are anything but clear. We submit that Scaevola's arguments were legally feeble and that he used rhetorical means to inflate them. To make our case, we first reconstruct the legal problem and then discuss Scaevola's arguments, including the *regula*.

---

6 Frezza (1962) 49–50, followed by Kaser (1971), 663 with note 40 and Zimmermann (1996) 125.

7 Zimmermann (1996) 791 note 52. Similarly, Kaser (1971) 515 note 13, who also refers to D. 50.17.88.

8 In *Inst*. 3.119, Gaius states that *sponsio* cannot be used for the promise by a pupil without his guardian authorising it, but in *Inst*. 3.119a he adds that *fideiussio* could be used to give surety for a natural obligation. There is no reason to suppose that Gaius' second observation excludes the applicability of *fideiussio* to unauthorised transactions made by a *pupillus*.

A *pupillus* had used a stipulation to promise someone the delivery of a certain slave. His guardian had not authorised this transaction, so no *obligatio civilis* had been created, but only a natural obligation, and such an obligation was not enforceable at law. However, a third party had guaranteed its performance by means of a *fideiussio*.[9] The *pupillus* did not deliver the slave in time, and then the slave died. While the natural obligation clearly was not an actionable ground for the creditor to sue the *pupillus*, he could sue the *fideiussor* for damages. Which he did, but the *fideiussor* refused to pay. The legal question at issue was whether the *fideiussor* was liable towards the creditor.

Counselling the *fideiussor*, Scaevola denied liability and relied on two facts: the *pupillus* was in delay and the slave had died. What would legally hold if the debtor had been an adult *sui iuris*? If such a person had to deliver a certain item which he had promised by *stipulatio* and if that item had subsequently been destroyed, then he could not be sued because the item could no longer be delivered. But if the destruction occurred while he was in delay, the creditor could sue him through a *condictio* including a *perpetuatio obligationis*, a fiction that the item and therefore also the obligation still existed. Obviously, this fiction could only be used for an obligation that was enforceable at law, an *obligatio civilis*. In D. 45.1.127, the debtor was a boy who had acted without his guardian's authorisation and who had therefore only created a natural obligation. Consequently, *perpetuatio obligationis* was impossible, the slave could no longer be claimed, and there was no *petitio* against the *pupillus*. Scaevola concluded that, since the *pupillus* was not liable and could not be in delay, the *fideiussor* was not liable for the *pupillus*' delay either.

We think this conclusion is anything but compelling. As Zimmermann formulates it: 'Suretyship is a way of ensuring that the creditor gets what the debtor owes him[.]'[10] The whole point of standing surety is to protect the creditor against the debtor defaulting. In this case, the *fideiussor* was liable if the *pupillus* did not deliver the slave in time. As that is precisely what the *pupillus* failed to do, the *fideiussor* was liable. But because Scaevola rejected the *fideiussor*'s liability, it fell to him to present cogent arguments. He first states that it does not count as delay when no action lies. Put plainly, one cannot be too late doing something when one is not responsible for doing it to begin with. This is a truism no one can disagree with and Scaevola clearly intended it to support the view that the *fideiussor* was not liable for the *pupillus*' delay. But the real legal issue did not concern delay; the actual question is whether the creditor

9 According to Gaius, *Inst.* 3.116, such a *stipulatio* would run as follows: *Idem fide tua esse iubes? Iubeo.*

10 Zimmermann (1996) 122.

could sue the *fideiussor* for damages because the *fideiussor* had stood surety. And that makes this argument, which is laid down as a *regula* in D. 50.17.88, rather misleading.

Scaevola then states that the *fideiussor*'s obligations were restricted to two scenarios: he could be sued during the slave's lifetime, or he was liable for his own delay afterwards, that is to say, after the slave's death. As neither situation had arisen, the *fideiussor* was not liable. This statement is also misleading. First, Scaevola implies that the *fideiussor* would have been liable if the slave had still been alive. He effectively makes out that the slave's death is as much the reason for the *pupillus*' non-liability as it is for the *fideiussor*'s. The fact of the matter is that the *pupillus* could not be sued because all he had created was a natural obligation, whereas the *fideiussor* could be sued because he had given the creditor a guarantee that the *pupillus* would deliver. The *fideiussor*'s liability arose from that guarantee; the slave being dead or alive was beside the point.

Scaevola also declares that the *fideiussor* would have been liable if he himself had been in delay after the slave had died. This appears to be a credible statement, because it stands to reason that a person is only liable for his own delay. And that is certainly how several Romanists, including Flume and Frezza, have come to see it. The consensus is that the *fideiussor* is liable for his own delay, not for that of the *pupillus*, and the word *postea* is generally brushed aside. And yet, it is relevant because it restricts the surety's liability for delay to the time after the slave's death. Passing the statement off as a *regula*, Scaevola was able to conclude that as the *fideiussor* was not guilty of delay he was for that reason not liable to the creditor. But like his other statements, this one too is misleading because it rests on the incorrect assumption that the *fideiussor* could be in delay, whereas in actual legal fact it is only the debtor himself who could be in delay. By going boldly off subject and making much of the *fideiussor* not being in delay, Scaevola cunningly propped up his position that in this case the *fideiussor* was not liable.

This reconstruction shows that Scaevola rather ingeniously used three rhetorical devices. First, for his argument 'Someone who is not liable cannot be in delay' he used the *topos e consequentibus*, more specifically the *modus tollendo tollens*.[11] Its immediate impression is that of a compelling argument because it is based on logic, but it is, in fact, a dud. The *pupillus* who acted without his guardian was never liable to begin with and the *pupillus*' delay simply had no bearing on the liability of the *fideiussor*. Yet by relating the slave's death to the

11 Cicero, *Topica* 54.

pupillus' delay, Scaevola managed to insinuate that this death was a relevant factor in settling the matter of the *fideiussor*'s liability.

Second, Scaevola used the *topos e contrario* as an argument to support the non-liability of the *fideiussor* in this case. He hinted at a contrast between the situation that the slave had died and the situation that he was alive. In the former scenario, the *pupillus* and, as a result, the *fideiussor* would not be liable; in the latter the *fideiussor* would be. He then suggested that this pointed to a contrast between the *pupillus*' delay and that of the *fideiussor*. But of course, both the *fideiussor*'s delay and the contrast were entirely of Scaevola's own devising.

Finally, Scaevola used the tactic of the *thesis*: he simplified and generalised his arguments to bolster their persuasive power. They may have helped him convince the judges, but they did not accurately reflect the law. They did, however, resonate with the doctrinal bias of some modern Romanists, who assumed Scaevola was describing, explaining, and applying a tenet of Roman law and who consequently failed to recognise the *regula* of D. 50.17.88 for what it is: a rhetorical argument deftly presented as a legal rule.

CHAPTER 8

The *status definitio*: The *topos a repugnantibus*

1 Ulpianus D. 50.17.4

Velle non creditur, qui obsequitur imperio patris vel domini.

Lenel appears to assume that D. 50.17.4 originally formed part of a *responsum* by Ulpian found in D. 29.2.6.4,[1] for he reconstructed the text as follows:

> D. 29.2.6.4 Ulpianus 6 ad Sab. Si is, qui putabat se filium familias, patris iussu adierit, eum neque sibi neque ei qui iussit quaesisse hereditatem constat:
>
> D. 50.17.4 Ulpianus 6 ad Sab. Velle non creditur, qui obsequitur imperio patris vel domini.
>
> [D. 29.2.6.4 cont.] quamquam is, quem pater iussit adire et decessit, si adierit iam mortuo patre, obliget se hereditati, ut Iulianus libro trigesimo primo digestorum scripsit: nam eum, qui dubitat, utrum filius familias an pater familias morte patris factus sit, posse adire hereditatem magis admittit.
>
> If a man, who thought that he was a son-in-power, has accepted on his father's instructions, it is agreed that he has acquired the inheritance neither for himself nor for the person who gave the instructions;
>
> Someone is not regarded as being willing if he obeys the command of a father or a master.
>
> although where a man who has been ordered to accept by his father, who then died, accepts, he binds himself to the inheritance if he accepts when his father is already dead, as Julian has said in the thirty-first book of his *Digest*; for he prefers to allow that a man who is in doubt as to whether he is[2] a son-in-power or has become head of a household on the death of his father can accept an inheritance.

1 Lenel (1889) II col. 1033, no. 2472.

2 Also according to Scott and d'Ors. Otto, Schilling, and Sintenis, Watson, and Spruit translate the phrase *utrum filius … factus sit* as 'has become a son in power or head of a household on the death of his father', thus connecting *filius familias* with *morte patris factus sit* – wrongly, in our view.

 | DOI:10.1163/9789004711020_009

Just like the first five books of Ulpian's commentary *ad Sabinum*, Book 6 deals with wills. Lenel inserted D. 29.2.6/D. 50.17.4 in this book under the heading *De adquirenda vel omittenda hereditate*, 'On taking up or failing to take up an inheritance'. Title D. 29.2 has the same heading.

D. 29.2.6.4 forms part of a long text in which Ulpian discusses all sorts of problems in connection with the acceptance of an inheritance by an heir who is not *sui iuris*. As a matter of legal principle, such a person does not acquire the inheritance for himself but for his *pater familias*. Because the inheritance may contain more debts than the latter is ready to accept, an heir who is *alieni iuris* can accept the inheritance only by virtue of a *iussum* (order) of his *pater familias*. In Romanist literature, opinions vary as to the legal problem Ulpian discusses in D. 29.2.6.4; we examine two, those of Voci and Hartkamp.

In his handbook on the Roman law of succession, Voci refers to D. 29.2.6.4 in the context of the requirements someone must meet to acquire an inheritance and from this text he deduces that the prospective acquirer should have *scientia* regarding his own *capacitas*.[3] Voci describes the case as follows. A son errs in thinking that he still is a *filius familias*, but in actual fact he is already *sui iuris*. His *pater familias* (who passed away without his son being aware of this) instructed him to accept a certain inheritance, and now the son thinks that by accepting it he carries out this instruction. In other words, while the son thinks he acquires it for someone else (his *pater familias*), he is legally capable of acquiring it for himself. Voci documents that the jurists before Julian regarded the acceptance as invalid, but that Julian advocated its validity.[4] The same held when the instituted heir was unsure of his status: Sabinus held that his acceptance or rejection of the inheritance was not valid, but Julian asserted it was.[5] Ulpian agreed with Julian.

Voci returns to this text when he examines it together with some other of Julian's texts on this topic.[6] Stating that in D. 29.2.6.4 the compilers did not fully reproduce Ulpian's text, he argues that D. 50.17.4 points to Ulpian discussing the significance of the paternal *iussum* in D. 29.2.6.4.

In our view, Voci's comments lack conviction. In the first case of D. 29.2.6.4, Ulpian states that the *aditio* by the erring *filius* is invalid, so he does not follow

3 Voci (1967) 626. Voci (1967) 621 derived the requirement of *vera et certa scientia* from Pap. D. 50.17.76; the other requirements concern the testator's personal situation, the validity of the will, and the basis of the *delatio*.

4 Voci refers to Jul. D. 35.1.21.

5 For Sabinus, Voci (1967) 626 quotes D. 29.2.23; for Julian's opinion, he refers to D. 29.2.6.4 (note 31).

6 Voci (1967) 631–637, particularly 633.

Julian; it is only in the second case (of the doubting *filius*) that he quotes Julian approvingly. Moreover, Voci's observation on D. 50.17.4 seems to be a shot in the dark. This *regula* does not show that in D. 29.2.6.4 Ulpian writes on the significance of the *iussum* of the *pater familias*; he examines two cases in which there is a problem concerning the person who has been given instructions. This all rather suggests that Voci cannot quite put his finger on the relationship between D. 50.17.4 and D. 29.2.6.4.

Hartkamp mentions D. 50.17.4 in his book on duress (*metus*) in Roman private law.[7] In the second chapter, titled '*Metus* und das Rechtsgeschäft', he examines whether a legal act was valid when it had come about under the influence of *vis/metus*, psychological force: Paul considered such an act valid, Ulpian thought differently. Celsus is known to have given two seemingly contradictory opinions. In D. 29.2.6.7, Ulpian quotes Celsus as saying that a man who accepted an inheritance under duress does not become the heir if he is a free person, and that he does not make his master the heir if he himself is a slave, but in D. 23.2.22 Celsus states that when a man marries someone because his father forces him to do so, the marriage will nevertheless be valid because he is held to have chosen this course of action.[8] Hartkamp suggests that Celsus' opinion about this second case may have inspired Ulpian to start a discussion about the question of whether someone who acts under duress can be considered as wanting to act,[9] and he suggests that D. 50.17.4 reveals a trace of this discussion.

First, Hartkamp assumes there is a connection between Ulpian's comment in D. 50.17.4 and Celsus' opinion in D. 29.2.6.7. He notes that the two texts resemble each other in that in D. 50.17.4 Ulpian uses the words *patris vel domini* and in D. 29.2.6.7 Celsus refers to a *filius familias* and a slave, and that Ulpian agreed with Celsus. Then, Hartkamp suggests that D. 50.17.4 is also connected to D. 23.2.22 in that it made Ulpian observe that 'Someone is not regarded as being willing, if he obeys the command of a father or a master' and so reject Celsus' opinion. Finally, Hartkamp ventures that the compilers may not have known what to do with Ulpian's remark in its original context – because of

7 Hartkamp (1971) 116–117. Remarkably, he does not refer to Voci.

8 Ulp. D. 29.2.6.7 *Celsus libro quinto decimo digestorum scripsit eum qui metu verborum aut aliquo timore coactus fallens adierit hereditatem, sive liber sit, heredem non fieri placet, sive servus sit dominum heredem non facere.* Cels. D. 23.2.22 *Si patre cogente ducit uxorem, quam non duceret, si sui arbitrii esset, contraxit tamen matrimonium, quod inter invitos non contrahitur: maluisse hoc videtur.*

9 In his own words (p. 116): 'ob im Falle der *vis compulsiva* ein auf Rechtsfolgen gerichteter Wille besteht oder nicht.'

D. 29.2.6.7's corrupt tradition[10] and because of the separation of the two Celsus texts – and, not wanting to remove it because of its fundamental significance, they may have included a shortened version as a general rule in D. 50.17.

We have three reasons for not subscribing to Hartkamp's interpretation of D. 50.17.4. The first reason is the plain fact that this text and the two texts by Celsus deal with completely different topics. D. 50.17.4 is about the question whether obeying the *iussum* of one's *pater familias* points to the instructed person *wanting* to carry out that instruction. D. 29.2.6.7 and D. 23.2.22, on the other hand, are about force exerted to make someone do something he clearly does not want to do, such as accepting an inheritance or contracting a marriage. Second, we do not agree with Hartkamp's reading of the phrase *imperio patris vel domini* in D. 50.17.4. It is generally assumed that the text refers to a *iussum* given by either a *pater familias* or a master. Like *aut*, *vel* means 'or', but that translation does neither word justice, because the two conjunctions are not synonyms: whereas *aut* is used to contrast two objectively and absolutely contradictory assertions (exclusive 'or'), *vel* is used to indicate that the contrast between two situations is based on a subjective opinion or choice (inclusive 'or').[11] Just as in D. 29.2.6.4, Ulpian here refers to a *filius familias* who was ordered by his *pater familias* to accept an inheritance to which the son was independently entitled. By adding *vel domini* Ulpian merely aimed to give this phrase a wider tenor. We will return to this point later. And finally, the compilers as likely as not knew what they were doing: they moved Ulpian's text to title D. 50.17 not because it contained a fundamental principle but because of its general wording.

With Lenel, we think that D. 50.17.4 aligns quite well with D. 29.2.6.4. In the latter text, Ulpian discusses two different cases. He begins with the case in which someone mistakenly thought he was in the power of his *pater familias* when, at the latter's instruction, he accepted an inheritance. It later turned out that at the moment of acceptance he was *sui iuris*, probably because in the meantime his *pater familias* had died. A conflict arose about the inheritance. The text does not mention the parties involved but it does tell us that the acceptance had been performed formally, by *aditio*. It is therefore safe to

10 In the first half of the 20th century, the authenticity of D. 29.2.6.7 was much discussed, cf. Hartkamp (1971) 109–115. He, too, thinks that D. 29.2.6.7 was changed in postclassical times and, following von Lübtow (1932) 23, he reconstructs the text as follows (p. 112): *Celsus … scribit eum qui a patre aut domino coactus creverit hereditatem sive liber sit, patrem sive servus sit, dominum heredem facere.*

11 According to Lewis and Short (1879) 210 (*aut*) and 1963 (*vel*). Also Glare (1968) 219 (*aut*) and (1982) 2021 (*vel*).

conclude that the intended heir was not a *heres necessarius*, a close relative of the testator's who would become heir *ipso iure*, and that he must have been appointed heir in a will. It was probably the intestate heirs who now claimed the inheritance, saying that the acceptance had mistakenly been based on the paternal *iussum* and that it was therefore invalid.[12] Ulpian supported them: he argued that the appointed heir did not acquire the inheritance, either for himself or for his *pater familias*.[13]

The next sentence – 'Someone is not regarded as being willing, if he obeys the command of a father or a master' – can be taken to be Ulpian's argument. It fits the following logical reasoning. Acceptance requires the will to accept. In this case, the heir only accepted being instructed to accept, and someone who accepts because he is under instruction to accept is not regarded as accepting of his own free will. Consequently, there was no valid acceptance and the inheritance should by rights go to the intestate heirs. This type of logical reasoning was first used by the Stoics. In *Topica*, Cicero ascribes it to the dialecticians,[14] explaining that such a reasoning can be formulated in various ways; the argument of D. 50.17.4 is of the second type of reasoning Cicero describes:

> When you deny what is connected, with the result that that statement with which it is connected must also be denied, this is called the second form.

In propositional logic, this inference rule is called the *modus tollendo tollens* and it takes this textbook form: if it is daytime, there is light; there is no light, so it is not daytime. Cicero calls this particular type of deductive argument the *topos a repugnantibus*.

Ulpian formulates his argument in general terms, as a *thesis*. He also uses other rhetorical means to lend persuasive colour to it: he amplifies the content by applying it not only to the *pater familias* but also to the *dominus*,[15] and by

12 Or one or more testamentary heirs may have claimed the contested share.

13 In the second part of D. 29.2.6.4, Ulpian describes a different case, that of the son who was instructed by his *pater familias* to accept an inheritance to which he had become entitled; he accepted it after his father had died. In this case, Ulpian states that the acceptance was valid. He does not explicitly say that the son knew his father had died, but he quotes Julian's argument that even when the son had doubts about his status and accepted all the same, his acceptance was valid.

14 Cicero, *Topica* 53–54; see also Hubbell's comments (1949) 422 under (a) on *Topica* 54.

15 Similarly, Buchwitz (2012) 48.

replacing the commonly used term *iussum* with the grand word *imperium*.[16] Finally, he embellishes the sentence by using consonance in *imperio patris*.

We conclude that the *regula* in D. 50.17.4 is not a normative rule; it is a rhetorical argument stemming from Ulpian himself. Neither Voci nor Hartkamp recognised it as such. This left the former at a loss what to do with the *regula* and cleared the way for the latter to interpret it in a sense that supported his reconstruction of D. 29.2.6.7. But that reading is far removed from what D. 50.17.4 is about. We believe Lenel had been right all along when he connected D. 50.17.4 to the first case discussed by Ulpian in D. 29.2.6.4 – as an argument.

2 Papinianus D. 50.17.74

> Non debet alteri per alterum iniqua condicio inferri.

This *regula* stems from the first book of Papinian's *Quaestiones* and Lenel inserted the text at the end of it.[17] In a footnote, he suggests that there is a connection with the preceding text, D. 4.8.33. Is it true that the two texts originally formed part of the same *responsum*? And if so, how do they relate?

> D. 4.8.33 Papinianus 1 quaest. Arbiter ita sumptus ex compromisso, ut et diem proferre possit, hoc quidem facere potest: referre autem contradicentibus litigatoribus non potest.
>
> D. 50.17.74 Papinianus 1 quaest. Non debet alteri per alterum iniqua condicio inferri.

> An *arbiter*, appointed by an agreement for arbitration with the understanding that he can also extend the time, can indeed do this, but he cannot shorten it if the parties disagree with each other on this point.[18]
>
> An unfair condition must not be imposed by one party upon another.

16 Heumann and Seckel (1907) 249 record that this is the only source of Roman law in which *imperium* is used in a private law context.

17 Lenel (1889) I col. 814, no. 66.

18 Otto, Schilling, and Sintenis (1830) I 544 incorrectly translate both *proferre* and *referre* as 'verschieben' although these words are antonyms: 'to extend' and 'to shorten', respectively. Scott (1932) III 130 translates them as 'extend' and 'defer', respectively, and so also ignores the contrast in meaning.

Lenel gave the first book of Papinian's *Quaestiones* the heading *De iurisdictione.* In the Digest, title D. 4.8 is called *De receptis: qui arbitrium receperint ut sententiam dicant,* 'On matters referred to arbitration and those who have undertaken to arbitrate in order to make an award'.

Of the first book of Papinian's *Quaestiones,* four texts have been preserved. The first two deal with *iurisdictio,* but the third and fourth texts do not – which explains why Lenel inserted them at the end of the book. The third text (D. 4.8.33) concerns a case of *compromissum,* a contract to have a conflict decided by an arbiter. In the fourth and last text (D. 50.17.74), there is no reference to arbitration, but the *regula* may relate to this legal concept even so.

In modern Romanist literature, these two texts have attracted but little attention. In her monograph on Papinian's *Quaestiones,* Babusiaux only mentions D. 50.17.74 and only for reasons of style.[19] Talamanca and Ziegler discuss D. 4.8.33 in their monographs on arbitration in Roman law.

Talamanca considers D. 4.8.33 when he contests the commonly held view that the *compromissum* had nothing to do with the penalty clauses the parties used to mutually guarantee performance of their obligations.[20] In his view, D. 4.8.33 shows the opposite, and he describes the case as follows. An appointed arbiter wants to shorten the term for settling the dispute.[21] This he is not allowed to do if the contract does not provide for it. However, the jurists allow for an exception when the parties involved agree to such a shortening. In this case, Papinian seems to assume that the *relatio diei* took place with both parties present, and that then and there they had to present any objections they might have: if they did not do so, they were considered to agree to the shortening of the term. According to Talamanca, it is plausible that the *stipulatio poenae* lapsed when the shortened term expired, and that this text consequently confirms the arbitration contract's close connection to the *stipulatio poenae*: if not, he puts forward, the text would not make any sense.

Ziegler mentions D. 4.8.33 in a discussion of typical *compromissum* clauses.[22] One such clause concerns the term within which the arbiter had to settle the dispute: if he exceeded that term, the *compromissum* expired. Because there could be all sorts of reasons why the arbiter could fail to settle the dispute in time, it was common practice to include a clause in the contract allowing him

19 Babusiaux (2011) 240 and 244 mentions the text as an example of *sententia,* which serves to embellish and to confer *ethos* to an argument, respectively, but she does not discuss its content.

20 Talamanca (1958), 37–39.

21 Talamanca (1958), 96–98.

22 Ziegler (1971), 129–130 (in note 433, he refers to Talamanca (1958)), and Ziegler (1992), 534.

to extend the stipulated term. According to Ziegler, D. 4.8.33 shows that this clause allows the arbiter to extend the term, but not to shorten it, unless the parties involved agreed to such a shortening.

We cannot help but feel that neither of these interpretations does justice to D. 4.8.33. Apart from the question of whether Talamanca was right to suppose that there was a close connection between the *compromissum* and the *stipulatio poenae*, his conclusion that D. 4.8.33 confirms this connection seems far-fetched: the penalty stipulation is not at issue in this text, and therefore neither is the connection between this stipulation and the *compromissum*. Nor does the text say that the parties tacitly agreed to the shortening of the term by the arbiter if they did not vocally object – all it says is that the arbiter cannot shorten the term if the contracting parties hold contradictory views on such a shortening: *contradicentibus*. Ziegler does not go as far as Talamanca, but like him he appears to assume that the initiative to shorten the term is taken by the arbiter. The text does not say so, and the word *contradicentibus* offers no support for that assumption either.

These authors' interpretations are problematic in that they do not solve a problem: if the contending parties consent to the arbiter settling the dispute earlier than agreed, then he does so and that is the end of the matter; if they do not consent, then the arbiter must wait for the stipulated term to expire. A problem arises only when the contending parties do not see eye to eye on the shortening of the term. It is this scenario that Lenel points to in his footnote at the beginning of D. 50.17.74.

Lenel here observes *Quaeri videtur, an consientiente litigatore altero, altero contradicente iudicii tempora possint prorogari*, 'The question seems to be whether the terms of the award can be extended if one party agrees to it but the other does not.' Lenel then refers to D. 4.8.33 and D. 5.1.2.2. In the latter text, the question is whether, if the contract contained only a term for settling the dispute, this term could be extended; according to Ulpian, it could be if the parties agreed to it.[23] In D. 4.8.33, the question is whether, if the contract allowed the term to be extended, it could also be shortened. Papinian said it could not if the parties did not agree to it. Sensing a substantive connection, Lenel submits that the words *alteri per alterum* in D. 50.17.74 refer to *contradicentibus litigatoribus* in D. 4.8.33 and that both texts originally formed part of the same *responsum*. Inspired by Lenel's observations, we reconstruct the case as follows.

---

23 D. 5.1.2.2 *Si et iudex ad tempus datus et omnes litigatores consentiant: nisi specialiter principali iussione prorogatio fuerit inhibita, possunt tempora, intra quae iussus est litem dirimere, prorogari.*

Two people locked in a dispute agree to call in an arbiter. As part of the arbitration contract, the arbiter will have to settle the dispute before a certain term expires, but he is allowed to extend the stipulated term. After a while, one of the parties for some reason wants to change the contract and shorten the arbitration term. This party may have argued that the shorter term falls within the term agreed earlier and therefore cannot be a problem; this would be the well-known argument *in maiore minus inest*.[24] The other party disagrees, for instance because there are witnesses yet to be heard or things to be done which may turn the arbiter's decision in its favour, and states that the proposed change goes against the contract. This party (or rather Papinian) puts forward the argument that the other party cannot impose an unfair condition. He formulates this argument as a *sententia* in which he uses rhetoric to make it more convincing. First, he formulates it in general terms as a *thesis*; second, he uses the word *condicio* in the sense of a general clause, thus amplifying the proposed shortening of the term;[25] and third, he embellishes his argument with the alliteration *alteri per alterum*.

In our view, the *regula* of D. 50.17.74 – an unfair condition must not be imposed by one party upon another – is a *thesis* based on the contrast between fair and unfair, or in other words, on the *topos a repugnantibus*.[26] If for one of the parties a shortened arbitration term were to boil down to an unfair contract amendment, mutual compliance with the original contract would be fairer all round. We conclude that the *regula* of D. 50.17.74 contains the legal and rhetorical argument Papinian uses in D. 4.8.33.

3 Papinianus D. 50.17.75

> Nemo potest mutare consilium suum in alterius iniuriam.

Lenel placed this text by Papinian between D. 4.4.30 and D. 37.6.8.[27] Since a *regula* usually pertains to the text that precedes it, we examine D. 50.17.75 in the context of D. 4.4.30 only. Are the two texts related and if so, how?

---

24 See also Chapter 3 (on D. 32.29.1) and Chapter 10 (on D. 50.17.9, 21, and 113).

25 In other words, the word *condicio* is used in a non-technical sense, as described by Heumann and Seckel (1907) 89.

26 Cf. Cicero, *Topica* 54.

27 Lenel (1889) I col. 817–818, no. 92.

D. 4.4.30 Papinianus 3 quaest. Si filius emancipatus contra tabulas non accepta possessione, post inchoatam restitutionis quaestionem, legatum ex testamento patris maior viginti quinque annis petisset, liti renuntiare videtur, cum et si bonorum possessionis tempus largiretur, electo iudicio defuncti repudiatum beneficium praetoris existimaretur.

D. 50.17.75 Papinianus 3 quaest. Nemo potest mutare consilium suum in alterius iniuriam.

An emancipated son, not having received *possessio contra tabulas* (possession against the will) after setting in motion an inquiry into restitution, claimed, when over twenty-five, a legacy under his father's will. He is held to have abandoned the action since, even though there was still time to obtain *bonorum possessio,* having chosen to abide by the wishes of the deceased, he is considered to have renounced the help offered by the praetor.

No one can change his mind to someone else's disadvantage.

The third book of Papinian's *Quaestiones* contains *responsa* on various topics, and Lenel placed both texts under the heading *De minoribus XXV annis*, 'On persons under 25'. In the Digest, title D. 4.4 carries the same heading: *De minoribus viginti quinque annis*.

In modern Romanist literature, the two texts are among those that have largely been ignored.[28] We make a first attempt to explain them. Although the context suggests that the legal problem in D. 4.4.30 turns on the fact that one of the parties is a *minor*, the law of succession is also relevant here, and particularly the *bonorum possessio contra tabulas*. Both topics are rather complicated, so we first briefly introduce them.

The term *minor XXV annis* denotes an adult who had not yet reached the age of 25.[29] As an adult – that is to say, a man or woman older than 14 or 12 years, respectively – they had full legal capacity. But as others might try to take advantage of these young adults' relatively limited life experience, around 200 BC the *lex Plaetoria* authorised the praetor to protect adults under 25 against the harmful consequences of a fraudulent transaction. He could grant a defence to an action brought to enforce the transaction and he could grant *restitutio in integrum* to set aside the transaction or undo any other disadvantage.

---

28 Babusiaux (2011) mentions D. 4.4.30 once (238) and D. 50.17.75 three times (240, 242, and 244) in the context of figures of style used by Papinian. Cervenca (1965) 617 refers to D. 4.4.30. Neither discusses the content of these entries.

29 Kaser (1971) 276–277.

Bonorum possessio contra tabulas (*bpct*) was a remedy the praetor could grant to the *liberi* and, if the testator was a freedman, to the testator's patron if the testator either had not instituted or had disinherited his child or his patron.[30] The *liberi* consisted of the *sui* (those who had become *sui iuris* upon the testator's death) and the *emancipati* that had not been adopted into another family. If the testator had passed over a *suus heres* in his will, then under the *ius civile* the will was invalid in its entirety and the praetor would grant *bonorum possessio* to the heirs upon intestacy. If an *emancipatus* had been passed over, the praetor would declare the institutions of heirs invalid, but he would maintain the disinheritances, the substitutions, legacies, and so on. The praetor could then grant *bpct* to the *emancipatus*. Not surprisingly, these complicated arrangements caused all sorts of problems in Roman legal practice.[31]

We now try to reconstruct the legal problem at issue in D. 4.4.30. Someone draws up a will, but there is no mention of whom he institutes as heir(s): *sui heredes* who are also heirs upon intestacy, or other persons (*extranei*). From the text, it appears that in his lifetime the testator emancipated a son who at that time had not yet reached the age of 25. The fact that this son now demands restitution for previously not having claimed *bpct* (see below) suggests that the testator neither instituted nor disinherited his emancipated son but passed him over. He leaves him a legacy, though, probably a *legatum per damnationem*.[32] The testator passes away and his will is opened.

The details of what happens next are a matter of conjecture, but one thing is clear: the testamentary heirs do not pay over the legacy to the *emancipatus*. What can he do? For him as a *minor*, it will not be easy to start proceedings against the heirs.[33] Papinian relates that the emancipated son at first does not receive *bpct* but he does not say why not: maybe the son is unaware of the fact that he can claim it. Later, he discovers that he could have done so, but by then the one-year term to claim *bpct* has passed.[34] Because he is still a *minor*, he petitions the praetor to restore him to the position of being able to claim *bpct*.[35] While this procedure is pending, he reaches the age of 25 and decides

30 Kaser (1971) 707–8; Voci (1963) 647–668.

31 The Digest contains two fairly extensive titles on this topic: D. 37.4 and 5.

32 The word *petisset* suggests as much.

33 A curator could be appointed to sue the *minor*'s debtors, cf. D. 26.7.1.3.

34 In Justinian's Institutes, it is stated that *bpct* had to be claimed within a year after the testator's death (*Inst.* 3.9.9).

35 On the basis of the word *lis* in D. 4.4.30, Cervenca (1965) 617 thinks that already in the *cognitio* procedure the *in integrum restitutio* was no longer regarded as a praetorian remedy but as a *iudicium*. His view may be correct, but it cannot be based on D. 4.4.30: there the word *lis* clearly refers to a procedure before the praetor.

to claim the legacy.[36] As a result, he now claims both his share upon intestacy and the legacy bequeathed to him by his father.

The legal question is whether the *emancipatus* can have it both ways. The praetorian edict offers no clues, but two texts in the Digest on a similar but less complicated case may shed some light. In D. 37.4.14 pr., Africanus quotes Julian as stating that an *emancipatus* who has been passed over in his father's will but who has been left a legacy cannot claim *bpct* once he has acquired the legacy. In D. 37.5.5.2, Ulpian describes the praetor's intention that in such a case the *emancipatus* has to choose between the legacy and *bpct*. In Papinian's case, the *emancipatus* first initiates proceedings to obtain *bpct* and then, after turning 25, he decides to claim the legacy. While legal practice dictates that the first choice is decisive, the *emancipatus*' first choice is not yet final when he claims the legacy, and Papinian can conceivably come to a different conclusion.

It is not clear whom Papinian advises in this case: the heirs, the *emancipatus*, or the praetor. What is clear is that in Papinian's view the option of granting *bpct* is no longer on the table. That option would be at variance with the testator's intention, and it would also be unfair to the testamentary heirs. But there is no law Papinian can invoke to support his opinion. He therefore turns to rhetoric and presents the following argument. By claiming the legacy, the *emancipatus* confirms that he accepts his father's will, and he must therefore be considered to have renounced the help offered by the praetor to claim *bonorum possessio* against his father's will. In other words, Papinian contrasts the son's claim on the basis of his father's will and his claim contrary to that will. Rhetorically, this device is the *topos a repugnantibus*.[37] Papinian uses a fiction to brush aside the *bpct* procedure and implicitly concludes that the testamentary heirs are to pay over the legacy to the *emancipatus*.

The next rhetorical step for Papinian is to formulate his argument in general terms, as a *thesis*: 'No one can change his mind to someone else's disadvantage.' It is clear that the person who is having a change of heart is the *emancipatus*. He first claims his intestate share, then the legacy, and then he claims both. This change of heart puts the heirs at a disadvantage: the *emancipatus* expects them to share the inheritance with him as well as pay over the legacy to him. That would be unfair, so Papinian assumes that the *emancipatus* renounced the *bpct* claim and that the heirs are prepared to pay over the legacy to him.

---

36 In his *Glossa Ordinaria*, Accursius mentions as an alternative that the *emancipatus* had repudiated *bpct* and had later regretted it. What we find difficult to reconcile is how one can repudiate something for which one has to ask.

37 Cicero, *Topica* 54.

This outcome has the effect of the father's testament being carried out as he had intended.

Our conclusion is that the *regula* of D. 50.17.75 is related to D. 4.4.30. As a stand-alone precept, the *regula* does not make sense: people often change their minds, and others may suffer as a result, but there is no legal rule to say that people cannot change their minds simply because their reversal might disadvantage others. But in connection with D. 4.4.30, the *regula* does make sense: the *emancipatus* cannot make two contradictory claims on the basis of his father's will if doing so is harmful to the legitimate interests of others. In later history, the *regula* of D. 50.17.75 was to enjoy something of a renaissance, albeit with a slightly different wording and purport,[38] but originally it was a rhetorical argument to support an opinion that lacked a legal basis.

---

38 In Canon law, it was referred to as the rule that a party cannot unilaterally change a procedure (*iudicium*) once it has been started unless such a change does not create a disadvantage for the other party. Cf. *Liber sextus* 5.13.33 (Bonif. VIII), mentioned by Liebs (1982) 124 no. 83. See also *Fiuris*. Later it became popular in Anglo-American legal theory as an argument against retroactive law: see Broggini (1966) 39 and 58.

CHAPTER 9

The *status qualitas*: The *topos comparatio*

1 Ulpianus D. 50.17.9

Semper in obscuris, quod minimum est sequimur.

Lenel added this text by Ulpian to D. 30.14.[1] Is there a connection between the two texts, as this grouping suggests, and if so, can it clarify the meaning of the *regula*?

> D. 30.14 Ulpianus 15 ad Sabinum. Si ita sit adscriptum: 'si cui legavero bis, semel heres ei dato' vel 'ut semel debeatur', et eidem duas quantitates adscripserit vel duos fundos, an utrumque debeatur? et ait Aristo unum videri legatum: nam quod ademptum est, nec datum videri secundum Celsi et Marcelli sententiam, quae vera est. 1. Sed Papinianus libro nono decimo quaestionum ait etsi post legata saepius adscripta idem hoc subiecit semel praestari velle et hoc ante impletum testamentum fecerit, ipso iure videri cetera legata adempta. Sed quo magis erit ademptum? Non enim apparet. Et ait posse dici exiguius esse praestandum.
>
> D. 50.17.9 Ulpianus 15 ad Sabinum. Semper in obscuris, quod minimum est sequimur.

> If a clause has been inserted in a will as follows, 'if I should make a bequest to someone twice, let my heir pay him once', or 'let one payment be due', and the testator then makes to the same person in writing a bequest of two sums or two tracts of land, are both of them due? Aristo said that it appears that only one was bequeathed; for what has been adeemed is judged not to have been given according to the opinion of Celsus and Marcellus; which is right.[2] 1. Papinian, in the nineteenth book of his *Questions*, says that if the testator, after having inserted several legacies, adds that he wishes only one to be paid and does this before completing the will, the other legacies are thereby held to be adeemed. But which

1 Lenel (1889) II col. 1054, no. 2532.

2 We do not follow Watson's translation of *fundus* by 'farms' and *vera* by 'true'; like the other translators, we prefer 'tracts of land' and 'right', respectively.

 | DOI:10.1163/9789004711020_010

one is adeemed rather than another? That is not evident. And he says it can be held that the smaller one should be paid.

In matters that are obscure we always follow what is the smallest.

Book 15 of Ulpian's commentary *ad Sabinum* deals with legacies, and Lenel gave it the heading *De his quae in testamento delentur vel adimuntur*. In the Digest, book D. 30 is titled 'On legacies and *fideicommissa*'. The legal problem in D. 30.14 concerns the cancellation (*ademptio*) of legacies in a will.

Mystifying though the *regula* of D. 50.17.9 may sound,[3] what is clear is that it is a variation on Papinian's last sentence in D. 30.14.1. In the *principium*, Ulpian describes a relatively simple case of revoking a legacy and in section 1 he gives the more complicated case as described by Papinian. It is eminently feasible that the first case serves as an introduction to the second one. Papinian's opinion in the second case returns in Ulpian's *regula* of D. 50.17.9 and it is not wild conjecture to suppose that the two texts are therefore somehow connected. This connection may help explain the meaning of the *regula*.

We first examine the problems Ulpian faces in D. 30.14 and how the text has been explained in modern literature. We then turn to D. 50.17.9 and its modern interpretations. Next, we discuss modern comments on the 'connectivity' of the two texts. And finally, we propose our own view on D. 30.14 read in tandem with D. 50.17.9.

In D. 30.14, Ulpian first deals with the following problem. A testator includes a note in his will stipulating that if he makes a bequest to the same person twice, only one will be owed. He then makes two bequests, for instance of money or land, to the same person. The general view, Ulpian asserts, is that only one bequest is owed because, so the argument runs, what has been revoked is regarded as not having been given.

Ulpian then quotes the case described by Papinian, in which the testator makes several, unequal bequests, probably to the same person, and then provides that only one of these bequests is owed. As a result, the other bequests will be regarded as having been cancelled. The question here is which bequest is owed, and Papinian contends it is the smaller one that should be paid.

3 This also shows in the translations, particularly of the word *minimum*: Watson translates it as 'the least difficult', Scott has 'the least ambiguous', Spruit 'het minst vergaande', and d'Ors 'el mínimo efecto', While these translations appear to express the translators' understanding of the word, we prefer Otto, Schilling, and Sintenis' literal translation: 'Bei Dunkelheiten befolgen wir immer Das, was das Geringste ist.'

In modern Romanist literature, D. 30.14 has featured mainly in discussions of how a testator could revoke a legacy. Originally, he would have to do this in a formal manner, by means of an *actus contrarius*; a *legatum per damnationem*, for instance, was revoked by the clause *heres meus ne dato*. In classical Roman law, the testator could also cancel a legacy informally, for instance by selling an object he had bequeathed in a *legatum per vindicationem*.[4] In our view, D. 30.14 does not really fit this context, because Ulpian's description concerns two different modalities of revocation: a condition preceding the legacies (pr.) and a statement following them (1). Moreover, the legal problem Ulpian discusses does not concern the proper form of the *ademptio legati* but the scope of its application. This mismatch in modern literature has not been conducive to a proper understanding of D. 30.14.[5]

And what about D. 50.17.9? Since the *regula* is quite cryptic, it will come as no surprise that it has invited a variety of readings in modern literature. A few examples will suffice here. Calero compares D. 50.17.9 with other texts of Roman jurists and considers it a variation on another *regula*, also from title D. 50.17: *In re dubia benigniorem interpretationem sequi non minus iustius quam tutius*, 'In any case which is uncertain, to follow the milder interpretation is no less just than safe.'[6] To our minds, however, these two *regulae* are essentially different: one advocates paying the smallest legacy, the other applying the most liberal interpretation. The comparison, then, does little to clarify D. 50.17.9.

Other Romanists have assumed that this *regula* could also be applied to ambiguous stipulations.[7] And yet others compare it to the modern law of contract. Michel, for example, connects it to Article 1602 of the French *Code civil*, which stipulates that in a contract of sale an undecided issue must be decided in favour of the buyer.[8] Trofimoff mentions D. 50.17.9 as one of the sources of Article 1190 of the French *Code civil*, which contains a rule of contractual interpretation: in case of doubt, a bespoke contract must be interpreted in favour of the person who assumed an obligation.[9] And Baldus suggests that the *regula* was used to interpret contracts in public international law in favour of the debtor.[10] None of these applications of D. 50.17.9, however, has the benefit

---

4 Knütel (1971) 78–79. On *ademptio legati* in general, see Kaser (1971) 755 with sources and literature.

5 Unfortunately, Babusiaux does not discuss D. 30.14.1 in her monograph on Papinian's *Quaestiones* (2011).

6 Calero (1988) 40–41. The other *regula* is D. 50.17.192.1 (see Chapter 11.3).

7 Backhaus (1981) 100, with literature.

8 Michel (1966) 325.

9 Trofimoff (1994) 212. At the time, Article 1190 of the French *Code Civil* was numbered 1162.

10 Baldus (1998) II 545.

of being obvious: it is quite a stretch to link 'follow what is the smallest' to the position of parties to a contract.

As for mentioning D. 50.17.9 and D. 30.14.1 together, only a few authors take the plunge. Voci refers to them in the chapter on interpretating dispositions *mortis causa*, and particularly in the section on problems of 'interpretazione oggetiva': if a clause in a will is factually, legally, or logically obscure, its interpretation must be based on the circumstances of the case.[11] In the category of legal obscurity, Voci discusses several types of cases, and one of these, he contends, concerned cases that were all resolved in favour of the heir. One of these cases is about the *ademptio legati*: if various bequests are made in favour of the same person and if it is not clear to which bequests the *ademptio* relates, the heir is allowed to pay over the smallest one. Voci then quotes Ulpian's *regula* and in a footnote he refers to D. 30.14 and D. 50.17.9.[12]

Wieling mentions both D. 50.17.9 and D. 30.14.1 in connection with an interpretation that relies on the wording (*verba*) of a text and is based on *topoi*, but he does not perceive the two texts as being connected.[13] Just like Voci, he thinks that in both cases the *favor heredis* was applied.[14] He does not discuss the *regula* of D. 50.17.9 and states that in the case of D. 30.14.1, in which the testator left several legacies of different sizes to one legatee and added that only one legacy would be valid, Papinian decided in favour of the heir in that he only need pay over the smallest legacy.

Backhaus refers to D. 30.14.1 and D. 50.17.9 in his paper on the *regula in maiore minus inest* (*immi*) in an attempt to answer the question whether in a case in which someone must choose between two different performances and he is allowed to opt for the smaller one (*quod minus est*), the jurist may have used an argument other than *immi*.[15] In D. 30.14.1, and maybe also in D. 50.17.9, the problem is caused by a *legatum per damnationem* which, according to the wording of the will, could refer to various objects belonging to the testator's estate and of which it was impossible to determine which one(s) the testator had meant to bequeath. Backhaus is struck by the fact that in other sources the same problem is solved by referring to the heir's right to choose. He concludes that in cases that are decided by *quod minus est*, the motivation is found in the

11 Voci (1963) 915–919.

12 Voci (1963) 919, note 14.

13 Wieling (1972) mentions D. 50.17.9 on p. 166 and D. 30.14.1 on pp. 167–168.

14 Wieling does not refer to Voci. On p. 25, he describes the *favor heredis* as a legal *topos*, but the Roman jurists did not use the term *favor heredis*, and in *Topica* there is no mention of the *favor heredis* as a *topos*, legal or otherwise.

15 Backhaus (1983) 158.

debtor's right to choose rather than in *immi*. Backhaus argues that this also holds for D. 30.14.1 and D. 50.17.9: they have nothing to do with *immi*.

While we agree with Voci, Wieling, and Backhaus that D. 30.14 and D. 50.17.9 hinge on the interpretation of an unclear will, we do not share their explanation that Papinian and Ulpian opt for the smallest legacy to favour the heir. For one thing, the heir's right to choose is mentioned in neither text. Both jurists may have decided in favour of the heir, but they did not use the heir's right to choose as an argument. In addition, Backhaus seems to base his conclusion that D. 30.14.1 and D. 50.17.9 have nothing to do with *immi* on an inexact summary of the case: he appears not to realise that D. 30.14.1 concerns various legacies of different sizes and the revocation of all but one of the legacies. We on the other hand do believe that the opinion expressed by Papinian and Ulpian coheres with the reasoning that the smaller is contained within the larger – in other words, with *immi*.

D. 30.14 is about two different cases. In D. 30.14 pr. Ulpian discusses the interpretation of an *ademptio*: the testator states that if he leaves two legacies to the same person, only one is owed. He then includes in his will two legacies for the same person. The question is whether both are owed. Ulpian quotes Aristo, who thought that only one was owed and referred to a *sententia* by Celsus and Marcellus: what has been taken away is judged not to have been given.[16] This argument is based on the contrast between giving and taking away, that is to say, on the *topos a contrario*, and it is formulated in general terms, as a *thesis*.

D. 30.14.1 concerns an ambiguous revocation: a testator leaves someone several, unequal legacies, adding that only one is owed but failing to specify which one. As a result of this omission, interpreting this part of the will is surrounded with uncertainty. No legal argument was available and theoretically the *ademptio* could even be declared invalid. Still, Papinian states that 'it can be held that the smaller one should be paid.' He does not give an argument, but as it is clear that he compares the different legacies, he may have reasoned that the smaller was contained within the larger. If he did, he would likely have used the *topos comparatio* and probably the argument *in maiore minus inest*.[17] Ulpian concurs, declaring that 'In matters that are obscure we always follow what is the smallest.'[18]

---

16 In a legal sense, *sententia* usually means opinion or judgment but in classical rhetoric it was used in the context of style to indicate an ornate, even sparkling text; see Tellegen-Couperus (2003) 213–215. Babusiaux (2011) 240–244 lists many examples from Papinian's *Quaestiones*.

17 For this argument, see Chapter 3.

18 It is possible that Papinian himself phrased this *sententia* but there is no conclusive proof that he did.

Ulpian turns Papinian's reasoning into a general proposition, and it is interesting to see how he does that. He reinforces the eloquence of the statement by hemming it in through alliteration: *Semper ... sequimur*. And by emphasising these two words in this way, their general tenor (*semper*) and broad scope (*sequimur* – first person plural) stand out. He also replaces Papinian's comparative *exiguius* (smaller) with *minimum* (smallest) and substitutes *Non enim apparet* with the dramatic *in obscuris*. Little wonder the compilers chose to include Ulpian's graceful dictum in D. 50.17.

2 Ulpianus D. 50.17.21

> Non debet, cui plus licet, quod minus est non licere.

Lenel inserted this text by Ulpian in a long *responsum* of his, D. 40.7.3, after section 15.[19] He may well have done so because of a perceived structural similarity the last sentence of D. 40.7.3.15 bears to D. 50.17.21. We examine whether the two texts can be credibly connected and whether such a connection can clarify the meaning of the *regula*.

> D. 40.7.3.15 Ulpianus 27 ad Sabinum. Si ita sit libertas servo data, si quinquennio heredi servierit, deinde eum heres manumiserit, statim liber fit, quasi per eum sit effectum, quo minus ei serviat: quamvis si non pateretur eum sibi servire, non statim perveniret, quam si quinquennium praeterisset. Ratio huius res evidens est: manumissus enim amplius servire non potest: at is quem quis non patitur sibi servire, postea pati potest intra quinquennii tempus. atquin iam quinquennio ei servire non potest: sed vel minus potest.
>
> D. 50.17.21 Ulpianus 27 ad Sabinum. Non debet, cui plus licet, quod minus est non licere.

> If freedom has been given to a slave on condition of his serving the heir as a slave for five years and the heir has then manumitted him, he becomes free at once on the footing that it is the heir's doing that the man ceases to serve him, although if he [simply] refused his service, he would only attain freedom after the passage of five years. The principle here is manifest; once a man has been manumitted, he cannot continue to serve as a

19 Lenel (1889) II col 1113, no. 2697.

slave; but if the heir [simply] refuses service, he can still accept it at any time within the five years. It is true that the man can no longer serve him for a *quinquennium*, but he can still serve for a shorter time.

He who is entitled to more must also be entitled to less.[20]

Book 27 of Ulpian's commentary *ad Sabinum* is titled *De statuliberis* and concerns slaves who are to be freed under a certain condition. In the Digest, D. 40.7 has the same heading, and D. 40.7.3.15 also concerns a conditionally freed slave.

Modern Romanist literature has largely ignored both D. 40.7.3.15 and D. 50.17.21, and no connection between them ever appears to have been suggested. Following a review of the available interpretations of the two texts, we examine whether they can be better understood when considered in tandem.

D. 40.7.3.15 is mainly quoted in works on the law of slavery. In his classic monograph on this subject, Buckland gives a full description of manumission,[21] the most common form of which was testamentary manumission, release from slavery by will. The owner could simply stipulate in his will that his slave be free, with the manumission taking effect after the instituted heir had accepted the inheritance, but the owner could also manumit the slave subject to a condition. This condition could, for example, be to serve the heir, pay the heir a sum of money, or perform services for the heir. Usually, the condition included a specified period of time (*dies*). Sometimes, the manumission took effect even though the condition had not been satisfied if, for example, the heir prevented the condition from being fulfilled. A conditionally freed slave, a *statuliber*, who was directed to serve the heir for some time and was manumitted or sold by the heir, was free *ex testamento* and at once, but this did not hold when the heir refused the *statuliber*'s service. Here, Buckland refers to D. 40.7.3.15, adding that it is not clear why in the first case the time was not required to elapse. To him, the reason Ulpian gives lacks logic: '[A]ll this amounts to is that refusal is only prevention of a part: the logical result would be that in the case where it

20 Our translation. D. 50.17.21 is hard to translate. Watson (1985) has 'Someone who has a greater entitlement is not under obligation, because not to be entitled is a less favorable state', which we find somewhat mystifying. Scott's translation (1932), too, goes slightly awry in rendering the text as 'He who is permitted to do more shall be allowed to do less'. Better translations are those by Otto, Schilling, and Sintenis (1832): 'Demjenigen, welchem das Mehrere erlaubt ist, muss nothwendig auch Das, was weniger ist, erlaubt sein'; by d'Ors (1975): 'El que puede lo más, debe poder lo menos'; and by Spruit (2001): 'Het mag niet zo zijn dat aan degene aan wie het meerdere vrijstaat het mindere niet vrijstaat'.

21 Buckland (1908) 449–597.

was made impossible the man is free at the expiry of the time with no further tender, not that he is free at once.'[22] To Buckland, then, D. 40.7.3.15 is nebulous.

Waldstein in his monograph on the *operae libertorum* also refers to D. 40.7.3.15. Like Buckland (to whom he does not refer), he discusses the question at which moment the *statuliber* became free.[23] Waldstein starts from D. 40.7.4.4, a text by Paul about a slave who must secure his liberty by serving Titius for three years; Paul states that if the heir prohibits the slave from serving Titius, the slave will be free immediately. Waldstein then compares this text with D. 40.7.3.15, considering in particular the second case (when the heir refuses the slave's service, the latter becomes free only after five years), and with two other texts,[24] but he does not follow up his comparison with a conclusion, nor does he take into account the explanation Ulpian gives in D. 40.7.3.15.

In our view, neither Buckland nor Waldstein does justice to D. 40.7.3.15. They both ponder the question when the conditionally freed slave will gain freedom if the heir prevents the condition from being fulfilled. Yet as becomes clear from the final part of the text, that is not the question occupying Ulpian. We think that for a proper understanding of D. 40.7.3.15 it is necessary to read the whole text.

Ulpian describes two scenarios. He begins with the elementary case of a slave who was freed on condition that he serve the heir for five years: after accepting the inheritance the heir manumits the *statuliber*, who then becomes free at once. At this point, Ulpian adds a complication: if the heir does not allow the *statuliber* to work for him but does not set him free either, the slave will be free only upon expiry of the period of five years stipulated in the will. To Ulpian, the reason for this difference is evident: when a man has been manumitted, he can no longer serve as a slave. However, a problem arises when the heir changes his mind and wants to accept the *statuliber*'s service after all. Although the text does not say so explicitly, it is conceivable that the *statuliber* refuses to serve the heir as his slave. The question then is of course whether

22 Buckland (1908) 493–494. On p. 493 note 14, Buckland states that manumission would only make him a Latin, certainly not a *libertus orcinus*. Waldstein (1986) 67 note 138, however, concludes that the *statuliber* would not become a freedman of the heir but a *libertus orcinus* of the testator. Earlier, Donatuti (1940) 187 assumed that the freedman became a citizen, even if the heir was an *extraneus*. We think the issue is academic, because the text does not deal with the status of the freedman.

23 Waldstein (1986) 113.

24 Paul. D. 40.7.4.2: If the slave works for the heir but the latter dies before the passing of the set time, then he will be free after the passing of that time. Ulp. D. 40.7.3.17: If, however, the heir by selling the slave makes fulfilment of the condition impossible, the slave will be free immediately.

the *statuliber* is at liberty to refuse, and it is probably this question that is the central issue of Ulpian's *responsum*. Ulpian asserts that the heir can claim the slave's service, provided he does so within the stipulated five years. The *statuliber* does not have to serve the full five years, but only as many years as are left within that period after the heir accepted the inheritance. Ulpian does not offer an argument for his position. Does D. 50.17.21?

D. 50.17.21 crisply states: 'He who is entitled to more must also be entitled to less.' As we observed above, no link between this *regula* and D. 40.7.3.15 ever appears to have been put forward, but the *regula* itself does get the occasional mention in Romanist literature. Stein, for instance, names D. 50.17.21 as an example of 'canons of interpretation derived from rhetoric', but he does not elaborate this qualification.[25] Schmidlin and Backhaus get closer, calling the text a derivative of the *argumentum a maiore ad minus*, but they, too, do not take the matter further.[26]

This leads us to consider whether D.40.7.3.15 and D. 50.17.21 can be better explained when combined: Does D. 50.17.21 contain the argument lacking in D. 40.7.3.15? Discussing the second case of D. 40.7.3.15, Ulpian states that the heir who had not manumitted the *statuliber* but had simply refused his service could still accept it, not for the full five years but for the time that was left. On the face of it, Ulpian does not substantiate his view, but in actual fact, the argument recorded in D. 50.17.21 fits the bill: 'He who is entitled to more must also be entitled to less.' This argument perfectly fits the case Ulpian describes: the heir who is entitled to the *statuliber*'s service for five years, must also be entitled to this service for a shorter period. The argument is even more convincing because it has been worded in general terms, as a *thesis*.

In this case, then, Ulpian probably won not by using a logical argument but by using a rhetorical argument based on the *topos comparatio*. In Cicero's view, under this *topos* all arguments are valid that are devised in this way: *Quod in re maiore valet valeat in minore*.[27] Combining D. 40.7.3.15 and D. 50.17.21 supplements Ulpian's statement with a fitting argument.

25 Stein (1966) 123.

26 Schmidlin (1970) 203 note 104; Backhaus (1983) 136 note 3. For this argument, see Chapter 3, Section 2. In an article about 'Konsequenz als Argument', Waldstein (1975) 53 note 108 refers to D. 50.17.21 to show that the Roman jurists used *consequens* in connection with the deduction from size, although neither the word *consequens* nor a synonym is to be found in this text.

27 Cicero, *Topica* 23 and 68–69.

3 Gaius D. 50.17.113

In toto et pars continetur.

Lenel inserted this *regula* between two other texts by Gaius stemming from his commentary on the provincial edict: D. 3.3.46.7 and D. 3.3.48.[28] In the Digest, the intervening text D. 3.3.47 is a *responsum* by Julian.[29] Lenel paraphrased this text and in his palingenesis of Gaius' work he included the paraphrase at the beginning of D. 3.3.48. We show these texts as reconstructed and explained by Lenel, and we then examine how they might relate to each other.

> D. 3.3.46.7 Gaius 3 ad ed. provinc. Si duobus mandata sit administratio negotiorum, quorum alter debitor sit mandatoris, an alter cum eo recte acturus sit? Et utique recte: non enim ob id minus procurator intellegitur, quod is quoque cum quo agitur procurator sit.
>
> D. 50.17.113 Gaius 3 ad ed. provinc. In toto et pars continetur.
>
> D. 3.3.48 Gaius 3 ad ed. provinc. [Iulianus autem ait alterum ab altero pecuniam petere non posse nisi hoc nominatim praeceptum sit] Itaque, si hoc specialiter mandatum est, tunc excipiente eo cum quo agitur 'si non mihi mandatum sit, ut a debitoribus peterem' actorem ita debere replicare 'aut si mihi mandatum est, ut a te peterem'.

> If a mandate for management of business has been given to two people of whom one is a debtor of the mandator, would it be right for the other to bring an action against him? It would certainly be right; for he is not deemed to be any the less a procurator because of the fact that the person he brings the action against is also a procurator.
>
> The part also is contained in the whole.
>
> [Julian says that the one cannot claim money from the other unless this is directed expressly.] Therefore, if a specific mandate for this has been given, then when the defendant introduces the defense, 'if I have not been given a mandate to claim from debtors', the plaintiff should counter thus, 'or if I have been given a mandate to claim from you'.

---

28 Lenel (1889) I col. 193, no. 81.

29 Iul. D. 3.3.47 *Qui duos procuratores omnium rerum suarum reliquit, nisi nominatim praecepit ut alter ab altero pecuniam petat, non videtur mandatum utrilibet eorum dedisse* ('If a person who has left two procurators with general powers over his estate has not expressly directed one to claim money from the other, he is considered not to have given a mandate to either of them.')

Lenel records that Book 3 of Gaius' commentary on the provincial edict carried the title *De cognitoribus et procuratoribus et defensoribus*, indicating that it dealt with representation in a court of law. In this book, the texts under scrutiny here are included under the subtitle *Ut alieno nomine sine mandatu agere non liceat*, 'That it is not permitted to sue in someone else's name without a mandate'. In the Digest, title D. 3.3 is called *De procuratoribus et defensoribus*.

When reconstructing the praetorian edict, and particularly the title *De cognitoribus et procuratoribus et defensoribus*, Lenel made ample use of Gaius' comment on the provincial edict. In a footnote, he wrote that Gaius' fragment 46.7 contradicts 48 and he offered the following explanation: D. 3.3.48 does not contain Gaius' own opinion but a 'Referat' on Julian's view (as worded in D. 3.3.47). Lenel added that Gaius supported his own opinion (as expressed in D. 3.3.46.7) with the argument contained in D. 50.17.113: *In toto et pars continetur*.[30]

In modern Romanist literature, Gai. D. 3.3.46.7 and 48 are usually discussed separately and often only the first text is referred to. They are mentioned in the context of the relationship between the *procurator omnium rerum* (with the *actio negotiorum gestorum* as a remedy) and the procurator by mandate (with the *actio mandati*).[31] Scholars are particularly interested in the difference of opinion between Julian and Gaius on this point and set Jul. D. 3.3.47 against Gai. D. 3.3.46.7, as, for instance, Miceli does in her 2008 monograph on representation in Roman law.[32] Only Behrends discusses D. 3.3.48 as well and, in a footnote, even mentions D. 50.17.113. We first discuss Behrends' interpretation and then turn to Miceli's reading.

Behrends refers to the texts in question in a 1971 paper that gives a historical overview of *procuratio* (agency) in Roman law.[33] He distinguishes two categories. First, there was the *procurator* who was engaged by a Roman magnate to manage his estate or to look after his interests otherwise, be it in Rome, in Italy, or overseas. Such agents acted on a contractual mandate and all sorts of powers could be transferred to them by contract. Cicero often wrote about them, particularly in his letters.[34] The other type of agency concerned the *procurator*

30 We do not know whether Lenel made this observation in the first edition of his *Edictum Perpetuum* (1883) but he certainly did in the third and final edition (1927) on p. 95 note 3.

31 In the sources and therefore also in modern literature, the latter is also called *procurator omnium bonorum*. For an overview, see Kaser (1971) 265–266 and 587; Zimmermann (1996) 53–54 and 417–418.

32 The sixteenth-century French jurist and classical scholar Cuiacius (Jacques Cujas) had already noticed the antinomy between the two texts and had tried to explain it. Cf. Angelini (1971) 118 with note 139.

33 Behrends (1971) 215–299, particularly 219–238.

34 For instance, Cicero, *Ad fam.* 13.72.1. See Behrends (1971) 221–225 for more references.

omnium rerum. In his speech in defence of Caecina, Cicero describes such an agent as *is qui legitime procurator dicitur omnium rerum eius qui in Italia non sit absitve rei publicae causa*.[35] From the word *legitime*, Behrends deduces that this form of *procuratio* may have been based on a law and reasons as follows. As of the third century BC, when Rome began to conquer the Mediterranean area, an increasing number of Roman citizens travelled the length and breadth of the expanding empire for the sake of trade or on state business. If in their absence a problem arose regarding their property in Italy, a neighbour or friend might step in of his own accord and act on the owner's behalf. To regulate the position of this non-authorised agent, a law was made by analogy with that for the *curator furiosi*.[36] In the early Empire, the number of people who were absent for a long time rose and while they could choose to appoint a mandated agent, the *procurator omnium rerum* remained popular, as appears from the numerous texts on the topic in the Digest. In Justinian's time, when Constantinople had become the capital of the Empire, there was no longer a need for the Rome-based *procurator omnium rerum*, and the compilers adapted the texts to create one type of agency that came with a general mandate and strictly limited powers, Behrends argues.[37]

It is in this context that Behrends discusses the texts of Julian and Gaius.[38] First, he presents Julian's case based on D. 3.3.47. Someone had appointed two *procuratores omnium rerum*, one of whom was also his debtor; Julian states that the other *procurator* could not sue the debtor-cum-*procurator* unless he had been expressly ordered to do so. In Behrends' view, however, Julian only states that the other *procurator* could not sue the debtor: the word *nisi* and the phrase *non videtur … dedisse* must have been interpolated.[39] Julian clearly based his decision on a formal legal ground that forbade a debt-free procurator from suing the debtor-cum-procurator, Behrends contends. He then presents the case Gaius discussed in D. 3.3.46.7. Two *procuratores* had been mandated to manage someone's affairs and as in Julian's case one of the *procuratores* was the principal's debtor. Gaius asserts that this debt could certainly be claimed because the 'Generalmandat' of the 'nichtschuldende' (unencumbered) procurator included the 'Teilmandat' to sue the debtor-cum-*procurator*. In D. 3.3.48,

35 Cicero, *Pro Caecina* 57, quoted by Behrends (1971) 229 note 55.

36 Behrends (1971) 231.

37 Behrends (1971) 238–239.

38 Behrends (1971) 235–238.

39 Behrends (1971) 236 with note 83. He reconstructs D. 3.3.47 as follows: *Qui duos procuratores omnium rerum suarum reliquit,* [*nisi*] *nominatim praecepit ut alter ab altero pecuniam petat,* [*non videtur mandatum utrilibet eorum dedisse*].

Gaius seems to contradict himself because now he requires a special mandate for one *procurator* to sue the other. Behrends solves this problem by assuming that the phrase *si hoc specialiter mandatum est, tunc* is an interpolation, too.[40] In a footnote he suggests that Lenel may well have been right when he construed Gaius' statement in D. 50.17.113 as an argument to support his view that the debt could be claimed.[41]

Miceli traces the origin of the *procurator* to the second half of the second century BC when Rome had consolidated its power in the Mediterranean area and Roman citizens acquired large estates (*latifundia*) in Italy and the provinces.[42] As the owners usually lived in Rome, they needed a trustworthy person to look after these estates. This person, the *procurator*, could have various duties and could act with or without a mandate. In the second century AD, the jurists began to use the *actio mandati* as an alternative to the *actio negotiorum gestorum*, but they continued to distinguish the mandatary from the *procurator omnium bonorum*. Miceli mentions Gai. D. 3.3.46.7 as an example of the procurator by mandate and Iul. D. 3.3.47 as an example of the *procurator omnium bonorum*,[43] but she ignores Gaius' other two texts, D. 3.3.48 and D. 50.17.113, which Lenel mentioned in this context.

While Behrends' and Miceli's interpretations of D. 3.3.46.7, 47, and 48 have merit, we believe neither does full justice to these texts. We concur with Miceli's historical observation that initially there was only *procuratio omnium rerum*, and we share her view that D. 3.3.46.7 and 47 deal with two different forms of *procuratio*. However, by not commenting on either D. 3.3.48 or D. 50.17.113 she leaves several relevant questions unanswered. We agree with Behrends that D. 50.17.113 may have served as an argument for Gaius' opinion in D. 3.3.46.7 and that D. 3.3.46.7 and 48 do not contradict each other, but we do not think D. 3.3.48 was adapted by the compilers, nor that in D. 3.3.47 Julian's decision that the debt-free procurator could not sue the debtor-cum-procurator was based on a law.[44]

40 Behrends (1971) 236 note 84.

41 Behrends (1971) 237 note 87.

42 Miceli (2008) 105–110. The extensive bibliography on p. 105 note 1 does not include Behrends' paper.

43 Miceli (2008) 324 and 226 note 27, respectively. She suggests that D. 3.3.47 concerns a *procurator ad litem*.

44 In our view, the word *legitime* in Cicero, *Pro Caecina* 57 does not refer to a particular law but gives – to quote Grose Hodge's translation (1927) – 'the word "agent" its legal sense of a man practically in the position of owner of all the property belonging to someone not in Italy or absent on State service, that is, one who possesses the rights of another as his representative'.

We conclude this section by returning to the question Gaius addresses in D. 3.3.46.7: Is a *procurator* entitled to sue his fellow *procurator* for owing a debt to their joint principal when they had both been mandated by the principal to manage his business? Gaius thinks he is, because his fellow *procurator*'s mandate does not reduce his own. As D. 3.3.48 shows, Gaius even gives the wording of the *formula*. The claimant, the *procurator* bringing the action, will have used the *condictio*. The defendant, the debtor-cum-*procurator*, is entitled to include an *exceptio* in the *formula* stating that the claimant's mandate to claim payment of debts only concerns other debtors, but the claimant in his turn is entitled to include a *replicatio* and say that the mandate authorises him to also claim payment from the debtor-cum-*procurator*.

Gaius phrases his argument in general terms: the part is also contained in the whole, that is to say, a *procurator* who can bring an action against all debtors of his *dominus* can do so, too, against the debtor who happens to be his co-*procurator*. Gaius is using the *topos comparatio* here, phrasing it as a variation on the *topos in maiore minus inest*.[45] Despite the resulting formulaic look and feel of Gaius' argument, it is a decidedly rhetorical argument intended to deliver a knock-down punch, not a characteristically legal one. We can only make an educated guess about whether Gaius originally included this *regula* between the case and the *formula* or inserted it after the *formula*; we are inclined to favour the former option because it generalises the *ad hoc* argument Gaius offers.

Our final point concerns the compilers' interference. They first removed Gaius' general argument from its original context, turning it into D. 50.17.113, and then inserted Julian's text into the open space in Gaius' text. In doing so, they were being overzealous, because the two jurists dealt with different cases: Julian's case concerns the traditional *procuratores omnium rerum*, who could act with or without a mandate, whereas Gaius dealt with *procuratio* based on a mandate (*si duobus mandata sit*). We believe Lenel was right to restore Gaius' text by adding D. 50.17.113 to D. 3.3.46.7, but we think he erred by including Julian's paraphrase D. 3.3.47 in D. 3.3.48.

---

45 Cicero, *Topica* 23.

4 Ulpianus D. 50.17.156.1

> Cui damus actiones, eidem et exceptionem competere multo magis quis dixerit.

This *regula* of Ulpian's is cited in the Digest twice: in D. 50.17 and at the end of D. 43.18.1.4.[46] We examine how the *regula* relates to this text.

> D. 43.18.1.4 Ulpianus 70 ad ed. Is autem, in cuius solo superficies est, utique non indiget utili actione, sed habet in rem, qualem habet de solo. Plane si adversus superficiarium velit vindicare, dicendum est exceptione utendum in factum data: nam cui damus actionem, eidem et exceptionem competere multo magis quis dixerit.
>
> D. 50.17.156.1 Ulpianus 70 ad ed. Cui damus actiones, eidem et exceptionem competere multo magis quis dixerit.

> But the person on whose land the *superficies* is located by no means needs an *actio utilis*: he has an *actio in rem* just as he has for the land. Plainly, if he wishes to vindicate against the superficiary, it is to be said that an *exceptio* must be used that is based on the facts. For when we grant an *actio* to someone, it has been said that he is all the more entitled to an *exceptio*.[47]
>
> It has been said that someone to whom we grant *actiones* is all the more entitled to an *exceptio*.

In Book 70 of his commentary on the edict, Ulpian deals with various interdicts, and Lenel states that D. 43.18.1 refers to the interdict *de superficiebus*, 'Concerning buildings on someone else's land'. In the Digest, title D. 43.18 carries the heading *De superficiebus*. It is reasonable to suppose that in D. 43.18.1.4 Ulpian does not refer to an actual legal problem but discusses the relationship between the superficiary and the owner of the land. The text is worded in fairly general terms and it is interesting because it contains an argument that has been repeated by the compilers in even more general terms, in D. 50.17. Not much is known about *superficies* under Roman law; title D. 43.18 contains only two texts, a long one by Ulpian and a short one by Gaius that stems from Gaius' commentary on the provincial edict. After briefly introducing the concept of

46 Lenel (1889) II col. 823, no. 1551.

47 Our translation.

superficies and succinctly reviewing Romanist literature about D. 43.18.1.4, we present our view on it.

In classical Roman law, the term *superficies* was used to indicate a tenant's hereditary right to use a building constructed on land belonging to the state or a town, or on privately owned land.[48] The building itself became the property of the owner of the land through accession. It was probably only in post-classical law that the superficiary acquired a real right to the building. *Superficies* was usually established by means of a lease contract with no time limit; the superficiary paid a rent to the owner that was called *vectigal* when paid to the state or a town and *solarium* when paid to a private person.

The legal protection of the superficiary was based on praetorian law. In D. 43.18.1 pr. Ulpian quotes the interdict *de superficiebus*, whose wording it shares with the interdict *uti possidetis*. This remedy was available to the superficiary to protect his use and enjoyment (*uti frui*) of the building in so far as that accorded with the lease contract and provided he had not acquired possession *vi, clam*, or *precario*. If the superficiary petitioned for another remedy, the praetor could grant it *causa cognita*. That remedy is indicated by Ulpian in D. 43.18.1.1 *in fine* as a *quasi in rem actio*. In section 3 he adds that an *actio de superficie* will be granted only to someone who has leased a building for a longer period.

In Romanist literature, D. 43.18.1.4 is construed in the context of the nature of the praetorian *actio de superficie*. From the phrase 'an *exceptio in factum* must be used', presumably by the superficiary, it has been inferred that in classical law the *actio de superficie* must have been an *actio in factum*, which just like the existing *actiones in rem* could be instituted by the superficiary against the owner as well as against a third party. The superficiary also had the *exceptio in factum* against the *reivindicatio* by a third party. Justinian was the first to qualify the *actio de superficie* as an *actio in rem*.[49]

We think this contextualisation of D. 43.18.1.4, especially the contention that the superficiary could also be granted the *exceptio in factum* against a third party's *reivindicatio*, is implausible. It is after all only the relationship between the owner of the land and the superficiary that Ulpian discusses. And more specifically, the clauses *Is autem in cuius solo superficies est* and *si adversus*

48 Kaser (1971) 456 with sources and literature. The traditional view is that *superficies* originated in the late Republic when the State or municipalities granted land to citizens for building purposes. Recently, Jusztinger (2017) 98–99 has suggested that this initiative was taken by patrician families who had bought huge tracks of land that had been confiscated during the civil wars of the first century BC.

49 Pastori (1962) 104–107; Pastori (1987) 335; Wesener (1995) 134 with literature in note 152.

superficiarium velit vindicare clearly and solely concern remedies open to the owner of the land against the superficiary. While it is conceivable that a third party, too, might have recourse to the *reivindicatio*, for instance, someone who acquired the land from the person with whom the superficiary had concluded a lease contract, the text only deals with the case of the praetor granting the remedy of *reivindicatio* to the owner of the land against the superficiary. There appear to be no leads in the text that justify extending its scope to granting the superficiary an *exceptio in factum* against a third party's *vindicatio*.

Given our reservations, what could be a more plausible reading of D. 43.18.1.4? In the context of Ulpian's discussion of the relationship between the owner of the land and the superficiary, the first sentence is clear: Ulpian states that the owner generally has an *actio in rem*, both concerning the *superficies* and concerning the land; he does not need an *actio utilis*. However, the second sentence (*Plane ... data*), despite claiming to state the obvious, is problematic, for two reasons.

First, the subordinate clause *si ... velit vindicare* is in the active voice, the subject being the owner, but the main clause (*dicendum est exceptione utendum*) is in the passive voice and does not specify by whom the defence is to be used. This syntactic difference has caused confusion among translators, most of whom chose to use the active voice for the main clause as well, but who then opted for different subjects: some for the superficiary, others for the owner.[50] We cannot think of a reason why the passive voice should not be retained in this clause.[51] Moreover, the subject of the verb *utendum* must be the superficiary: he will need the defence to try and block the owner's *reivindicatio*.

The word *utendum* is also at the heart of the second problem. Most translators render it as 'can use' or 'may use'.[52] We think the connotation of optionality is incorrect because the verb form of *utendum* is a gerundive, meaning that the defence *must* be used. With this translation the whole text becomes meaningful: whereas the owner does not need an *actio utilis* because the praetorian edict contains an *actio directa in rem* for him, the superficiary must use an *exceptio in factum* because the praetorian edict does not contain a defence for him.

The third sentence of D. 43.18.1.4 now makes more sense, too: it contains the argument why, in Ulpian's view, the superficiary is entitled to an *exceptio in*

50 Otto, Schilling, and Sintenis (1832) and d'Ors (1975) for the superficiary; Scott (1932) and Watson (1985) for the owner.

51 Similarly, Spruit (2001).

52 Otto, Schilling, and Sintenis (1832): 'kann'; Scott (1932) 'can'; Watson (1985) 'may'; Spruit (2001) 'kan'; d'Ors (1975) 'tendrà' (will have).

factum: 'For when we grant an *actio* to someone, it has been said that he is all the more entitled to an *exceptio*.' To lend greater weight to the argument, Ulpian formulates it in general terms, as a thesis. He gives the argument a still wider scope by using the term *actio* instead of interdict and by turning the *exceptio in factum* into an edictal *exceptio*.[53] Ulpian also uses rhetoric to find his argument: the words *multo magis* suggest the *topos comparatio*, and particularly the argument *in maiore minus inest*, the larger contains the smaller: someone who is entitled to file a legal claim is all the more entitled to put forward a defence against someone else's claim.

When the compilers included Ulpian's argument in D. 43.18.1.4 as a *regula* in D. 50.17, they omitted the word *nam* and changed the word *actionem* into *actiones*, stretching the meaning of the *regula* to breaking point. These liberties did not pose practical problems, because in the sixth century AD the formulary procedure of classical law had long been replaced by imperial jurisdiction: Justinian's classicism restored the *actio* and *exceptio* in terminology but not in form and function.[54] Even so, what in D. 50.17.156.1 purports to be a *regula* is in actual fact a rhetorical argument that makes sense only in its original context.

53 Earlier, in D. 43.18.1 pr. and 3, he also refers to the interdict *de superficiebus* as the *actio de superficie*. According to Lenel (1927) 477, it was common practice to indicate interdicts with the term *actio*, cf. Ulp. D. 44.7.37 pr. *in fine*: *interdicta quoque actionis verbo continentur*.

54 Kaser and Hackl (1996) 577–578 and 583–584.

CHAPTER 10

The *'status' ambiguitas*

1 Pomponius D. 50.17.20

> Quotiens dubia interpretatio libertatis est, secundum libertatem respondendum erit.

Lenel included D. 50.17.20 as the last text in Book 7 of Pomponius' commentary on Sabinus.[1] In Lenel's arrangement it is preceded by two texts, D. 40.4.11 and D. 40.5.44, but in modern literature another order has been suggested. How do these three texts relate and what function does D. 50.17.20 have here?

> D. 40.4.11 Pomponius 7 ad Sab. Si legato servo fideicommissa libertas relicta est, vel heres vel legatarius eum cogitur manumittere. 1. 'Si Stichus et Pamphilus decem dederint, liberi sunto': potest alter quinque dando liber esse, quamvis alter non dederit. 2. Cum testamento servus liber esse iussus est, vel uno ex pluribus heredibus institutis adeunte hereditatem statim liber est.
>
> D. 40.5.44 Pomponius 7 ad Sab. De libertate fideicommissaria praestanda servus cum domino recte contendit.
>
> D. 50.17.20 Pomponius 7 ad Sab. Quotiens dubia interpretatio libertatis est, secundum libertatem respondendum erit.

> If a slave has been legated but fideicommissary freedom is left to him, the heir or legatee is compelled to manumit him. 1. 'If Stichus and Pamphilus have given ten, let them be free'; one of them can be free by giving five, though the other has not given. 2. When the will orders that a slave be free and several heirs have been instituted, he becomes free as soon as even one of them enters on the inheritance.
>
> When fideicommissary freedom is due, the slave has a right to bring proceedings against the master.
>
> Whenever there is any doubt over liberty in an interpretation, a reply must be given in favor of liberty.

1 Lenel (1889) II col. 106, no. 520.

 | DOI:10.1163/9789004711020_011

Lenel notes that Book 7 of Pomponius' commentary on Sabinus is about legacies. The last three texts in this book are combined under the heading *De libertate relicta*, 'On bequeathing liberty'. In the Digest, title D. 40.4 concerns testamentary manumissions and D. 40.5 is about grants of freedom by *fideicommissa*. In the three texts shown above, Pomponius deals with both forms of manumission. It may be helpful to first briefly describe them.

A testator could in his will manumit one or more of his slaves; the gift of freedom had to be expressed in imperative words (for example, *liber esto*) and took effect when the instituted heir accepted the inheritance. The testator himself then became a *patronus*, the freedman a *libertus orcinus*.[2] Alternatively, the testator could make the gift of liberty by means of a *fideicommissum*.[3]

Originally, the *fideicommissum* was a request made by the testator to a beneficiary of a will or a codicil to do something for or give something to a third party. The obligation entrusted to the beneficiary had no legal force until the Emperor Augustus made the *fideicommissum* enforceable by law, under the *cognitio extraordinaria* procedure. However, when a testator had asked in a *fideicommissum* to manumit a certain slave, a problem would arise if the fiduciary did not honour the request: the slave could then not enforce fulfilment because as a slave he could not bring an action against the person encumbered to set him free.[4] As from the second century AD, a series of *senatusconsulta* authorised the praetor to, in certain cases, declare the slave free as if he had been manumitted directly by the testator. Later that century, the slave himself was probably allowed to enforce the manumission that had been bequeathed to him by *fideicommissum*.

The sources are not clear on when exactly the slave was allowed to claim his freedom and in Romanist literature opinions vary. Most authors adhere to the view that only in exceptional cases were slaves able to sue their master, and they refer to Pomponius D. 40.5.44 and to D. 5.1.53, a text by Hermogenian.[5] In this connection, another question was raised in Romanist literature: Was the so-termed *favor libertatis* already a leading principle in classical Roman law or did it become valid only in postclassical law, under the influence of Stoic philosophy and Christianity? The latter view was the *communis opinio* among

2 Voci (1963) 408–410.

3 Voci (1963) 410–430. The manumittor would then become a *patronus* and in that capacity could claim services from the freedman.

4 This was not the only type of *fideicommissum* that was hard to enforce. Cf. Tellegen (2010) 297–321.

5 Cf., e.g., Impallomeni (1963) 67 note 34; Kaser and Hackl (1996) 452; Knütel (2006) 134. For an overview, see Silla (2008) 2–6.

Romanists until the middle of the twentieth century, when Castello argued that this concept was used as early as the second century AD and included the capacity of slaves to go to court; his view gained precedence.[6] Later, Wieling claimed that the *favor libertatis* became an important principle even earlier, in the first century AD, and his is now the commonly held view. Unfortunately, Wieling did not venture whether the principle also applied to fideicommissary manumissions.[7] In 2008, Silla dedicated a monograph to the '*cognitio* sulle *libertates fideicommissae*'. As, to our knowledge, he is the only modern Romanist to have discussed the three Pomponius texts in relation to each other, we now explore this work in more detail.

Silla holds that it was only by the end of the second century AD that slaves were allowed more room to exact performance of a fideicommissary manumission.[8] He argues that the *favor libertatis* was not the fundamental interpretative principle it has been made out to be in modern literature. To be sure, it was important to respect the testator's intention, but for a long time it was culturally, socially, and legally unthinkable that a slave should bring an action against his master.

Turning to the three texts by Pomponius, Silla examines them in the context of the second century AD interventions in the fideicommissary manumission. In his view, D. 40.5.44 is the central text of the three.[9] First, Silla places this text in the context as reconstructed by Lenel, so between D. 40.4.11 and D. 50.17.20. He assumes that the *principium* of D. 40.4.11 concerns the fideicommissary manumission of a slave who had been bequeathed: either the heir or the legatee was obliged to manumit him. Following Talamanca, Silla thinks that the question of who eventually had to manumit the slave depended on the type of legacy the testator had chosen.[10] In D. 40.4.11.1 and 2, Pomponius discusses two cases of testamentary manumission. In D. 40.5.44 he returns to

6 Castello (1956) 348–349 with an overview of older literature. For modern literature, see Bretone (2009) 817.

7 Wieling (1972) 79–81. He consequently does not mention the texts by Pomponius and Hermogenian either.

8 Silla (2008) 4–18.

9 Silla (2008) 64–68.

10 Talamanca (1965) 368–370 reasons as follows: when the slave had been bequeathed in a *legatum per vindicationem*, he became the property of the legatee as soon as the inheritance was accepted, and the legatee then had to manumit the slave under the *fideicommissum*. Had the slave been bequeathed in a *legatum per damnationem* or a *legatum sinendi modo*, the heir had to transfer the slave to the legatee; as long as he did not do so, the heir had to manumit the slave on the basis of the *fideicommissum*; once the heir had transferred the slave to the legatee, it was incumbent on the legatee to manumit the slave.

the fideicommissary manumission, and in D. 50.17.20 he concludes by confirming that if there was any doubt, a reply must be given in favour of liberty.

Silla contends that this order is illogical and he suggests it should be reversed: it is conceivable that in Pomponius' original work D. 40.5.44 preceded D. 40.4.11. If it did, Pomponius first confirmed that in case of a fideicommissary manumission the slave rightly brings an action against the *dominus* (D. 40.5.44), and then he identified the *dominus* as the heir and the legatee, respectively (D. 40.4.11 pr.). The question of whether the heir or the legatee was the *dominus* depended on the type of legacy in which the slave had been bequeathed. That is why, in Silla's view, Pomponius had to elaborate on the various types of legacy and on their effects on the obligation to manumit the slave. As to the other two texts, Silla thinks that the reversed order makes it easier to understand the combination of the apparently dubious situations in D. 40.4.11.1 and 2 with the interpretation *pro libertate* proposed in D. 50.17.20.

At first sight, Silla's idea to reverse the order of the texts may seem ingenious, but we suspect it does not hold. Silla claims that his order is more logical because now the first two texts (D. 40.5.44 and D. 40.4.11 pr.) deal with fideicommissary manumissions and the last three texts (D. 40.4.11.1 and 2, and D. 50.17.20) with ambiguous testamentary manumissions. In our view, this (re)construction is not a matter of logic but rather of dogmatics. There is nothing in D. 40.4.11 pr. to suggest that Pomponius elaborated on the various types of legacy and their consequences, and it is hard to see how the last three texts connect with the first two texts. In sum, our understanding of the three Pomponius texts does not benefit from the reversal Silla proposes.

We prefer the order Lenel chose. He gave the three texts separate numbers, implying that there is no obvious connection between them.[11] He placed them in the order in which they appear in the Digest, as he customarily did when further particulars were lacking. We follow Lenel's order, but we do think there is a case to be made for the three Pomponius texts being connected.

We submit that Pomponius dealt with the following problem. A testator instituted someone as his heir and to someone else he bequeathed his slave, requesting in a *fideicommissum* that the slave be manumitted (D. 40.4.11 pr.). Somehow, the legatee did not acquire the slave; perhaps he had died before the heir accepted the inheritance.[12] The legacy lapsed, and ownership of the

11 Lenel (1889) II col. 106, nos. 518, 519, and 520 respectively.

12 If the legatee dies after having become owner of the slave but before having manumitted him, it is incumbent on the legatee's heirs to free the slave. Cf. D. 40.4.20 *in fine*.

slave passed to the heir as soon as he entered upon the inheritance.[13] The slave now claimed his freedom from the heir, who refused, arguing that the *fideicommissum* was not addressed to him (D. 40.5.44). Pomponius states that the slave could claim freedom from his master, be he the legatee or the heir, and his view probably prevailed.[14]

D. 50.17.20 contains Pomponius' argument. It shows that he regards this case as one of *dubia interpretatio*, that is to say, as turning on a written text which could be interpreted in two different ways. The *status* is that of *ambiguitas.*

Cicero asserts that in cases of *ambiguitas* it can be useful to show that approval of an opponent's view disregards a more useful, honourable, or compelling view.[15] In the case at hand, the opponent is the heir who refuses to manumit the slave because in the *fideicommissum* the testator had not asked him to do so. The slave, or Pomponius for him, could then argue that this interpretation of the *fideicommissum* was not honourable. Rather, the testator had chosen the *fideicommissum* to ensure that either the legatee or the heir would become the slave's *patronus* after having manumitted him. That is a more honourable view and it should prevail.

Perhaps the two cases Pomponius describes in D. 40.4.11.1 and 2 also formed part of the argument. They concern the interpretation of an ambiguous direct testamentary manumission. Pomponius may have used them by way of comparison. In the first case, the testator had added a condition to the manumission: 'If Stichus and Pamphilus have given ten, let them be free.' If one of them gives five, will he be free? Yes, he will, even if the other has not given. This is an interpretation in favour of liberty and it is an honourable interpretation. In the second case, the testator had instituted more than one heir. The question is: Does a direct manumission take effect as soon as one heir has accepted his share or only after all the heirs have done so? Pomponius takes the position that acceptance by one heir is sufficient for the will to take effect; this is an interpretation in favour of liberty and it is an honourable interpretation.[16] The parallel with the *regula* of D. 50.17.20 is clear: if there is any doubt over a direct manumission and a decision is made in favour of liberty, the same must

13 In our view, the question who the slave's master is does not depend so much on the type of legacy as on what happened with the legacy.

14 Cf. Ulpian in D. 40.5.24.21: *ad quemcumque enim pervenerit is servus, cui fideicommissa libertas relicta est, cogi eum manumittere: et ita est saepissime constitutum.*

15 Cicero, *De inv.* 2.120. A perfect example of such a case is provided by Trebatius in D. 35.1.40.4; for a comment on this text, see Tellegen and Leesen (2016) 120–124.

16 Neither text raises the question of whether and by whom freedom could be claimed for the obvious reason that it was not a problem: any *adsertor in libertatem* could do this for the slave. Cf. Kaser and Hackl (1996) 218.

happen if there is any doubt over a fideicommissary manumission. Or, whenever there is any doubt over liberty in an interpretation, a reply must be given in favour of liberty.

In D. 50.17.20, Pomponius formulates his opinion in general terms, as a *thesis*, to make it more convincing. In his *Topica*, Cicero regards a *thesis* as a *quaestio*, but as we have pointed out in connection with *Topica* 21,[17] a *thesis* is not formulated as a question but as a statement when it forms part of an argument. We conclude that the *regula* in D. 50.17.20 may have been the rhetorical argument Pomponius used to support and connect his *responsa* in D. 40.4.11. and D. 40.5.44.[18]

2 Iulianus D. 50.17.64

> Ea, quae raro accidunt, non temere in agendis negotiis computantur.

Lenel placed this text by Julian from Book 29 of his *Digesta* after D. 28.2.13 pr. and under the same entry number, suggesting that the two texts originally belonged together.[19] We attempt to find out whether they did and how D. 50.17.64 may have fitted in.

> D. 28.2.13 pr. Iulianus 29 Digesta. Si ita scriptum sit: 'si filius mihi natus fuerit, ex besse heres esto: ex reliqua parte uxor mea heres esto. Si vero filia mihi nata fuerit, ex triente heres esto: ex reliqua parte uxor heres esto', et filius et filia nati essent, dicendum est assem distribuendum esse in septem partes, ut ex his filius quattuor, uxor duas, filia unam partem habeat: ita enim secundum voluntatem testantis filius altero tanto amplius habebit quam uxor, item uxor altero tanto amplius quam filia: licet enim suptili iuris regulae conveniebat ruptum fieri testamentum, attamen cum ex utroque nato testator voluerit uxorem aliquid habere, ideo ad huiusmodi sententiam humanitate suggerente decursum est, quod etiam Iuventio Celso apertissime placuit.

---

17 See Chapter 2.

18 It would appear he did so successfully, for D. 50.17.179 contains a comparable *propositio* by the jurist Paul: *In obscura voluntate manumittentis favendum est libertati.* This *regula* derives from Book 16 of Paul's commentary *ad Plautium*, which deals with manumissions in general. It is not clear which specific type of manumission Paul refers to there.

19 Lenel (1889) I col. 392, no. 420.

> D. 50.17.64 Iulianus 29 Digesta. Ea, quae raro accidunt, non temere in agendis negotiis computantur.
>
> If a will was drawn up as follows, 'If a son is born to me let him be heir in respect of two thirds, let my wife be heir in respect of the remaining part; but if a daughter is born to me, let her be heir to the extent of a third; let my wife be heir in respect of the remaining part,' and both a son and daughter were born the decision must be that the whole inheritance should be divided in seven parts, so that the son gets four of them, the wife two, and the daughter one; for in this way, in accordance with the wishes of the testator, the son will have as much more again as the wife and the wife as much more again as the daughter; for although it was agreed that by a subtle[20] rule of law the will was broken, yet, as the testator wished his wife to have something against both children, humanity suggested that a decision of this kind should be reached, which very clearly had the approval also of Iuventius Celsus.
>
> Those things which occur rarely are not lightly to be reckoned with in the conduct of affairs.

In Julian's *Digesta*, Book 29 is titled *De testamentis*. In Justinian's Digest, title D. 28.2 is called *De liberis et postumis heredibus instituendis vel exheredandis*, 'On instituting as heirs or disinheriting children and *postumi*'.

D. 28.2.13 pr. relates an interesting scenario. A testator had included two conditional institutions of heirs in his will, one in case a son was born to him and one in case the child born to him was a daughter. If the former happened, his son should inherit two thirds of the estate, and his wife the remaining third part. If the latter occurred, his daughter should inherit one third and his wife the remaining two thirds. The apparently unanticipated contingency that arose after the will had been drawn up and probably after the testator had died was that twins were born, a boy and a girl to be precise. As the will only made

20 The word *subtilis* is hard to translate. Heumann and Seckel contend it could be used in a positive sense ('fein, scharfsinnig') as well as in a negative sense ('spitzfindig, streng'). And the various translations of the Digest bear witness to this split: Watson ('nice') and Otto, Schilling, and Sintenis ('feinen') versus Scott ('strict'), d'Ors ('estricto'), and Spruit ('rigoureuze'). Heumann and Seckel also point out that the classical jurists used the term *subtilis* for pedantic interpretation and explication of the law, 'Buchstabenjurisprudenz', whereas the compilers did so to indicate the severity of classical law that was mitigated by the mildness (*humanitas, benignitas*) of the Byzantines. See Kleiter (2010) 21–23 with literature.

provision for either a son or a daughter being born, it was unclear how the inheritance ought to be divided.

Julian argues that in deference to the testator's intentions the inheritance should be divided into seven parts: four for the son, one for the daughter, and two for the mother. Elaborating his argument, he contends that while under a *subtilis iuris regula* the will should be regarded as invalid, *humanitas* favoured the outcome he arrived at, because the testator had wanted his wife and any children to benefit. Celsus, he adds, fully concurred.

There can be little doubt that freak occurrences indicated by the phrase 'Those things which occur rarely' in the *regula* of D. 50.17.64 could easily refer to the birth of boy/girl twins as described in D. 28.2.13 pr. Such a phenomenon would likely have been such a rare occurrence as to make it unlikely that it would be taken into account in 'the conduct of affairs' like drawing up a will.[21] It follows that D. 50.17.64 more likely than not contains a second argument Julian uses to support his opinion in D. 28.2.13 pr.

While in modern literature D. 50.17.64 has hardly merited a mention, D. 28.2.13 pr. has not lacked for attention, most of which has been directed to its final sentence (*licet enim ... placuit*) where Julian seems to offer an explanation for the solution he suggests. For a long time, it was assumed that for reasons of content, grammatical inconsistencies (*iuris regulae conveniebat*), and the use of such terms as *subtilis* and *humanitas* this phrase is an interpolation.[22] Today, however, the text is commonly regarded as shortened but essentially classical.[23] We agree. Below we first review scholarly discussion of it and subsequently present our view on D. 28.2.13 pr. in its entirety as well as in connection with the *regula* of D. 50.17.64.

The last sentence of D. 28.2.13 pr. juxtaposes two concepts: the *subtilis iuris regula*, which in earlier times would have made the will *ruptum*, and *humanitas*, which now suggests that the will is nevertheless valid. How are they to be explained? With regard to the *subtilis iuris regula*, Julian does not say which rule exactly he is referring to. Of the various explanations offered in modern literature we mention a few. Nörr states that under the *ius civile* the will was

21 We believe Spruit's translation of *in agendis negotiis* as 'bij het sluiten van contracten' (at the moment of concluding contracts) is too specific to fit this context.

22 Levy and Rabel (1931) 181; some Romanists regarded the text as almost entirely interpolated, i.e., as of *dicendum*.

23 Lombardi (1963) 74 note 78 does see clear traces of interference by the compilers but he nonetheless regards the text as a summary of a more elaborate motivation by Julian. Similarly, e.g., Voci (1963) 137 note 116, Nörr (1974) 114, Palma (1992) 26, and Kleiter (2010) 121.

invalid because it only took into account the possibility that there would be one *suus heres*, whereas after the will had been drawn up there appeared to be two *sui heredes*.[24] Schmidlin, on the other hand, surmises that Julian refers to the rule of jurists' law described by Gaius in *Inst.* 2.131 that the birth of a *postumus/postuma* who was passed over in the will would make that will invalid.[25] Scarano Ussani similarly assumes that a *postumus* had to be either instituted as an heir or disinherited for the will to be valid. He argues that in a D. 28.2.13 pr. scenario, a rigorous use of logic would turn the two *postumi* into *praeteriti*: the birth of the daughter would have invalidated the conditional institution of the son, and the birth of the son would negate the conditional institution of the daughter. Julian, Scarano Ussani concludes, would have rejected such a literal interpretation of the will.[26]

As for *humanitas*, the once commonly held view that it stemmed from Justinian's time[27] has given way to the appreciation that the words *humanitate suggerente* in D. 28.2.13 pr. trace back to classical law. Scarano Ussani, for instance, explains the phrase as follows. If the will were invalid, the law of intestacy would apply, in which case the son and the daughter would each receive one half of the estate and their mother would come away empty-handed. Julian used the term *humanitas* to salvage the mother's share in accordance with the testator's intention.[28] Palma adds that the testator wanted his wife to inherit at all events, in gratitude for a life in solidarity.[29] He believes that, in doing so, Julian extended the scope of the *regula* of D. 50.17.64 that extraordinary circumstances should not invalidate a legal act.

The persuasiveness of these explanations of the concept of *subtilis iuris regula* strikes us as being tentative. First, there is no compelling reason to concur with Nörr in thinking that the will was invalid under the *ius civile* merely because there were two *sui heredes* instead of the scenario (one heir)

24 Nörr (1974) 114.

25 Schmidlin (1976) 100–101. Arguing along similar lines, Hausmaninger (1984) 42, who asserts that the will is invalid because the two *postumi sui* have neither been instituted nor disinherited, and Kleiter (2010) 121.

26 Scarano Ussani (1987) 141–142. He writes (141): 'In entrambi i casi previsti dal defunto era infatti *praeteritus*, nè *exheredatus*, un postumo.'

27 E.g., Robbe (1937) 189–192.

28 Scarano Ussani (1987) 142–143. Similarly, Montañana Casani (2000) 430, referring to *aequitas* instead of *humanitas*. According to Kleiter (2010) 123–124, this is a case of a real 'Entscheidungskorrektur' by Julian.

29 Palma (1992) 26: 'per privilegiare una voluntà che attesta gratitudine per una vita solidale.'

envisioned in the will: no other *responsum* dealing with the same problem concludes that the will is invalid.[30]

Second, Schmidlin's argument that Gaius, *Inst.* 2.131 applies does not hold: Gaius (*Inst.* 2.130) states that just like other *liberi postumi* must either be instituted as heirs or be disinherited on the understanding (*Inst.* 2.131) that only the birth of a *postumus* who had not been instituted as an heir invalidates the will. The facts of the case stated in D. 28.2.13 pr. belie the applicability of the rule Gaius refers to: both *postumi* have been instituted as heirs and have been born, and their births therefore cannot have invalidated the will. Scarano Ussani's appeal to logic does not hold either because in both conditional institutions the condition has actually been fulfilled.

We do subscribe to the explanation of the use of the concept of *humanitas*. It is humane for a man to want his estate to be divided among his children and his wife, and that is what Julian's solution achieves. Interesting though Palma's comparison of Julian's solution with the *regula* of D. 50.17.64 is, he unfortunately does not clarify in what sense Julian went beyond the *regula* of D. 50.17.64.

This leaves the question how D. 28.2.13 pr. should be explained and how it relates to the *regula* of D. 50.17.64. The facts are clear. A testator institutes as heir his as yet unborn son or daughter, and he also and unconditionally institutes his wife as heir. After the testator passes away, both a son and a daughter are born. One of the testator's surviving male relatives, for instance a brother, will have been appointed their legal guardian. It is not clear whether a conflict arose about who was entitled to what part of the inheritance; no contesting parties are mentioned. Possibly, the guardian turned to Julian asking him how the inheritance should be divided. Julian suggests that the inheritance should be divided among the son, the mother, and the daughter in the proportion of 4:2:1. Celsus, who also may have been consulted, agrees with Julian.

D. 28.2.13 pr. is particularly interesting because it contains Julian's argument. He contrasts an old rule of law that used to invalidate such a will and the principle of *humanitas*, which now allows the will to remain valid. The first reflex of Romanists (us included) has predictably been to try and discover which *subtilis iuris regula* Julian is referring to. Not finding the solutions put forward in modern literature persuasive, we submit an alternative explanation. Julian suggests that if there are several heirs, the testator should divide his estate into twelfths (*unciae*) and that after his death the division should

30 E.g., Afr. D. 28.5.48.1, which contains a *responsum* by Julian; Tryph. D. 28.2.28.4; Paul. D. 28.5.82 pr.

also be in portions of twelfths. If such a division turns out to be impossible, the will should be regarded as invalid. As he did not have recourse to law, Julian refers to former legal practice and uses it to show a striking contrast with contemporary considerations,[31] proposing that the modern principle of *humanitas* is a legitimate basis for keeping the will intact and respecting the testator's intention. We believe it is highly likely that Julian provides this contrast for rhetorical reasons only.

The thing is, the testator's intention has nothing to do with the validity or invalidity of the will. It is reasonable to assume that Julian was aware of this and realised he needed another kind of argument. The *regula* of D. 50.17.64 furnishes that argument: when drawing up his will, a testator cannot possibly take into account a wide range of scenarios most or even all of which may not exist at the moment of his death. If a testator in his will broadly indicates how he wants his estate to be divided and if after his death the particulars of the situation that has arisen do not dovetail seamlessly with the wording of the will, it is perfectly justified to propose a humane outcome that captures the spirit of the will (the testator's intention) rather than rigidly sticking to the inconclusive wording of the will. Julian formulates this argument in general terms, as a *thesis*: 'Those things which occur rarely are not lightly to be reckoned with in the conduct of affairs.' That, too, is *humanitas*. We conclude that the *regula* of D. 50.17.64 is a rhetorical tactic that supports Julian's argument in D. 28.2.13 pr.

That only leaves the question howJulian may have shaped this argument. The case turns on the interpretation of a will in which the institution of the heirs does not accord with the factual situation after the testator has died. It is not clear what the testator would have wanted if he had been aware of this situation, but it is clear that the meaning of the will can be construed in different ways. A clear case of *ambiguitas*.

In *De inventione*, Cicero explains that if a written text has two or more meanings, the way forward is to assert that the text is anything but ambiguous: that in ordinary language the allegedly ambiguous word or phrase is always used in the sense proposed.[32] And we believe that is exactly what Julian does: he reconciles the family relationships indicated by the testator in his will with the actual situation after the testator's death by arguing that it is impossible for a testator to phrase the institution of his heirs in such a way that the wording will cover any and all situations that can potentially exist when he dies. In sum,

31 It is no coincidence that Julian is using the simple past form *conveniebat*.

32 Cicero, *De inv.* 2.118.

the *regula* of D. 50.17.64 is not a legal rule but a rhetorical argument that is an excellent fit with the case presented in D. 28.2.13 pr.

3 Marcellus D. 50.17.192.1

> In re dubia benigniorem interpretationem sequi non minus iustius est quam tutius.

This *regula* by Marcellus has been preserved in Justinian's Digest twice: in title D. 50.17 and in D.28.4.3 pr., in the middle of a long text from Marcellus' *Digesta*.[33] We examine how the *regula* relates to the case set out in this text.

> D. 28.4.3 Marcellus 29 Digesta. Proxime in cognitione principis cum quidam heredum nomina induxisset et bona eius ut caduca a fisco vindicarentur, diu de legatis dubitatum est et maxime de his legatis, quae adscripta erant his, quorum institutio fuerat inducta. Plerique etiam legatarios excludendos existimabant. Quod sane sequendum aiebam, si omnem scripturam testamenti cancellasset: nonnullos opinari id iure ipso peremi quod inductum sit, cetera omnia valitura. Quid ergo? Non et illud interdum credi potest eum, qui heredum nomina induxerat, satis se consecuturum putasse, ut intestati exitum faceret? Sed in re dubia benigniorem interpretationem sequi non minus iustius est quam tutius. Sententia imperatoris Antonini Augusti Pudente et Pollione consulibus. 'Cum Valerius Nepos mutata voluntate et inciderit testamentum suum et heredum nomina induxerit, hereditas eius secundum divi patris mei constitutionem ad eos qui scripti fuerint pertinere non videtur'. Et advocatis fisci dixit: 'Vos habetis iudices vestros'. Vibius Zeno dixit: 'Rogo, domine imperator, audias me patienter: de legatis quid statues?' Antoninus Caesar dixit: 'Videtur tibi voluisse testamentum valere, qui nomina heredum induxit?' Cornelius Priscianus advocatus Leonis dixit: 'Nomina heredum tantum induxit'. Calpurnius Longinus advocatus fisci dixit: 'Non potest ullum testamentum valere, quod heredem non habet'. Priscianus dixit: 'Manumisit quosdam et legata dedit'. Antoninus Caesar remotis omnibus cum deliberasset et admitti rursus eodem iussisset, dixit: 'Causa praesens admittere videtur humaniorem interpretationem, ut ea dumtaxat existimemus Nepotem irrita esse voluisse, quae induxit.'

33 Lenel (1889) I col. 631, no. 263.

1. Nomen servi, quem liberum esse iusserat, induxit. Antoninus rescripsit liberum eum nihilo minus fore: quod videlicet favore constituit libertatis.

D. 50.17.192.1 Marcellus 29 Digesta. In re dubia benigniorem interpretationem sequi non minus iustius est quam tutius.

Very recently in a *cognitio* held by the emperor, when someone had erased the names of his heirs and his property was claimed as caduciary by the imperial treasury, there was a long discussion about the legacies and especially about those legacies which had been assigned to those whose institution had been erased. The majority thought that the legatees also should be excluded. Which, indeed, should follow, I said, if [the testator] had canceled all the writing in the will: some think that by operation of law what has been erased is removed but all the rest will stand. What then? Is it not sometimes credible that someone who had erased the names of his heirs had thought that he would have done enough to bring about an intestacy? But, in a doubtful matter, to follow the milder interpretation is not only more just, but safer. The judgment of the Emperor Antoninus Augustus, in the consulship of Pudens and Pollio: 'As Valerius Nepos, having changed his mind, both cut open his will and erased the names of his heirs, in accordance with a *constitutio* of my deified father, his inheritance is not regarded as belonging to those who were appointed [heirs].' And he said to the advocates of the imperial treasury: 'The judges are for you.' Vibius Zeno said: 'I ask you, lord emperor, to hear me patiently: What do you decide with regard to the legacies?' The Emperor Antoninus said: 'Does it seem to you that someone who erased the names of his heirs intended his will to stand?' Cornelius Priscianus, advocate of Leo, said: 'He erased only the names of the heirs.' Calpurnius Longinus, advocate of the imperial treasury, said: 'It is not possible for any will to stand, which does not have an heir [in it].' Priscianus said: 'He manumitted certain [slaves] and gave legacies.' The Emperor Antoninus, having sent everyone away, when he had considered the matter and had ordered [them] to be admitted once more, said: 'The present case seems to admit of a more humane interpretation, in that we think that Nepos intended that only those provisions which he erased should be ineffectual.' 1. He erased the name of a slave whom he had ordered to be free. Antoninus in a rescript said that he [the slave], nevertheless, would be free; and the reason why he laid this down was in order to favor freedom.

> In any case which is uncertain, to follow the milder interpretation is no less just than safe.[34]

Lenel states that Book 29 of Marcellus' *Digesta* was headed *Ad legem Iuliam et Papiam* and concerns legislation of the Emperor Augustus regulating marriage. The rewards and penalties stipulated in this legislation mainly related to the law of succession and served as a model for other interventions by the emperor in that area of law, as in the case under discussion. In Justinian's Digest, this text features in a different context: it is included in title D. 28.4, *De his quae in testamento delentur inducuntur vel inscribuntur*, 'On matters which are obliterated, erased or written over in a will'.

D. 28.4.3 pr. consists of two parts: in the first part (up to and including the statement in bold type), Marcellus describes the discussion that took place in connection with a trial before the Emperor Marcus Aurelius;[35] the second part, which Marcellus appears to quote from an official report of that trial, records arguments and ends with the emperor's judgment. Contextual details about the discussion are unclear: Did it take place in the emperor's *consilium*? Did it precede the actual session (as in this text) or did it unfold during that session?[36] And did the case recorded in D. 28.4.3.1 form part of the same trial? What is clear is that the *regula* in D. 50.17.192.1 repeats Marcellus' opinion as he expressed it at the end of the first part of D. 28.4.3 pr.

Marcellus recounts the following problem. One Valerius Nepos had made a will in which, apart from instituting the heirs, he included a number of legacies and manumissions. Some of the legacies were in favour of the instituted heirs: they were legacies *per praeceptionem*. Precisely when and why is unknown, but the testator at some later point changed his mind: he opened the deed of the will and erased the names of the heirs. After his death, a conflict arose about the will. The imperial treasury claimed the estate in its entirety: having had their names erased in the *heredis institutio*, the erstwhile

34 Watson's translation of the *regula* in D. 28.4.3 differs from that in D. 50.17.192.1: Book 28 was translated by Lewis, and Book 50 by Crawford. Cf. Watson (1985) vol. 1, Preface XII–XIII.

35 As the adoptive son of the Emperor Antoninus Pius, M. Aurelius went by the official name of M. Aurelius Antoninus. Pudens and Pollio were consuls in the year 166. The name Antoninus has caused some confusion among Romanists; cf. Müller-Eiselt (1982) 188 note 121.

36 It is generally assumed that the discussion took place in the *consilium* but the text does not explicitly say so. On the relationship between the discussion and the trial, see Wankerl (2009) 72–75 with literature. Querzoli (2013) 180–183 focuses on the position of Ulpius Marcellus.

heirs were considered to be *indigni*, unworthy to inherit from the testator, and the estate they had originally stood to inherit became *bona caduca*.[37] This claim was discussed, presumably in the imperial *consilium*. The emperor first decided that the inheritance should not go to the instituted heirs. When subsequently asked what was to be done about the legacies and manumissions, he narrowed down his decision and citing a humane interpretation ruled that only those provisions that had been erased should be invalid. This could be taken to mean that the emperor regarded the *legata per praeceptionem* as valid.

In modern Romanist literature, D. 28.4.3 pr. has been widely discussed, unlike D. 28.4.3.1 and D. 50.17.192.1.[38] It was particularly Marcellus' *regula* at the end of the first part and Emperor Marcus Aurelius' judgment at the end of the second part that have prompted much comment, and two recent studies, a monograph by Wankerl and a paper by Hendel, connect D. 28.4.3 pr. and the *regula* of D. 50.17.192.1. It is to these two publications that we now turn.

In her 2009 monograph *Appello ad principem*, Wankerl takes up the 'Urteilsstil und Urteilstechnik in kaiserlichen Berufungsentscheidungen (Augustus bis Caracalla)'. She discusses two judgments by Marcus Aurelius, one of them being that recorded in D. 28.4.3 pr. Wankerl notes that this judgment is also mentioned in two texts by Papinian, D. 34.9.12. and D. 34.9.16.2.[39] From the former, she infers that Marcus Aurelius remitted the case of the legacies *per praeceptionem* to the *praefecti aerarii* and, from the latter, that the other legacies could be claimed from the imperial treasury. We now look at her reading of that text in more detail.

Wankerl first examines the discussion in the emperor's *consilium*[40] about the validity of the legacies.[41] Most members of the *consilium* were of the opinion that crossing out the names of all the heirs in the will had rendered the entire will, legacies included, void. Marcellus objected that erasure would only have this effect if all provisions had been crossed out. Some opined that only what had been crossed out was lost but that the remainder was valid. To this, Marcellus also objected because, he said, the testator may have thought that by erasing the institution of the heirs he had invalidated the whole will. Wankerl

37 Cf. Voci (1967) 475 and 482; similarly, Serangeli (1982) 255, Reimundo (1983) 47–51, and recently Wankerl (2009) 75; not so Calero (1988) 41–42.

38 *Fiuris* gives 99 hits for D. 28.4.3 pr., against 9 for D. 50.17.192.1 and 3 for D. 28.4.3.1. Modern monographs show a similar pattern. The most recent paper we know is that by Stagl (2020), with literature.

39 Wankerl (2009) 68–94, referring to Calero (1988) 28f.

40 But see note 36.

41 Wankerl (2009) 76–78 with literature. She mentions Volusius Maecianus, Bassaeus Rufus, and Cervidius Scaevola as other well-known members of Marcus Aurelius' *consilium*.

concludes that Marcellus's reasoning shows that he believes the testator's intention to be essential for the validity of the testamentary provisions. If the intention cannot be assessed, as in this case, then he proposes to interpret the will mildly and keep it intact as much as possible. In Wankerl's opinion, Emperor Marcus Aurelius' decision about the legacies (in D. 34.9.12 and 16.2) also shows that he regarded the testator's intention as important and therefore opted for the *benignior interpretatio*. Referring to D. 50.17.192.1, Wankerl suggests that this milder interpretation was also supported by the *favor testamenti*.[42]

At the trial presided over by the emperor, the litigants put forward the same arguments that had been used by the jurists in the *consilium*. Wankerl points out that Priscianus, one of the defendants' advocates, raised the manumissions to steer the discussion to the *favor libertatis* and to save at least the other provisions of the will.[43] In Wankerl's view, the *consilium* had correctly presented the testator's intention as the central element and the advocate's choice to invoke the *favor libertatis* was legally incorrect.

Linking D. 28.4.3 pr. to D. 34.9.12 and 16.2, Wankerl concludes that Marcus Aurelius' judgment applied to three cases with different defendants.[44] He delegated the decision on the *legata per praeceptionem* to the *praefecti aerarii* with the instruction that the legacies should be paid out if it could not be proved that the testator had changed his mind (D. 34.9.12); this decision, Wankerl contends, was in complete agreement with the 'Grundaussage' in D. 28.4.3 pr. that only what had been erased should be regarded as invalid. Regarding the other legacies, Marcus Aurelius concluded that it was impossible to assess the testator's intention and he therefore, in accordance with Marcellus' *benignior interpretatio*, decided in the legatees' favour (D. 34.9.16.2 and D. 50.17.192.1). The manumissions he declared valid on account of the *humanior interpretatio* (D. 28.4.3 pr.).

Finally, Wankerl deals with the rhetorical dimension of the trial.[45] In her view, the conflict turns on the interpretation of the will, and the litigants discuss it in the context of the *genus legale*, which is divided into four *status*. The interpretation of a will, Wankerl asserts, would normally fall under the *status scripti et voluntatis*. She argues that the treasury and the majority in the *consilium* saw the crossing out of the heirs' names as a *pars pro toto* and concluded that the testator had intended to annul the entire will. The opposing side, and in the end the emperor himself, wanted to restrict the consequences of the

42 Wankerl (2009) 78 note 425.
43 Wankerl (2009) 84–85, referring to Wieling. Similarly, Finkenauer (2010) 20.
44 Wankerl (2009) 85–87.
45 Wankerl (2009) 92–93.

crossing out to what actually had been crossed out, and they therefore referred to the *favor libertatis* and the *favor testamenti*. These, too, Wankerl contends, were common principles of interpretation.

The second Romanist to connect D. 28.4.3 and D. 50.17.192.1 is Hendel.[46] He addresses the 'Sicherheitsgedanken bei der benignior interpretatio', and particularly the word *tutius* (safer) in the *regula*. The jurist Marcellus uses the words *non minus iustius est quam tutius* to explain his view that in case of doubt a *benignior interpretatio* should be followed. Hendel contends that such a motivation is exceptional, and he examines it to clarify what Marcellus could have meant with *benignior interpretatio*. He thinks that the term *iustius* in general does not add much to the concept of *benignitas* but that the term *tutius* does.

Giving a series of examples, Hendel demonstrates that the Roman jurists not only used the term *tutus* (and variants) in the general meaning of protecting someone or something against damage and danger but that they also applied it to ambiguous stipulations, intending to keep intact as much of the legal act in question as possible. The case in D. 28.4.3 pr. turns on the validity of a will whose later revision by the testator resulted in ambiguity of interpretation. Hendel postulates that here *tutius* must be taken to mean the greater safety that is provided if a clear testamentary provision is retained even when the testator may have changed his mind.[47]

Hendel also considers why the compilers of the Digest may have included Marcellus' view as expressed in D. 28.4.3 pr. in title D. 50.17.[48] He points out that it has been suggested that they did so in error because this maxim could be applied to unilateral provisions only: in case of bilateral legal acts, it would not be clear to whose advantage the *benignitas* should be applied. Hendel, however, believes that D. 50.17.192.1 can be quite easily understood as a general rule of interpretation that does not aim at favouring one party over another, but at retaining as much as possible the integrity of the original content of a legal act for the sake of certainty of proof and protection of trust, and at preserving the intention expressed in it.

Hendel ends his paper with a discussion of Marcus Aurelius' *humanior interpretatio*.[49] Although the emperor arrived at the same conclusion as Marcellus, he used a different argument. First, the emperor had established that the instituted heirs were unworthy of inheriting, and he had declined succession upon

46 Hendel (2013) 419–431.
47 Hendel (2013) 424–427.
48 Hendel (2013) 427–428.
49 Hendel (2013) 428–431.

intestacy. As to the legacies, upon due consideration he had decided that the *humanior interpretatio* should be followed and that the legacies that had not been erased should be maintained (pr. *in fine*). Finally, Marcellus added that in keeping with the *favor libertatis* the emperor had also ruled that a slave whose name had been crossed out was yet to be manumitted (section 1).[50]

Wankerl and Hendel interpret D. 28.4.3 pr. and D. 50.17.192.1 quite differently and while their deliberations offer valuable insights, we believe they are not entirely satisfactory. We dissent from Wankerl's interpretation on two points. The first concerns her linking Marcus Aurelius' judgment in Marce. D. 28.4.3 pr. with Pap. D. 34.9.12 and 16.2. These two texts concern a testator who in his will erased the name of one of the heirs, so they deal with a different case – the name of one heir being erased as against the names of all heirs in D. 28.4.3 pr. – and with different legal questions.[51] Moreover, Wankerl does not explain why in D. 34.9.12 the case concerning the *legatum per praeceptionem* is assigned to the *aerarium*, the state treasury, whereas in D. 34.9.16.2 the case of the other legacies is to be dealt with by the imperial treasury.

The second point on which we disagree with Wankerl is her rhetorical analysis of the trial.[52] It appears to be based on the assumption that the trial turned on the *status scripti et voluntatis* because it is about the interpretation of a will. We reject that assumption. The *status* Wankerl refers to could apply if there were an observable discrepancy between what the testator wrote and what he meant but in this case it is not at all clear what the testator wanted when he erased the names of the instituted heirs. There consequently is not a clear will which the *fiscus* and *plerique* could interpret in accordance with the testator's intention. The will is a *res dubia* and the more obvious candidate for interpreting the will is the *status ambiguitas*.

---

50 Stagl (2014) 868–869 and (2020) 9–10 assumes that D. 28.4.3 pr. and 1 concern the same case because both texts mention manumissions and because both texts stem from Marcellus' comment on the *lex Iulia et Papia*. We tend to think that the two texts concern different cases: in the case described in D. 28.4.3 pr. the heirs' names were erased and their shares were declared invalid, whereas in the case referred to in section 1 the name of the slave was erased but his manumission was declared valid.

51 In D. 34.9.12 the question is whether the testator still wanted this heir to have his *legatum per praeceptionem*, while in D. 34.9.16.2 it is whether the legacies owed by this heir could now be claimed from the imperial treasury; the legal question in D. 28.4.3 pr. turns on the validity of the legacies and manumissions, and particularly of the *legata per praeceptionem*.

52 In his review of Wankerl's monograph, Mantovani (2015) 658 considers the rhetorical analysis of the decisions to be the most relevant and most innovative aspect of her book, yet he does not discuss Wankerl's rhetorical explanation of D. 28.4.3 pr.

Nor do we share Wankerl's understanding of the rhetorical argumentation. We believe it is unlikely that the *fiscus* and *plerique* regarded the crossing out of the heirs' names as a *pars pro toto*. This literary device is a figure of speech, a rhetorical trope, that serves to embellish. True, the *fiscus* and *plerique* argue that the erasure of the heirs' names invalidates the entire will, but that is a legal rather than a rhetorical point.

We also differ with Hendel on two points. First, we do not think that in D. 28.4.3 pr. *in fine* Marcus Aurelius only decided on the validity of the legacies in Valerius Nepos' will; if he did, why then did Marcellus not say so? The second point concerns the discussion about the compilers being right or wrong to include Marcellus' opinion in title D. 50.17. In our view, Hendel errs in ignoring its rhetorical character. D. 28.4.3 pr. clearly shows that Marcellus supports his opinion that the legacies in Nepos' will can be regarded as valid with the *regula* that a milder interpretation is more just and safe. Expressing an opinion in general terms is not tantamount to creating a general rule of interpretation. Whether the compilers were right or wrong to include Marcellus' opinion in title D. 50.17 is not an easy question to answer because it depends on what a *regula* is and why the compilers created this title in the first place. We return to this issue in the final chapter.

Having reviewed Wankerl's and Hendel's theories about D. 28.4.3 pr. and its connection to the *regula* of D. 50.17.192.1, we now present our view. We submit that the main bone of contention in the case set out in D. 28.4.3 pr. is whether the *legata per praeceptionem* can be considered valid despite the testator having erased the names of the heirs in the *heredis institutio*. This is the central topic of discussion in the *consilium*, and we think it is also the fundamental if unrecorded reason for the case to have been brought before the emperor.

In D. 28.4.3 pr., the question is whether the *fiscus* was entitled to claim the entire estate of the deceased testator, Valerius Nepos, after he had erased the names of the heirs he had instituted in his will. In the *consilium*, there had been a long discussion (*diu ... dubitatum*) about the validity of the legacies and particularly of those legacies left to the instituted heirs. The majority argued they were not valid, some said they were. Marcellus presented arguments against either position and concluded that the case was a *res dubia* because it was not clear what the testator had wanted when he erased the heirs' names. The case consequently turned on the *status ambiguitas*.

Marcellus does not mention the arguments the two parties put forward, but he does refute them. These rebuttals were possibly based on the arguments presented by the other party. The majority took the view that the will had become invalid in its entirety (legacies and all), the minority held that only the erased provisions had been invalidated. Marcellus refuted the minority opinion with a rhetorical question: 'Is it not sometimes credible that someone who had erased the names of his heirs had thought that he would have done enough to bring about an intestacy?' This argument may well have been the reason for the majority to consider the entire will void. The majority opinion that the legatees should also be excluded Marcellus refuted by arguing that such an exclusion would follow if the testator had erased all the writing in the will. This may well have been the point made by the minority: since the testator had only erased the heirs' names, he must have wanted to preserve the rest of the will.

Both of Marcellus' arguments can be traced back to rhetorical textbooks for questions turning on *ambiguitas*. The second argument Cicero mentions in *De inventione* is to deduce from the context what the testator wanted.[53] It is this type of argument the majority used: the context – the heirs' names have been erased – shows that the testator wanted to invalidate the will in its entirety. The minority used the same type of argument: from the context –only the heirs' names have been erased – it can be deduced that the testator wanted the rest of the will to stand.

Marcellus sides with the minority arguing that when in doubt, following the milder interpretation is both fairer and safer. This argument echoes Cicero's suggestion a little further on in *De inventione*: 'By stating that our interpretation is honourable, useful, and necessary, we make clear that the interpretation of the other party fails in this respect.'[54] The milder interpretation is more honourable because it is safer and more just.

Marcellus then quotes Marcus Aurelius' judgment that the original heirs could not inherit Valerius Nepos' estate. As this ruling does not specify whether it applies to everything the testator had bequeathed in his will, Vibius Zeno asks the emperor what his decision implies for the legacies. The emperor's immediate answer is a rhetorical question: 'Does it seem to you that someone who erased the names of his heirs intended his will to stand?' The obvious answer is 'No', confirming that the emperor's mind is still attuned to the ruling he has just handed down, but Cornelius Priscianus is quick to point out that while Nepos had indeed erased the heirs' names, he had left the manumissions and the legacies intact.[55] The counsel for the treasury objects that it is not possible

53 Cicero, *De inv.* 2. 117. Also, for instance, Cicero, *De oratore* 2.110 and Cicero, *Topica* 96.

54 Cicero, *De inv.* 2. 119.

55 It is not clear how Zeno and Leo are involved in this trial. Wankerl (2009) 81 note 447 suggests that Zeno had been manumitted in the will and that Leo was entitled to a *legatum per praeceptionem*. Stagl (2014) 866, on the other hand, believes Zeno was a legatee and in fact the same person as Leo. With Wankerl, we think it is impossible to know who they were. It is not especially relevant either.

for any will to stand that does not have an heir in it, but the emperor, after due consideration, decides that only the provisions that had been erased should be ineffectual and that for the case at hand a more humane interpretation is the more appropriate one. With his initial decision thus qualified, the emperor squarely lands on Marcellus' side.[56]

There is, however, one notable difference between the decision handed down by the Emperor Marcus Aurelius and Marcellus' opinion: whereas the emperor uses the *benignitas* argument for this particular case only, Marcellus expresses it in general terms, as a *thesis*. Undoubtedly, this difference originates in the difference in purpose. While the emperor needs to substantiate his judgment in this specific case (*Causa praesens*), Marcellus needs to convince the emperor of his point of view, and using words that suggest a universal scope is likely to add to the persuasiveness of his argument. It is not stretching probability to assume that the compilers noticed this difference and for that reason included Marcellus' *thesis* as a *regula* in title D. 50.17.

56 In our view, Palma (1992) 42 is wrong when he states that Marcellus agrees with the emperor. It is the other way round: Marcellus presents an argument that the emperor, having reflected on it, acknowledges and endorses in his ruling.

CHAPTER 11

D. 50.17.1 and the *regula Catoniana*

The first text in the final title of the Digest, D. 50.17 *De diversis regulis iuris antiqui*, is puzzling: while to the casual eye the compilers included it as an introduction to the 210 *regulae* listed in that title, the *regulae* themselves are rather different from one another. In modern literature, no attempts have been made to explain D. 50.17.1 in relation to the texts that follow it. Some scholars have connected D. 50.17.1 with the *regula Catoniana* even though that *regula* does not occur in title D. 50.17. Having demonstrated that twenty *regulae* in D. 50.17 are rhetorical arguments formulated in general terms, we now aim to find out whether D. 50.17.1 fits the same mould. We then do the same for the *regula Catoniana* and see how it compares with D. 50.17.1.

1 Paulus D. 50.17.1.

> Paulus 16 ad Plautium. Regula est, quae rem quae est breviter enarrat. Non ex regula ius sumatur, sed ex iure quod est regula fiat. Per regulam igitur brevis rerum narratio traditur, et, ut ait Sabinus, quasi causae coniectio est, quae simul cum in aliquo vitiata est, perdit officium suum.
>
> A *regula* is what briefly clarifies what a case is about. The law is not to be derived from a *regula*, but a *regula* must follow from the law as it is. By means of a *regula*, therefore, a brief narrative of the facts is provided and, as Sabinus says, as it were, the summary of the question at issue, which loses its function as soon as it is falsified in any way.

The *inscriptio* communicates that this fragment stems from Book 16 of Paul's commentary on Plautius, a jurist who lived at the time of the Emperor Vespasian's reign. In his palingenesis of this work, Lenel indicated that Book 16 deals with manumissions but – not knowing how D. 50.17.1 fitted in – he included it at the end of this book.[1]

In what may be an attempt to describe the concept of *regula*, D. 50.17.1 has attracted a lot of attention from Romanists, beginning in 1833 and culminating

1 Lenel (1889) I col. 1173, no. 1230. In a footnote he remarks *Quo haec spectent, ignoro.*

 | DOI:10.1163/9789004711020_012

in the methodological studies of around 1970.[2] A major point of debate was whether the *regula* was a normative rule or a definition, and two monographs have been dedicated to the *regulae iuris*: one by Stein dating from 1966, the other by Schmidlin published in 1970. We first review their interpretations and then present our reading.

Stein contends that D. 50.17.1 reflects a difference of opinion among the classical jurists about what a *regula* is. He begins his analysis by placing this text in its original context, that of manumissions.[3] He then refers to Daube who 'has shown that the text originally formed part of a discussion of the validity of legacies given to manumitted slaves and, in particular, to the effect on such legacies of the *regula Catoniana*.'[4] Stein states that its designation as a *regula* implied that the *regula Catoniana* was generally applicable to cases of legacies to manumitted slaves and that some classical jurists, led by Sabinus, allegedly challenged this notion and tried to circumvent the *regula*. In this connection, Stein refers to Dietrich Behrens who had 'observed that the three sentences of which D. 50.17.1 is composed do not fit well together. The beginning of the third sentence merely repeats the point made by the first and the *igitur* which connects the third sentence to the second has little meaning.'[5] Stein is not surprised that the fragment is a patchwork since three jurists were involved in wording D. 50.17.1: Paul, Plautius, and Sabinus. The last sentence of the text gives Sabinus' own view: '*regula* = *definitio* = statement of facts (*rerum narratio*): if it conflicts with the facts it has no value whatever.'[6]

Next, Stein argues that Sabinus' view was shared by Iavolenus, who was a leader of the Sabinian school at the end of the first century AD. But as other jurists regarded a *regula* not just as a neutral statement of facts but as normative, Stein suggests that this difference of opinion was actually one of the controversies between the Sabinian and Proculian schools. To support his view, he refers to a text by Celsus in which this leader of the Proculian school regarded the *regula Catoniana* as still having some value even if in certain cases it is false (D. 34.7.1 pr.).

Stein finds this difference between the two ways of regarding *regulae* reflected in D. 50.17.1: in the first sentence the verb *enarrare* is used in connection with *regula,* whereas in the third sentence a *regula* is referred to as a

2 For an overview of the older literature, see Schmidlin (1970) 8 note 16. In *Fiuris*, D. 50.17.1 gets 117 hits.

3 Stein (1966) 67.

4 Stein (1966) 67 referring to Daube (1959) 205–206.

5 Stein (1966) 69–70 referring to Behrens (1958) 353–354.

6 Stein (1966) 70.

narratio.[7] Citing Varro and Quintilian, Stein observes that the verb *enarrare* not only means 'to expound', 'to relate', but also 'to interpret'. In his view, 'a *regula* which *enarrat*, does not merely summarise the law; it brings out its hidden significance and gives it a certain tendency. By the choice of words of which it is composed, it hints at the *ratio*, the principle or policy, of the law.'[8] The phrase *per regulam … narratio traditur*, on the other hand, refers to a *regula* as a bald statement of facts. Stein suggests that the first sentence stems from Plautius, who would regard a *regula* as something of a normative rule, whereas in the second and third sentences Sabinus gives his own interpretation of a *regula* as a juristic rule which merely reflected the actual state of the law and had no independent normative force.[9]

Schmidlin pursues a different path of perception.[10] While he concedes that Daube's suggestion about D. 50.17.1 referring to the *regula Catoniana* may be correct, he believes there is more to it. He reasons that the *regula Catoniana* was regarded as a normative rule, which as such claimed general validity and tended to be rigorous, and that Paul as well as the other classical jurists turned away from such normative rules, preferring an elastic casuistry.[11] When stating *non ex regula ius sumatur, sed ex iure quod est regula fiat*, Paul made it clear, Schmidlin postulates, that in general he rejected normative rules and the law to be deduced from them; he may have had in mind the *regula Catoniana* but also some other *regula*, Schmidlin contends. Moreover, Schmidlin continues, the structure of the text does not give any information about either the original context or the specific rules Paul may have had in mind. To Schmidlin's mind, the compilers shortened the text drastically to make it fit for purpose as an introduction to the *regulae* gathered in title D. 50.17.

Like Behrens, Schmidlin thinks that D. 50.17.1 consists of three sentences that are not an easy fit, but he explains the gaps between the sentences as resulting from interference by the compilers. He suggests that the three sentences refer to three types of *regula*: the definition type, the normative *regula*, and the casuistic one. The first sentence refers to the definition type; it can be regarded as a remote descendant of the 'Definitionsregel' stemming from Stoic logic. The second sentence, Schmidlin argues, is essential, for it deals with the relationship between *regula* and *ius*. Here, Paul allegedly contrasted two types

7 Stein (1966) 71.
8 Stein (1966) 72.
9 Stein (1966) 73.
10 Schmidlin (1970) 7–18.
11 Schmidlin (1970) 11: 'Gerade ihre Starrheit weckt den Widerspruch der eine elastische Kasuistik vorziehenden klassischen Juristen.'

of *regula*: the normative one that lays down the law (*ex qua ius sumatur*, like the *regula Catoniana*), and the casuistic one that only presents and summarises the law: *qui ex iure sumatur*. In Schmidlin's view, Paul rejected the first one, just as Sabinus and later jurists had done, and he approved of the second one. In the third sentence, he confirmed his position by quoting Sabinus' comparison of the *regula* with the *causae coniectio:* such casuistic rules can be easily abolished when legal opinion changes. Schmidlin recognises this type of *regula* in the *libri regularum* to which Paul himself contributed a volume.

Well-organised though they are, these interpretations, we feel, do not significantly clarify matters. Stein's argument that D. 50.17.1 contains a difference of opinion is based on the supposed contrast between the words *enarrat* and *narratio*, but we do not think these words have contradictory meanings. True, it is conceivable that in this text *enarrare* is used in the sense of 'to interpret', for in the *regula* the advocate or jurist will give his view of the case, but it is unlikely that *enarrare* is used in the sense of 'hinting at the *ratio* of the law', because the object of *enarrat* is *rem quae est*, not *ius quod est*. *Enarrat* simply means 'expounds', stating the facts of the case, just as the words *rerum narratio* in the third sentence mean 'a narrative of the facts'.

Schmidlin's suggestion that each of the three sentences of D. 50.17.1 contains a different type of *regula* is not entirely plausible either. The first sentence does not say that a *regula* is a definition; if it had been meant to say that, Paul certainly would not have used *enarrat*. This in turn weakens the connection Schmidlin makes with Stoic logic. Nor is he on firm ground with his contention that the second sentence refers to a normative and a casuistic *regula*; indeed, it says that the *regula* should not set a legal standard (*non ex regula ius sumatur*) but should follow from the law as it is.[12] The very expression 'casuistic rule' – which Schmidlin alleges is confirmed in the third sentence – would appear to be a *contradictio in terminis*.

Both Stein and Schmidlin follow Behrens' criticism of D. 50.17.1, but neither of them explains why the compilers ought to have placed such a complicated and even intrinsically contradictory text at the beginning of title D. 50.17. If Stein's theory is correct, there should be traces of the supposed 'difference of opinion among the classical jurists about the meaning of *regula*' in the rest of title D. 50.17. We cannot find them, and Stein himself does not mention them either in his discussion of the content of D. 50.17. If Schmidlin's theory is

12 Nörr (1972) 29 follows Schmidlin's interpretation of the first sentence but on p. 30 he does not think that the second sentence refers to two types of *regulae*.

correct, then it should be possible to find three types of *regula* in this title. We cannot find those either.

How then do we explain D. 50.17.1? As we mentioned in Chapter 4, the preface to the Digest does not provide any clue about the purpose of title D. 50.17. That leaves the content of the title for us to go by. In Chapters 5 through 10, we showed that twenty *regulae* in D. 50.17 are rhetorical arguments, *topoi*, meant for a specific case formulated in general terms, as *theseis*; it is possible and to our mind likely that the same holds for many of the other *regulae* in that title.[13] If that is the case, then D. 50.17.1 arguably contains a description of the concept of *regula* in this rhetorical sense and the compilers may for that reason have been moved to place it at the beginning of title D. 50.17. Starting from this hypothesis, we interpret D. 50.17.1 as follows.

D. 50.17.1 relates to the wording of a convincing argument in a legal conflict, to be used before the praetor and/or the judge. The first sentence introduces the concept of *regula* as the summary of someone's view of the conflict in short and general terms. A good example may be the *regula* in D. 50.17.4: *Velle non creditur qui obsequitur imperio patris vel domini*. The second sentence indicates that the law cannot be inferred from that summary because it is not a normative rule but a rhetorical argument; hence, the *regula* must follow the law. In D. 50.17.4, for instance, this law would be that a *filius* is subject to the *patria potestas*. In the third sentence, Paul concludes that a *regula* is a statement of the key facts and the legal question concisely rolled into one. In D. 50.17.4 the *regula* in this sense would be: Is someone who accepts an inheritance at the order of his *pater familias* regarded as wanting to do so himself? Paul approvingly quotes Sabinus, who said that a *regula* loses its function as soon as one fact of the case is changed. In our view, that could happen if a *regula* is used as an argument in another case than it had originally been invented for. This interpretation leaves the Latin text completely intact: it is not intrinsically contradictory and it suits the Justinian context quite well.

As we mentioned in the opening of this chapter, some scholars have linked D. 50.17.1 to the *regula Catoniana*, and if our reading is correct, then D. 50.17.1 should be applicable to that *regula*, too. To put this hypothesis to the test, we must first find out more about the *regula Catoniana*: What is known about it and what are the relevant sources (Sections 2 and 3)? Next, we reconstruct the case Cato dealt with and interpret the *regula* in this context (Section 4), and finally, we apply D. 50.17.1 to the *regula Catoniana* (Section 5).

13 In Chapter 4, we explained there are 137 *regulae* that could very well be *theseis* but that cannot be identified as rhetorical arguments because their original context has been lost.

2 The *regula Catoniana*

Dating from the second century BC, the *regula Catoniana* is the oldest surviving *regula*. The oldest source is D. 34.7.1, a text by Celsus *filius* from his *Digesta*, a work that was written more than 250 years later.[14]

> D. 34.7.1 pr. Celsus 35 Dig. Catoniana regula sic definit, quod, si testamenti facti tempore decessisset testator, inutile foret, id legatum quandocumque decesserit, non valere. Quae definitio in quibusdam falsa est.
>
> The Catonian Rule is as follows: 'A legacy which would have been invalid if the testator had died immediately after making his will is invalid whenever he dies.' In some cases, this statement of the rule is misleading.[15]

Uncertainty surrounds the origins of the *regula Catoniana*. It may stem from Cato *Censorius* or from his son. It may be based on a *responsum* by Cato or it may have been drawn up by him as a *regula*. Its original context is unknown,[16] and Book 35 of Celsus' *Digesta* is titled *Ad legem Iuliam et Papiam*, but the *regula Catoniana* obviously cannot refer to these laws. The heading of title D. 34.7 in Justinian's Digest is *De regula Catoniana*.

In modern Romanist literature, the *regula Catoniana* is generally regarded as an important legal rule from the time of the Republic, when it has long been assumed Roman legal science came into being. In his manual, Kaser describes Roman private law as case law which had only partially been formulated in norms, such as *leges*, *plebiscita*, and *senatusconsulta*, and he adds: 'Normativ gefaßt sind aber auch gewisse von den Juristen entwickelte *regulae*, die von ihnen in ähnlicher Weise als feststehend behandelt werden wie Gesetze.'[17] In a footnote, he refers to the *regula Catoniana*.

From the sixteenth century onwards, the *regula Catoniana* has generated an extensive literature, and the main question has always been in what cases

---

14 Lenel (1889) I col. 166, no. 250.

15 Watson's translation of the rule begins with 'Any legacy', a choice we believe exaggerates the general character of the rule. Otto, Schilling, and Sintenis have 'dasjenige Vermächtnis' and d'Ors has 'El legado'. Like Spruit ('een legaat') we prefer 'A legacy'. The words *testamenti facti tempore* are commonly translated as 'at the time of the making of the will'. We think this translation is wrong, because it takes no account of the perfect tense of *facti*. Only Scott does and we follow his translation.

16 Lenel (1889) I col. 126 combined this text with four other texts containing quotes from Cato under the heading *Laudatur non indicato libro*.

17 Kaser (1971) 211 with note 8.

and how this *regula* was applied. One scholar to address the question was Jacques Lambert in his monograph on the *regula Catoniana*.[18] He severely criticised older research for tending to recognise the *regula Catoniana* in many texts in Justinian's Digest which he thought had nothing to do with it. He himself assumed that the *regula Catoniana* was a legal rule that applied to one case only, namely that of the *legatum per vindicationem* of something already belonging to the legatee, in which case the legacy would be invalid.[19] Lambert believed that the *regula* dated back to the time when a will could only contain *legata per vindicationem* that transferred ownership to the legatee as soon as the testator died,[20] and he postulated that Cato used other *responsa* to coin the principle that later came to be known as the *regula Catoniana*.[21]

Even though Lambert's interpretation has not been widely accepted,[22] we think he was right to assume that the *regula Catoniana* concerned only one case. Yet we do not think this case concerned a *legatum per vindicationem*: Celsus' definition in D. 34.7.1 pr. does not imply it nor do other sources confirm it.[23] Moreover, there are no sources to support Lambert's view that Cato based his *regula* on older *responsa*.

If, as we believe we have demonstrated in the previous chapters, twenty *regulae* in D. 50.17 were rhetorical arguments meant for a specific case but formulated in general terms and if in D. 50.17.1 the *regula* was described in that sense, the question arises whether this also holds for the *regula Catoniana*: was it a normative rule or an argument for a specific case formulated in general terms?

As the extensive Romanist literature about the *regula Catoniana* is, in the main, associative and as a result somewhat diffuse, we prefer to start from the primary sources. The Digest contains a limited number of texts that deal with the *regula Catoniana* and that we divide into three categories. Title D. 34.7 (*De regula Catoniana*) consists of five texts (Section 3.1). Three texts in the Digest outside this title mention the *regula* (Section 3.2). And finally, there are a few texts in the Digest (and elsewhere) whose phrasing is reminiscent of the *regula Catoniana* but that do not explicitly mention it (Section 3.3).

18 Lambert (1925) 7–8.
19 Lambert (1925) 104–118.
20 This would have been the transition period between the primitive will *per mancipationem* and the *testamentum per aes et libram*.
21 Lambert (1925) 20.
22 Cf. Voci (1963) 998–1000; Kaser (1971) 754 with note 7.
23 In his review of Lambert's book, Kreller (1927) 436–439 does not consider these issues.

3 Primary Sources on the *regula Catoniana*

3.1 *The Five Texts in Title D. 34.7* De regula Catoniana

The first text in this title is the one by Celsus we mentioned before. Above, we quoted only the *principium* of D. 34.7.1. The whole text runs as follows.

> Celsus 35 Dig. Catoniana regula sic definit, quod, si testamenti facti tempore decessisset testator, inutile foret, id legatum quandocumque decesserit, non valere. quae definitio in quibusdam falsa est. 1. Quid enim, si quis ita legaverit: 'si post kalendas mortuus fuero, Titio dato?' An cavillamur? Nam hoc modo si statim mortuus fuerit, non esse datum legatum verius est quam inutiliter datum. 2. Item si tibi legatus est fundus, qui scribendi testamenti tempore tuus est, si eum vivo testatore alienaveris, legatum tibi debetur, quod non deberetur, si testator statim decessisset.
>
> The Catonian Rule is as follows: 'A legacy which would have been invalid if the testator had died immediately after making his will is invalid whenever he dies.' In some cases, this statement of the rule is misleading. 1. For suppose someone makes a legacy in the following terms: 'If I die after the Kalends, let such-and-such a sum be given to Titius.' Are we going to quibble about this? The more correct view is that in the event of the testator's immediate death, the situation is one in which the legacy does not take effect rather than one in which it was invalidly made. 2. Similarly, if a piece of land which at the time of the making of the will was your property is legated to you and if you would then have alienated it[24] during the testator's lifetime, the legacy is owed to you, but it would not have been owed in the event of the testator's immediate death.

Celsus points out that in some cases the *regula Catoniana* is false, and instead of giving examples of cases to which the *regula* would apply, he gives two examples of cases to which he says it does not apply.[25]

---

24 Watson translates the phrase *si eum … alienaveris* as 'on the understanding that you will alienate it', suggesting that this phrase referred to a condition in the will. In our view, the phrase describes only what might happen after the will has been drawn up. Similarly, Otto, Schilling, and Sintenis, d'Ors, and Spruit. We have modified Watson's translation accordingly.

25 Somewhat astonishingly, Voci (1963) 998 states that the rule would apply, for instance, when the object of the legacy belonged to the legatee, and he adds that such a legacy would not become valid if, after the will had been made, the object became someone else's property. Moreover, when quoting D. 34.7.1 pr. Voci omits to include the phrase *quae definitio in quibusdam falsa est*; nor does he refer to Celsus' example in D. 34.7.1.2. On

The first example concerns a testator who makes a legacy on the condition that he dies after the Kalends, that is to say, after the first day of the next month. When the testator dies immediately after his will has been drawn up, the legacy lapses, not, as Celsus rather testily observes, because it has been invalidly made but rather because it does not take effect. Opinions on what precisely Celsus means vary.[26] We believe Celsus' view is that the legacy is not owed because the condition has not been fulfilled, in which case the *regula Catoniana* does not apply.

The second example concerns the bequest of a piece of land that belonged to the legatee; that legacy would be invalid because one cannot leave something to someone who already owns it, but if during the testator's life the legatee alienated the land, then, Celsus says, the legacy is valid and owed. It would, however, not be owed if the testator had died immediately after drawing up his will, in which case the *regula Catoniana* would not apply.

Both examples, then, concern cases to which the *regula Catoniana* on reflection does not apply. Stein and Hausmaninger present them as two exceptions to the rule, confirming that the *regula Catoniana* was normative rather than descriptive,[27] but this reasoning strikes us as being at variance with Celsus' observation that, in some cases, the rule is misleading: an argument can be misleading, but a normative rule cannot. It would appear, then, that Celsus regarded the *regula Catoniana* as an argument meant for a specific case and formulated in general terms.

The second text in D. 34.7 is by the jurist Paul. It runs as follows:

> Paulus 4 ad Plautium. Sed et si sic legaverit: 'si filia mea Titio nupta erit', sufficere visum est, si mortis tempore nupta inveniatur, licet testamenti facti tempore fuerit impubes.
>
> But if someone makes a legacy on the condition that 'my daughter will marry Titius', it has been held sufficient that she is shown to be married at the time of the testator's death, even if at the time of the making of the will she was *impubes*.

Lenel notes that this text does not derive from Book 4 of Paul's commentary on Plautius but from Book 9, which concerns legacies.[28] A testator had included in his will a legacy for his daughter on the condition that she marry Titius. At

---

p. 999 note 10 he does refer to D. 34.7.1.1 and 2 to illustrate his statement that the rule does not apply to a conditional legacy but that case is dealt with in D. 34.7.1.1 only.

26 For an extensive comment, see Hausmaninger (1968) 477–480.

27 Stein (1966) 71; Hausmaninger (1968) 481.

28 Lenel (1889) I 1164 note 1: in the *Florentina* manuscript, VIIII is written as IIII.

the time he made the will, his daughter was not yet of age and therefore unable to contract a valid marriage. However, when the testator died, she was Titius' wife. It seems the heir refused to pay over the legacy to her, using the *regula Catoniana* as an argument: when the will was drawn up, the testator's daughter was not married to Titius and therefore the condition imposed on the legacy was not fulfilled. Paul, on the other hand, argued that for the validity of the legacy it was sufficient for the daughter to be married to Titius by the time her father died. His argument amounts to a rejection of the *regula Catoniana*.

The remaining three texts in D. 34.7 derive from the jurists Papinian and Ulpian. They exclude the use of the *regula Catoniana* in various situations:

> D. 34.7.3 Papinianus 15 Dig. Catoniana regula non pertinet ad hereditates neque ad ea legata, quorum dies non mortis tempore, sed post aditam cedit hereditatem.
>
> The Catonian Rule does not apply to inheritances or legacies whose *dies cedens* is not the time of death, but the acceptance of the inheritance.

This text deviates from the *regula Catoniana* as worded by Celsus in two ways. First, Papinian discusses the *regula* in connection with both inheritances and legacies, whereas Celsus refers only to legacies. Second, for the *dies cedens* (the day when the legacy falls due), Papinian distinguishes between the time of the testator's death and the time of the heir accepting the inheritance, while Celsus does not mention either time but refers to the time immediately after the testator had made his will. Possibly, Papinian was inspired by the distinction which in his day was made in connection with the *regula Catoniana* between the *heres necessarius* and the *heres voluntarius*: the former (a *filius* or a manumitted slave) acquired the inheritance as soon as the testator died, whereas the latter acquired the inheritance only after formally accepting it. (Two texts referring to this distinction, by Maecianus and Paul, belong to the second category and we discuss them there.)

> D. 34.7.4 Ulpianus 10 ad Sab. Placet Catonis regulam ad condicionales institutions non pertinere.
>
> It is agreed that the Catonian Rule does not apply to conditional appointment of heirs.

It is not clear what this *responsum* by Ulpian is about: the *regula Catoniana*, after all, does not pertain to the appointment of heirs, conditional or otherwise. Referring back to the French humanist A. Faber, Lenel thought the word *condicionales* could not derive from Ulpian.[29] He assumed that this text referred to the well-known opinion of the *Sabiniani* mentioned in Gaius, *Inst.* 2.123 that passing over a *filius* would make the will invalid *ab initio*. In Ulpian's case, the legal question would then have been whether a will would also be invalid *ab initio* if a *filius* had been conditionally appointed heir. For an affirmative response, a comparison would have been made with conditional legacies, and Ulpian would have countered with the argument that 'the *regula Catoniana* does not apply to the appointment of heirs'. The compilers, Lenel surmised, did not fully understand Ulpian's answer and would have added the word *condicionales*.

We do not believe this to be a plausible explanation, nor do we believe the word *condicionales* to obfuscate matters.[30] The straightforward question Ulpian deals with is whether the Catonian rule applies to the conditional appointment of heirs. The equally straightforward answer is no because the rule simply does not apply to the appointment of heirs at all, be they conditional or not.

> D. 34.7.5 Ulpianus 22 ad Sab. Regula Catoniana ad novas leges non pertinet.
>
> The Catonian Rule does not apply to new laws.

The 'new laws' mentioned in this text are probably the *leges Iulia et Papia Poppaea*.[31] In these laws, which were introduced in the context of Augustus' population policy, the law of succession was used to enforce observance. Non-observance could lead to reduced *capacitas* to inherit. Whether someone was *capax* was determined at the moment the inheritance devolved. Someone had probably tried to use to their advantage the fact that an heir or legatee was *incapax* when the testator drew up his will, but Ulpian made short work of that argument: the *regula Catoniana* does not apply.

These five texts create the impression that in the early Empire the *regula Catoniana* was sometimes used to argue that a legacy or some other testamentary disposition was invalid. In D. 34.7.1, Celsus pointed out that such arguments were misleading: they seemed to be convincing but they were legally wrong – in other words, they were rhetorical arguments. The other four texts in this title suggest that those arguments did not meet with success. We now turn to texts outside D. 34.7.

---

29 Lenel (1889) II 1041 note 1.

30 Heirs could be appointed conditionally, as the *causa Curiana* shows. Even so, Voci (1963) 999 note 13 believes Lenel's explanation to be plausible.

31 According to Voci (1967) 433 with note 12 and 444 with note 63.

3.2 *The* regula Catoniana *Outside Title D. 34.7*

Outside D. 34.7, three texts have been preserved in the Digest that explicitly mention the *regula Catoniana*. These are texts by Ulpian, Maecianus, and Paul.

> D. 30.41.2 Ulpianus 21 ad Sabinum. Tractari tamen poterit, si quando marmora vel columnae fuerint separatae ab aedibus, an legatum convalescat. Et si quidem ab initio non constitit legatum, ex post facto non convalescet, quemadmodum nec res mea legata mihi, si post testamentum factum fuerit alienata, quia vires ab initio legatum non habuit. Sed si sub condicione legetur, poterit legatum valere, si exsistentis condicionis tempore mea non sit vel aedibus iuncta non sit, secundum eos, qui et emi rem meam sub condicione et promitti mihi stipulanti et legari aiunt. Purum igitur legatum Catoniana regula impediet, condicionale non, quia ad condicionalia Catoniana non pertinet.
>
> However, the question may arise whether, if at some time marbles or columns became separated from buildings, the legacy becomes valid. Well, if the legacy is not valid from the beginning, it does not become valid after the event, just as the bequest of my own property to me, if it is alienated after the will has been made, remains invalid because it had no effect in the first place. But if it is bequeathed under a condition, the legacy may be valid if at the time when the condition is fulfilled the property is not mine, or the thing is not joined to buildings, according to those who hold that I can buy my own property under a condition and that it can be promised and bequeathed to me under a stipulation. The rule of Cato will therefore prevent an unconditional legacy but not a conditional one, because it does not apply to conditional bequests.

In the first of the three texts, Ulpian raises the topic of the *regula Catoniana* in the context of legacies and particularly asks what things can be the object of a legacy. In the preceding text, D. 30.41.1, he states that all kinds of things can be bequeathed, but things that are attached to buildings cannot, due to a *senatus consultum* to that effect. Ulpian now turns to the question of whether, if at some time marbles or columns have become separated from buildings, they can be validly bequeathed. He thinks not, and he compares this case with that of a bequest of his own property to himself if he has alienated it after the will has been made. Ulpian argues that such a legacy is invalid because it was invalid from the start, when the will was made; only if his property has been bequeathed to himself under a condition and if the property is not his when the condition is fulfilled can the legacy be valid. He concludes with a summary: the *regula Catoniana* does block an unconditional legacy but not a conditional one.[32]

It is clear that Ulpian makes no bones about using the *regula Catoniana*. He argues that the legacy in question is invalid, and he supports his argument by contrasting this unconditional legacy with a conditional one. If the legacy had been made under a condition, it would have been valid. It has not been, so it is invalid. In rhetorical terms, he uses the *topos e contrario*. He uses exactly the same example that Celsus uses in D. 34.7.1.2 (the bequest of one's own property to oneself) but unlike Celsus he does apply the *regula Catoniana* to this case.

The second text in the category of *regulae Catonianae* outside D. 34.7 derives from the second century jurist L. Volusius Maecianus.

> D. 35.1.86.1 Maecianus 3 fideic. Cum vero libertas sub condicione, legatum autem praesenti die datum est, in hoc quaestio est, an constiterit legatum: etenim nec Catonianae sententiae locum in proposito esse, quia etsi statim testator decessisset, non tamen omnimodo inutile esset legatum, cum posset condicio libertatis ante aditam hereditatem impleri et legatum manumisso deberi, nisi forte necessarius heres exstitisset: tunc enim omnimodo inutile erit legatum iure ipso, quia sub condicione acceperit libertatem.
>
> Now when freedom is granted subject to a condition but a legacy is[33] presently due, the question is whether the legacy is effective: Cato's sentence[34] has no place here because even if the testator were to die forthwith, the legacy would not become wholly ineffective, since the condition of the slave's freedom could be realized before the heir's acceptance of the inheritance and the legacy so become due to the freedman, that is, of course, if there were no *heres necessarius*; in this latter case, the legacy would be quite invalid by operation of law,[35] since the gift of freedom was conditional.

Maecianus argues that the *regula Catoniana* does not apply to a legacy left to a conditionally freed slave, because the legacy will be valid if the condition is fulfilled before the heir accepts the inheritance, making the testator's immediate death irrelevant. However, he continues, the legacy will be invalid if the heir

32 Similarly, Paul. D. 35.1.98.

33 The Watson translation (mistakenly) here has 'as'.

34 Watson translates *Catonianae sententiae* as 'the rationale of the *regula Catoniana*'. In our view, the word *sententia* is used here in a rhetorical sense, as a synonym of *regula* (cf. Quintilian, *Inst. Or.* 8.5).

35 Here, Watson mistranslates *iure ipso* as 'at civil law'.

is a *heres necessarius* because he then acquires the inheritance *iure ipso* at the testator's death and does not have to formally accept.[36] In this scenario, there simply is no time for the condition to be fulfilled and the slave consequently is incapable of acquiring the legacy. In other words, the legacy will not be invalid because of the *regula Catoniana* but because of an unfulfilled condition.

The third and final text in this category is by Paul.

> D. 33.5.13 pr. Paulus 8 ad Plautium. Si optio servi data mihi fuerit et Sticho aliquid testator sine libertate legasset, tunc sequens legatum consistit, cum tota familia ad unum, id est Stichum recciderit, ut quasi pure legato utiliter sit legatum. Nec adversatur Catoniana, si voluntarius heres institutus sit, quia potest ante aditam hereditatem, etiamsi statim decesserit, familia minui: quod si necessarius heres institutus sit, sequens legatum propter Catonianam inutile est.
>
> If the option of a slave has been given to me and the testator has left something to Stichus without granting him freedom, the second legacy stands only when the entire household is reduced to one individual, namely Stichus, so that the legacy is valid just as if it had been made unconditionally. Cato's rule does not tell against this, if a *heres voluntarius* has been instituted, because the household can be diminished before the inheritance is accepted, even if the testator dies immediately. But if a *heres necessarius* has been instituted, the second legacy is invalid on account of Cato's rule.

The legacy left to a slave belonging to the estate (Stichus) without setting him free is invalid unless he becomes the property of a third person, for instance, another legatee. In this case, a legatee has been given the right to choose a slave from the estate. If he chooses Stichus, then he will acquire Stichus' bequest as well, but it is not certain that he will choose Stichus. Only if Stichus is the only slave left to the estate will the legatee's choice inevitably fall on Stichus and will the legacy become valid. In other words, the legatee's right to choose a slave functions as a condition for Stichus to acquire his legacy.

But of course, it takes time to reduce the number of slaves, for instance by selling them, and it is here that Paul introduces the *regula Catoniana*. It will not affect the legacy left to Stichus if the appointed heir is a *heres voluntarius*, someone who can acquire the inheritance only after formally accepting it, because the required acceptance will not take place for some time after the

36 Voci (1967) 577.

testator has died. Selling the slaves of the estate except Stichus in the interim fulfils the condition, and Stichus together with his legacy will go to the legatee. However, if the heir is a *heres necessarius* there is no time to reduce the number of slaves and then the *regula Catoniana* invalidates Stichus' legacy.

In the case Paul relates, the appointed heir may have refused to pay over Stichus' legacy to the legatee and resorted to the *regula Catoniana* as an argument. Paul defends the legatee's claim by contrasting the actual situation of a *heres voluntarius* (Stichus' legacy is valid) with the hypothetical situation of a *heres necessarius* (Stichus' legacy is invalid) to conclude that Stichus' legacy was valid. In rhetorical terms, he uses the *topos e contrario*. It would appear that both sides used rhetorical arguments rather than the less appealing legal argument that a slave cannot acquire a legacy.

What we believe these three texts show is that the *regula Catoniana* was widely known and frequently if not always successfully raised as an argument in legal conflicts. Depending on the context, both Ulpian and Paul either rejected or endorsed its application. Ulpian dismissed it in D. 34.7.4 and 5 but affirmed it in D. 30.41.2; Paul denied it in D. 34.7.2 but favoured it in D. 33.5.13 pr. From this we infer that the *regula Catoniana* cannot have been a normative rule of law but was used as a rhetorical argument formulated in general terms.

3.3 *Texts Whose Wording Recalls the* regula Catoniana

Both in the Digest and elsewhere, there are a few texts whose wording brings to mind the *regula Catoniana* without explicitly mentioning it. We discuss two of the best-known ones, one by Julian and one by Gaius.[37]

> D. 36.2.17 Julianus 36 Dig. Cum legato servo aliquid legatur, dies eius legati quod servo datur non mortis tempore, sed aditae hereditatis cedit: et ideo impedimento non est regula iuris, quo minus manumisso legatum debeatur, quia etsi confestim pater familias moreretur, non in eiusdem personam et emolumentum legati et obligatio iuris concurreret. Perinde igitur est hoc, de quo quaeritur, ac si filio herede instituto patri legatum esset: quod consistere intellegitur eo, quod, quamvis statim pater familias moriatur, potest emancipatus adire hereditatem, ut patri legatum debeat.
>
> If a slave be left by legacy, and a legacy be left to him, the legacy given to the slave vests not at the time of the death, but when the inheritance is accepted, and thus no rule of law impedes the legacy to be due to him after

37 Two other well-known texts are *Ulpiani Epitome* 24.23 and Just. *Inst.* 2.20.32.

> manumission; for even if the *pater familias* had died forthwith, the benefit of the legacy and the legal obligation would not concur in the same person.[38] The case in question, therefore, is the same as if a son were instituted heir and a legacy left to the father, which is taken to be valid because, though the *pater familias* should die forthwith, the son may accept the inheritance after emancipation, and thus owe the legacy to his father.

Julian compares the case of a legacy left to a slave who was himself bequeathed with the case of appointing another man's *filius* as heir to whose father was left a legacy. In both cases, the validity of the legacy is questioned. Julian asserts that there is no 'rule of law' to prevent either legacy from becoming due. The generally held view is that *regula iuris* refers to the *regula Catoniana*. But does it?

In modern Romanist literature, the first case has as good as monopolised attention. It has been interpreted in various ways, but always in connection with the *regula Catoniana*, and Daube's view has become the leading one.[39] He assumes that the testator first bequeathed a certain slave to whom he also left a legacy, and that later, before he died, he manumitted the slave. Prior to the manumission, the *dies cedens* (vesting date) of the legacy would have been the time when the testator died and the *regula Catoniana* would have barred the freedman from claiming his legacy, for if the testator had died immediately after drawing up his will, the legacy, having been left to a *servus hereditarius*, would be void. If the testator had not died immediately after drawing up his will and had manumitted the slave later, the result would have been the same. Daube contends that Julian set aside the *regula Catoniana* by moving the *dies cedens* from the testator's death to the acceptance of the inheritance. In that way, the legacy became due to the slave after he was set free.

In our view, this reading of the case is debatable because it does not fully take account of Julian's argument. Julian states that there is no rule of law to prevent the legacy from becoming due after manumission, because 'even if the *pater familias* had died forthwith, the benefit of the legacy and the legal obligation would not concur in the same person.' From this argument, Daube lifts the phrase 'even if the *pater familias* had died forthwith' to make the connection with the *regula Catoniana*. In doing so, he fails to consider that Julian makes a

38 In the modern translations, this sentence has been translated and explained in very different ways, but the *regula iuris* is generally interpreted as the *regula Catoniana*. We prefer to translate as literally as possible.

39 Daube (1959) 207. Similarly, Stein (1966) 68 and Hausmaninger (1968) 475. Schmidlin (1970) 31–32 offers a minor variation.

point of stating which rule of law he means, that is, that the person who is to benefit from the legacy should not be the same one as the person who has a legal obligation (probably to pay over the legacy), and that particular rule has nothing to do with the *regula Catoniana*. Moreover, Daube's understanding of the case does not link up with the second case Julian mentions and which he says deals with the same problem.

We think the first case of D. 36.2.17 should be interpreted in such a way that it parallels the second case. Because Julian added the second case to explain the first one, we start with the second, easier case. A testator appoints another man's *filius* as heir and he includes a legacy for the heir's *pater familias*.[40] When the testator dies and his will is opened, the *pater familias* has to decide to either emancipate his son to enable him to accept the inheritance for himself and pay over the legacy to his father or authorise his son to accept the inheritance on his behalf. In the latter scenario, the legacy is void because the *pater familias* acquires the inheritance including the property left to him in the legacy: he cannot claim the legacy from himself. In the former scenario, the legacy is valid because the emancipated son acquires the inheritance for himself and is obliged to pay over the legacy to his father. There is then no concurrence of benefit and obligation.

Now to the first case of D. 36.2.17. A testator bequeaths a slave to someone, probably requesting the legatee to manumit the slave, and includes a legacy for that slave.[41] After the testator's death, the instituted heir accepts the inheritance and transfers the slave to the legatee who can then manumit him. The freedman claims the legacy from the heir, but the heir refuses to pay. He may have argued that he cannot pay over a legacy to someone who was a slave at the time the testator died. Julian, however, states that the legacy is not due until the instituted heir has accepted the inheritance: it is then that the legatee acquires the slave and, once he has been manumitted, the freedman can claim the legacy from the heir. So, the benefit of the legacy falls to the freedman and the legal obligation to pay over the legacy rests on the heir. The parallel between the two cases is that, after having been manumitted, the freedman can claim the legacy left to him, just as the *pater familias* can after he has

40 Both here and in the first case, the term *pater familias* is used to indicate the testator. It is not clear why this is.

41 It is unlikely that, as Daube assumes, the testator himself would have manumitted the slave, because that would invalidate the slave's legacy. This to us suggests that the testator asked the legatee by *fideicommissum* to manumit the slave. The legatee would then become the freedman's *patronus*.

emancipated his son. In neither case is there concurrence in the same person of the benefit of the legacy and the obligation to pay it over.[42]

We conclude that *regula iuris* in D. 36.2.17 refers to a rule stipulating that a legacy is invalid if the person who is obliged to pay it over is the same as the person who is entitled to it. This rule rests on the legal principle that one cannot owe something to oneself. It certainly is not the *regula Catoniana*.

The second text whose wording is reminiscent of the *regula Catoniana* without explicitly mentioning it stems from Gaius' Institutes:

> Gaius, Inst. 2. 244 An ei, qui in potestate sit eius, quem heredem instituimus, recte legemus, quaeritur. Seruius recte legari putat, sed euanescere legatum, si quo tempore dies legatorum cedere solet, adhuc in potestate sit; ideoque siue pure legatum sit et uiuo testatore in potestate heredis esse desierit, siue sub condicione et ante condicionem id acciderit, deberi legatum. Sabinus et Cassius sub condicione recte legari, pure non recte putant; licet enim uiuo testatore possit desinere in potestate heredis esse, ideo tamen inutile legatum intellegi oportere, quia quod nullas uires habiturum foret, si statim post testamentum factum decessisset testator, hoc ideo ualere, quia uitam longius traxerit, absurdum esset. Sed diuersae scholae auctores nec sub condicione recte legari, quia quos in potestate habemus, eis non magis sub condicione quam pure debere possumus.
>
> The question is raised whether a legacy bequeathed to someone who is in the *potestas* of the person whom we have instituted as heir is valid. Servius thinks that the legacy is valid, but that it becomes void if the legatee is still in *potestas* at the moment of the *dies cedens*. And that, therefore, the legacy is due, either when a legacy has been bequeathed unconditionally and he has ceased to be in the *potestas* of the heir during the testator's lifetime or that this [i.e., the legatee ceases to be in the heir's *potestas*] has happened in case of a legacy under a condition before the condition is fulfilled. Sabinus and Cassius hold such a legacy to be valid if conditional and void if unconditional. For though a legatee can cease to be in the *potestas* of the heir during the testator's lifetime, nevertheless the legacy should be regarded as void, since it would be absurd that

42 In the translations of Otto, Schilling, and Sintenis, d'Ors, and Spruit, the words *in eiusdem personam* are explained as 'the heir'. Nörr (1972) 54 appears to do the same: he mentions this text in connection with another rule, namely that a legacy cannot be given to the heir who has to pay over this legacy (*heredi a semet ipso legatum dari non potest*, Flor. D. 30.116.1).

> something which would have no force if the testator died immediately after making the testament should be valid because he had a longer span of years. But the authorities of the other school hold the legacy invalid even if conditional, because we do not owe anything to those we have in our *potestas* no more under a condition than directly.[43]

Perhaps signalling a trend in modern literature, some authors appear to regard this passage as the most important source of the *regula Catoniana*.[44] That to us is slightly curious, because in this text Gaius does not explicitly mention the *regula*. He first outlines the legal problem, then quotes Servius' opinion, and concludes by describing the controversy between the *Sabiniani* and *Proculiani* on this problem. It is only Ulpian who in D. 30.41.2 (the first of the second category texts we discussed above) follows the opinion of Sabinus and Cassius and in that context mentions the *regula Catoniana*.[45]

The legal question here is whether a legacy bequeathed to someone in the instituted heir's *potestas* is valid. Servius thinks it is, except if the legatee is still in the instituted heir's *potestas* at the moment of the *dies cedens*. The legacy is therefore owed either if the legacy is an unconditional legacy and the legatee has ceased to be in the heir's *potestas* while the testator is still alive, or if the legacy is conditional and the legatee is no longer in the heir's *potestas* before the condition has been fulfilled. In describing these outcomes, Servius not so much as whispers the *regula Catoniana*.

The same legal question sparked a controversy between the *Sabiniani* and the *Proculiani*. The problem may have arisen when a testator instituted two heirs and bequeathed a legacy to a *filius* of one of them.[46] The other heir disputed the validity of the legacy. Sabinus and Cassius considered such a legacy valid if it had been left conditionally and void if it had been left unconditionally. Although the *regula Catoniana* is not explicitly mentioned, it is clearly implied in the phrase that the unconditional legacy 'would have no force if the testator died immediately after making the will' and that it would be absurd to consider something valid that was intrinsically invalid because the testator happened to live longer. Ulpian later followed the Sabinian view in D. 30.41.2 (discussed above).

Proculus and Nerva on the other hand thought that such a legacy was also invalid if it had been left conditionally, arguing by analogy when they state that

---

43 Translation by Leesen (2010) 153.

44 Hausmaninger (1968) opens his paper about the *regula* with this text.

45 On D. 30.41.2, see also Leesen (2010) 166–167.

46 As Leesen (2010) 161 contends.

the principle that 'we do not owe anything to those we have in our *potestas*' applies to both types of legacy. As far as we know, the view of the *Proculiani* did not prevail.

Looking back on the texts we have reviewed in this section, we believe a case can be made for arguing that the jurists did not treat the *regula Catoniana* on a par with formal legislation, as Kaser believed they did. On the contrary, in many cases the *regula* was declared inapplicable and in the remaining cases the jurists did not agree with each other. On the one hand, Servius, Celsus, and sometimes Paul held on to the traditional rule that a legacy had to be valid when the will was opened. The *Proculiani* on the other hand argued that only those legacies were valid which were valid when the will had been made. In between were the *Sabiniani* followed by Ulpian and sometimes by Paul. Given these 'fluctuations', it is highly improbable that the *regula Catoniana* was rated as a normative and generally binding legal rule. We think it more plausible that it was appreciated foremost and possibly even purely as a rhetorical device.

4 The *regula Catoniana* as a Dubious *thesis*

We believe the *regula Catoniana* was a dubious argument geared to a specific case but phrased in general terms, as a *thesis*. To clarify our view, we reconstruct the earliest case to which the *regula* refers and analyse its rhetorical and legal elements.

Although no details are known about the case in whose context the *regula Catoniana* was originally phrased, Celsus' definition in D. 34.7.1 justifies the supposition that the validity of a legacy was disputed. And the context of D. 50.17.1, with which D. 34.7.1 is usually connected, suggests that the disputed legacy was intended for a slave who was manumitted in the same will. It is conceivable that on learning of the contents of the will, the heir had no desire to pay over the legacy, and he turned to Marcus Cato for advice. We think it likely this was Cato the Elder, for two reasons.

In his biography, Plutarch relates that, as a young man, the elder Cato (234–149 BC) developed his powers of speech, practising and perfecting his oratory in the towns and villages near Rome where he acted as an advocate for all who needed him.[47] Later, he became known as the Roman Demosthenes and even

47 Plutarch, Marcus Cato, 1. 4–5; 3.3, and 4.1 on Cato's activities in court. According to Plutarch, Marcus Cato (1.2, 'His third name was not Cato at first, but Priscus. Afterwards, he got the surname of Cato for his great abilities. The Romans call a man who is wise and prudent *catus*.' Translation Perrin (1914), 303 . On the Elder Cato as orator, see Sciarrino (2007), 55–60.

after a distinguished military career he did not withdraw from public life but offered his services to his friends and fellow countrymen in the courts of law, now also in Rome. It is not stretching the imagination to suppose that in this case Cato both counselled and represented the heir in the litigation the manumitted slave pursued against him.

Plutarch also chronicles that the elder Cato lived frugally, working his own land when not away on military duties. One of the many examples he gives of Cato's frugality is how he treated his slaves.[48] He bought only sturdy labourers such as grooms and herdsmen, and when they became too old to work, he felt it his duty to sell them rather than feed so many useless mouths. Plutarch regarded this conduct as 'the mark of a very mean nature', but Cato's work ethic does suggest that he himself may have felt that leaving a legacy to a manumitted slave was wasteful.

Preparing the defence, Cato naturally had to conceive and construct arguments benefiting his client, the heir. Not knowing which arguments he brought forward, we only have his conclusion as worded in the *regula*: 'A legacy which would have been invalid if the testator had died immediately after making his will is invalid whenever he dies.' This *regula* is worded as a *thesis*: it refers to legacies in general and it does not mention that the legatee used to be a slave – the very reason Cato would want to prove the legacy to be invalid. Yet we may be able to reconstruct the underlying argument.

The crucial element in the *regula* is the moment when the testator dies, either immediately after making his will or at some later point in time. The testator's death marks the tipping point between the two phases in the timeline of a will: the first one is the making of the will, the second one its taking effect.

When in a will liberty and a legacy were granted to a slave, he obtained liberty when the will took effect and having thus become *capax* the freedman could now acquire the legacy. In the deed of the will, this legatee was referred to as 'slave', because that was after all what he was when the will had been drawn up. To use that status as an argument, Cato brought forward the moment at which the slave had to be *capax* to when the will had just been drawn up. If the testator died at that time, the slave would still be *incapax* and the legacy would therefore be invalid. Cato could then compare this time of death with any later moment of death and neatly conclude that the legacy would then also be invalid.

Taking a closer look at this clever argument, we think it is interesting to note the two things Cato neglects to do. He does not refer to the first phase in the

48 Plutarch, Marcus Cato 4.4, 5.1, and 21.1–4 on Cato and slaves.

timeline of a will, its making, because the text does not have any formal status; it is just a written document containing the wishes of the testator regarding what should happen to his estate after his death. It is not a final text because the testator can decide to change it. That being so, it would not make sense for Cato to qualify a legacy in this document as either valid or invalid. He also does not refer to the second phase in the timeline of a will, when it has taken effect. At that point, the validity of a legacy or of another stipulation in the will can become a bone of contention, but at the same time, the manumission will also have taken effect and the freedman will be *capax* to claim his legacy. That being so, it would not make sense for Cato to argue that the legacy was invalid once the will had taken effect. So what does he do? By referring to the moment of the testator's death, Cato opts for a specific point in time when the legacy could be regarded as invalid: the will is final but the legatee is not yet *capax*. In itself, this precise moment has no legal effect on the validity or invalidity of the legacy, but Cato suggests that, since the will has become final, the legacy is invalid because the slave has not yet been manumitted.

Cato's next step is to boost the persuasive quality of his reasoning and he likely chooses the *topos ex consequentibus*: one thing follows necessarily from another.[49] He then draws up an ostensibly logical argument in general terms – as a *thesis* – by stating that 'a legacy which would have been invalid if the testator died immediately after having made the will would also be invalid if the testator died at any moment of time.' Put simply, as soon as a legacy becomes invalid, it remains invalid. On the face of it, this reasoning is impeccable, but on reflection it is not quite so watertight, for in the time between the making of the will and the actual death of the testator, both the will and the situation can be subject to change. Cato disregards this eventuality and adds weight to the time of death by using the word *quandocumque*, 'whenever'. The result is a canny argument, and Cato's clever use of it shows that he was well acquainted with both Roman law and rhetoric.

The *regula Catoniana* was well known in classical Roman law and it was used in a variety of cases, and yet the Digest contains several texts dealing with a legacy left to a slave who was manumitted in the same will without reference being made to the *regula Catoniana*.[50] Does that mean that the testators when formulating their will took account of the *regula Catoniana*? The Digest texts do not give a clue, but one specific document may help answer that question, namely the will of one C. Longinus Castor. His is one of the wills drawn up by

---

49 Cicero, *Topica* 53. Cato the Elder died long before Cicero was born, but he may have known the Greek source Cicero used. See Reinhardt (2003) 306–307.

50 E.g., D. 33.8 *De peculio legato* and D. 34.1 *De alimentis vel cibariis legatis*.

Roman soldiers who in the second century AD were stationed in Egypt and it is one of the very few wills that have been preserved in their entirety.

Longinus Castor was a Roman army veteran. Around 190 AD, he made a will to which he later added a codicil. At the end of the codicil it says that after the will was opened a *scriba* translated both documents from Latin into Greek. It is these Greek copies of both that have been preserved on papyrus.[51] In his will, Longinus Castor manumitted his slaves Marcella and Cleopatra and appointed them heirs for equal shares of his estate.[52] He also manumitted his slave Sarapias, the daughter of his freedwoman Cleopatra, and left her a substantial legacy.[53] For our purposes, the two distinct words Longinus Castor uses to identify Cleopatra hold particular relevance. When appointing her heir, he calls her *serva mea*. This makes sense, for when he drew up his will she was his slave and would remain so until the moment she and her co-heir Marcella learned that they had been manumitted in the will. In the section of the will that frees Sarapias and leaves her a legacy, her mother, Cleopatra, is called *liberta mea*, my freedwoman. This to us suggests that the testator was aware of the difference between the first and the second phase in the timeline of his will.

Sarapias' legacy is also interesting for another reason. If the *regula Catoniana* were to apply to Longinus Castor's will, this legacy would be invalid because if Longinus Castor had died immediately after making his will, Sarapias would have been *incapax*. According to Castor's contemporary Ulpian, the *regula Catoniana* could be avoided only by making the legacy depend on a condition: *purum igitur legatum Catoniana regula impediet, condicionale non* (D. 30.41.2). Longinus Castor articulated the manumission and Sarapias' legacy without a condition but by inserting the words *cui insuper* between the manumission and the legacy he made it difficult to isolate and invalidate the legacy. Anecdotal though this evidence may be (it is after all only one will),

51 On this *scriba* (Greek: *nomikos*), see Crook (1995) 69. In *FIRA* (1964) 147–153, Arangio Ruiz translated the Greek text back into Latin. We quote from this new Latin translation.

52 *FIRA* (1964) 147–148 (*Liberas esse iubeo*) *Marcellam servam meam maiorem annis* (*triginta et Cleopatram*) *servam meam* (*maiorem*) *annis triginta,* (*et ambo*) *mihi heredes* (*sunto*) *ex aequis partibus.* It is unclear why reference is made to the age of the two slaves. Amelotti (1966) 144 suggests this may have been done in view of the *lex Aelia Sentia,* but we think it could refer to a senatorial decision requiring a minimum age for manumission, cf. Gaius, *Inst.* 2.276.

53 *FIRA* (1964) 149 *Sarapias ancilla mea, Cleopatrae libertae meae filia, libera esto,* (*cui*) *insuper do lego aruras frumentarias quinque, quas habeo prope vicum Caranidem in loco qui dicitur Strutho* ('Sarapias my servant girl, the daughter of my freedwoman Cleopatra, must be free, and to her I also bequeath five pieces of corn-producing land which I own near the village of Caranides at the place called Strutho.' Our translation).

the testator's careful choice of words strongly indicates that testators more likely than not took account of the *regula Catoniana* in drawing up their wills. And if, as we have argued, the *regula Catoniana* is a dubious argument, that makes it all the more likely that testators had good reason to be wary of it and through the language used in their will took pains to reduce the risk of a legal battle whose outcome might not reflect their intentions, especially one in which one of parties was represented by as formidable and ingenious an adversary as Cato the Elder.

Cato, as we suggested early on in this section, may well have litigated on behalf of the heir against the manumitted slave. If Cato did indeed do this, he would undoubtedly have worked his argument to the full and would have made the most of suggesting that the combination of a testamentary manumission and a legacy was legally impossible. For his opponent, representing the legatee, it might have been difficult to refute such an argument when it was convincingly presented in court. Cato's opponent might have replied that in the framework of the will the legacy was valid and that it could not be void as long as the will had not come into effect. To which Cato then might well have retorted that the slave was not free yet and that a legacy could not at the same time be valid and invalid. *Falsa* though it is, Cato's quasi-legal reasoning may have swayed his audience and carried the day for his client: it certainly has in modern times.

5 The *regula Catoniana* and D. 50.17.1

In this chapter, we have argued that in D. 50.17.1 Paul describes the concept of *regula* as a thetical argument and that the compilers placed this text at the beginning of title D. 50.17 *De regulis iuris antiqui* by way of introduction. And we have put forward arguments why the *regula Catoniana* – which is often connected with D. 50.17.1 – is such a thetical argument. We conclude this chapter by comparing the *regula Catoniana* with the three sentences that comprise Paul's description of the *regula* in D.50.17.1 to establish whether the two texts align.

Paul opens as follows: *Regula est, quae rem quae est breviter enarrat*, 'A *regula* is what briefly clarifies what a case is about.' The *regula Catoniana* says that every legacy which would have been invalid if the testator had died immediately after he had made his will is invalid when the testator dies at a later moment in time. The *regula* hinges on the temporal aspect of a legacy's validity.

The second sentence consists of two parts: *Non ex regula ius sumatur, sed ex iure quod est regula fiat*, 'The law is not to be derived from a *regula*, but a *regula* must follow from the law as it is.' As the *regula Catoniana* does not create law, it is not normative. What is more, far from following the Roman law of succession, the *regula Catoniana* is in fact at variance with it by insinuating that a legatee must be *capax* at the time of the making of the will.

In the third sentence, Paul presents his conclusion and wraps up with a word of caution: *Per regulam igitur brevis rerum narratio traditur, et, ut ait Sabinus, quasi causae coniectio est, quae simul cum in aliquo vitiata est, perdit officium suum*, 'By means of a *regula*, therefore, a brief narrative of the facts is provided and, as Sabinus says, as it were the summary of the question at issue, which loses its function as soon as it is falsified in any way.' The various texts we discussed in this chapter clearly show that that is precisely what fate had in store for the *regula Catoniana*. Citing Sabinus, Paul reminds his audience that it is risky to use a *regula* in another case than the one for which it was originally designed.

We believe it is reasonable to submit that the *regula Catoniana* fits Paul's description of the *regula* concept in D. 50.17.1, namely as a thetical argument fashioned for a specific case. We do not claim that all *regulae* in D. 50.17 are *theseis* – about 30 are not – but we do think it plausible that most of them are and that there are *theseis* outside this title. One of them is the *regula Catoniana*. Given how this *regula* is a textbook example of the *regula* concept Paul describes, it is remarkable that the compilers did not include it in D. 50.17. It is impossible to say for certain, but perhaps they chose to exclude it because they regarded it as not entirely correct or reliable. Instead, whether acting on misgivings or not, they created title D. 34.7, which contains five *responsa* rejecting the application of the *regula Catoniana*. The compilers could of course hardly leave out an argument that in the early Empire had been popular in legal practice, but by inserting it in a separate title they took care that it was only outside that title that a few *responsa* could be found that confirmed the applicability of the *regula Catoniana*.

Perhaps the compilers' decision also throws some light on why in modern Romanist literature the *regula Catoniana* has attracted so much attention and why it has been explained in so many ways. By isolating it, the compilers gave the *regula* the appearance of a rule of law that had been created by a celebrated Roman statesman. In this respect it is understandable that modern Romanists felt they had to try and fit the stand-alone *regula Catoniana* into what they regarded as the system of Roman law. This endeavour may have kept them from recognising the *regula* as an ingenious if flawed rhetorical ploy.

CHAPTER 12

So Long to a Paradigm?

The main question we addressed in this book is whether the Roman jurists used the rhetorical devices *topoi* and *theseis* when substantiating their opinion on a thorny legal problem and if so, whether evidence of these devices can be found in Justinian's Digest. Modern Romanist literature sidesteps this question because it traditionally regards the jurists as being different from orators and indifferent to rhetoric. This view dates from the 19th century, when in Germany the jurists of the Historical School constructed a system of modern civil law as a science which they held to be based on ancient Roman law. Consequently, Roman law itself came to be regarded as a *scientia* and, as such, as having nothing to do with the *ars* of rhetoric. This view is typical of the second history of Roman law, whereas in actual fact there is no continuity between the first and the second histories of Roman law. We demonstrated that Roman jurists did use *topoi* and *theseis* and that these rhetorical devices can be found in the *regulae iuris* that have been preserved in the Digest, particularly in title D. 50.17.

The *regulae iuris* in this title are generally assumed to be general rules or principles. We identified the original context, the *leges geminatae*, of twenty of these *regulae* elsewhere in the Digest, and they form the principal part of this book. We have discovered that originally these *regulae* were rhetorical arguments for one particular, complicated case that the jurist in question had formulated in general terms to make his *responsum* more convincing. These arguments often did not comfortably fit the modern system of Roman law and sometimes they even had no connection whatsoever with Roman law. By explaining them in the context of rhetoric, and of Cicero's *Topica* especially, we were able to recognise and reconstruct the original tenor of the twenty *responsa*. The fact that this approach also works for the celebrated *regula Catoniana* convinced us that Roman jurists from Cato to Ulpian – when they felt it necessary to do so – used rhetorical devices to support their opinions. In this final chapter, we summarise the steps we took to arrive at this conclusion.

1 Cicero's *Topica* and Trebatius Testa (Chapter 2)

Starting with Cicero's *Topica*, we showed that this work has nothing to do with Aristotle's *Topike* but that Cicero may have been inspired by another work of Aristotle's, *Rhetorike*, and particularly by *Rhetorike* B II 23. This section

 | DOI:10.1163/9789004711020_013

originates in an older layer of *Rhetorike* and contains, in a rather haphazard order, some 30 *topoi* that could be useful in a political or juridical debate. In his *Topica*, Cicero does something similar, by selecting seventeen *topoi* that Aristotle had discussed, but Cicero adds his own touch by presenting them in a clearly structured overview: for each *topos* he explains how it could be applied to a particular legal problem, first at a basic level and then more in detail.

In modern Romanist literature, Cicero's references to Roman law are generally regarded as inadequate both legally and rhetorically. We analysed one of them, *Topica* 21, where Cicero demonstrates how to use the *topos a repugnantibus* to great effect in a case that appears undecidable on its legal merits alone. The legal problem is whether a *pupillus'* death invalidates the legacy paid over by him, or in other words, whether the pupillary substitute is the heir of the testator or of the *pupillus*; this problem was also debated among the Roman jurists of the time. We concluded that the argument Cicero deduces from the *topos* ('For what has once been given to someone by will cannot be taken from him to whom it has been given without his consent') is legally sound and rhetorically effective.

Next, we considered the question of whether Cicero's *Topica* may have inspired the jurist Trebatius, at whose request Cicero says he wrote this book. We showed that in one of his *responsa* Trebatius himself used a *topos* and a *thesis*. In D. 2.14.10.2, Ulpian quotes Trebatius as saying that if a debtor's procurator has made a *pactum de non petendo* with a creditor and if that creditor then sues the debtor all the same, the debtor can defend himself with an *exceptio doli*. Ulpian agrees and even quotes Trebatius' argument: 'Just as a pact made by my procurator will prejudice me it will also benefit me.' This argument derives from the *topos e contrario* and Trebatius may have been inspired by Cicero's description of it in *Topica* 47. By formulating the argument in general terms, as a *thesis*, Trebatius lent it greater persuasive force.

2 Quintus Mucius Scaevola *pontifex*: Jurist and Orator (Chapter 3)

Earlier, the jurist Quintus Mucius Scaevola also used *topoi* and *theseis*, as we demonstrated with two examples. The first one concerns Scaevola's role as an advocate in the famous *causa Curiana*. This case, we believe, turned on the question of whether the condition of a pupillary substitution could be regarded as fulfilled if no son had been born to the testator. Scaevola, speaking for the intestate heir, contends it could not, because 'someone had to be born before he could die': this was a logical argument derived from the *topos a consequentibus* and formulated as a *thesis*.

The second example concerns Scaevola's use of a *topos* and a *thesis* in one of his *responsa*. In D. 32.29.1, Labeo describes how Scaevola dealt with a legacy in which a testator had left to his wife 'a share just as great as what little share has been left to one heir.' In our reconstruction of the case, the testator had initially left equal portions to the various heirs but had later altered that allocation to the effect that the heirs no longer stood to inherit equal portions. His wife then wondered what that meant for her legacy and she turned to Scaevola. He answered that her legacy would be as large as the largest portion, using the argument *quia in maiore minor quoque inesset*. Aristotle already mentioned this argument in his *Rhetorike* as the *topos* 'of more and less' and Cicero discusses it as an example of the *topos comparatio* (*Topica* 23 and 68–71). This to us strongly suggests that in this case Scaevola used a topical argument and formulated it in general terms, as a *thesis*.

3 The *regulae* in D. 50.17 (Chapter 4)

The argument *in maiore minus inest* Scaevola uses in D. 32.29.1 led to a breakthrough in our research because this argument also appears in title D. 50.17 *De diversis regulis iuris antiqui*, several times in fact. This emboldened us to formulate the hypothesis that this title contains *regulae* that are topical arguments worded as *theseis*. Putting this hypothesis to the test required us to identify *regulae* in the Digest whose original context, the *leges geminatae*, has been preserved elsewhere in the Digest. Using Lenel's *Palingenesia iuris civilis* we identified the *leges geminatae* of twenty *regulae* and these allowed us to reconstruct the legal problem, the opinion of the jurist(s), and the argument to substantiate it. We found that these cases turned on four different rhetorical *status: coniectura, definitio, qualitas*, and *ambiguitas*, and that five *topoi* were used. We parsed the twenty *regulae* in their original context per *status*, and then per *topos*, and we now summarise our exegeses in that order.

4 *Coniectura* (Chapter 5)

The *status coniectura* pertains to disputes about *sit ne* (whether something is), suits five *regulae*, and in each case the argument derives from the *topos causa*.

Ulpianus D. 50.17.13 Non videtur cepisse, qui per exceptionem a petitione removetur. Viewed in isolation, this *regula* is impenetrable, but considered together with D. 30.28 pr. it attains clarity. It concerns the case of a creditor who could not collect a debt because the debtor was able to fend off the claim with an *exceptio*. In his will, the debtor had bequeathed to the creditor the money owed, but after the debtor's death the heir refused to pay over the legacy to the creditor. His argument probably was that the legacy was invalid because if it were not, the creditor could collect the same debt twice. Ulpian, insisting the legacy was valid, makes short work of that argument: although the *exceptio* had been the legal basis for precluding the creditor from receiving the money owed to him, the legacy was the legal basis for the debt being settled.

Ulpianus D. 50.17.31 Verum est neque pacta neque stipulationes factum posse tollere: quod enim impossibile est, neque pacto neque stipulatione potest comprehendi, ut utilem actionem aut factum efficere possit. Lenel inserted this *regula* after the first sentence of D. 21.2.31, where Ulpian comments on a stipulation guaranteeing that a slave was healthy, and neither a thief nor a corpse bearer. Some jurists held that such a stipulation is invalid because it cannot effect a factual change such as turning an unhealthy slave into a healthy one, and D. 50.17.31 contains the argument *ex causa* supporting their view. Ulpian agrees with them.

Ulpianus D. 50.17.35 Nihil tam naturale est quam eo genere quidque dissolvere, quo colligatum est. Ideo verborum obligatio verbis tollitur: nudi consensus obligatio contrario consensu dissolvitur. In modern Romanist literature, the classical origin of this *regula* has been called into question, but we agree with Lenel that it is the link between D. 46.4.8.3 and D. 46.2.2. Ulpian states that what is contracted by formal words is also discharged by formal words: the words are the *causa* of the contract's creation as well as of its discharge. He then formulates the *regula* of D. 50.17.35, and by including, by way of example, both formally concluded contracts (*stipulatio*) and informal contracts (for which informal consent suffices), he clears the way to D. 46.2.2 about *novatio*, a process to annul an obligation however contracted and to replace it by a new one, created by *stipulatio*.

Paulus D. 50.17.167.1 Qui iussu iudicis aliquid facit, non videtur dolo malo facere, qui parere necesse habet. The context of this *regula* has not been preserved, but a striking resemblance to Ulp. D. 39.3.4 pr. prompted Lenel to conclude that it pertained to a case turning on the *actio aquae pluviae arcendae*. In this text, Ulpian quotes Labeo as stating that if someone has built a tomb and water from it causes damage, he is liable to an action to ward off rainwater and that if, by judicial order, he restores the site to its previous condition, he is not liable for violating the tomb, because it was the judicial order that caused the tomb to be violated. Paul's *regula* may have provided the argument for a similar case, because the action for violating a tomb only lies against someone who acted with evil intent, as the reference to *dolus malus* suggests. This supports our view that the *regula* was created as an argument in a particular case and not as the general rule modern Romanists have conventionally assumed it to be.

Paulus D. 50.17.180 Quod iussu alterius solvitur, pro eo est, quasi ipsi solutum esset. Lenel inserted this *regula* in D. 12.4.9 as its penultimate sentence. In this *responsum*, Paul discusses four situations in which someone procures a dowry for a woman to her future husband and then something goes wrong. The *regula* concerns the third case: at the request (*iussum*) of a woman, someone promises to pay to her fiancé a sum of money which he erroneously thinks he owes her, and after the wedding the husband successfully claims the money. Paul asserts that the money could be considered as unduly paid to the wife and could be reclaimed. The *regula* provides the argument why: the woman's *iussum* is the cause of the undue payment.

5 *Definitio* (Chapters 6–8)

The second *status, definitio*, pertains to the question *quid sit* (What is it?), suits eight cases, and the arguments involved derive from three different *topoi*: four from *e contrario*, one from *e consequentibus*, and three from *e repugnantibus*.

Pomponius D. 50.17.7 Ius nostrum non patitur eundem in paganis et testato et intestato decessisse: earumque rerum naturaliter inter se pugna est 'testatus' et 'intestatus'. This *regula* is generally regarded as a fundamental principle of the Roman law of succession. With Lenel, however, we think that it probably concerns a *responsum* by Pomponius quoted by Ulpian in D. 28.5.19 where he describes the following case. Someone had made a will in which the sum of the twelve shares did not make up the full estate, but the testator did include a substitution for a person who had not been instituted as heir. This person was probably an intestate heir whom the testator mistakenly thought did not have to be instituted as heir. When the will was opened, this person had already died, and in the conflict that arose the testamentary heirs would have challenged the validity of the substitution. Ulpian records that this view was supported by Aristo, who argued that a non-existing share had been given to the substitute. Other jurists, including Pomponius and Ulpian himself, agreed with Aristo. We submit that Pomponius also provided another argument, namely that the substitution was invalid because otherwise part of the inheritance would be due to a substitute heir upon intestacy. Pomponius formulated the argument in general terms, as a *thesis*, contrasting testate and intestate succession, and the compilers eventually included this rhetorical argument as a *regula* in D. 50.17.7.

Paulus D. 50.17.10 Secundum naturam est commoda cuiusque rei eum sequi, quem sequentur incommoda. Lenel proposes a connection between this *regula* and D. 36.1.20.2 because both seem to deal with the legacy of a portion of an inheritance. D. 36.1.20.2 revolves round the legal question of who has to pay the costs of selling and preserving assets belonging to an inheritance: only the instituted heir or both the instituted heir and the legatee, who is after all the beneficiary of a portion of the inheritance? The legatee in the underlying case as we reconstructed it presumably refused to pay his share of the costs, possibly arguing that these costs should be charged to the heir because it is the heir who acquires the inheritance. He may have strengthened this argument by contrasting the advantages and the disadvantages, and by phrasing it in general terms. When they moved the argument to D. 50.17, the compilers, inadvertently or not, suggested that the *regula* deals with the question of who should have an advantage whereas originally it dealt with the question of who should have a disadvantage. It is only in the latter context that the *regula* makes sense.

Paulus D. 50.17.29 Quod initio vitiosum est, non potest tractu tempore convalescere. In his palingenesis of Paul's commentary *ad Sabinum*, Lenel included this *regula* after D. 26.8.3, but it is unclear whether the two texts are connected. In D. 26.8.3 Paul states that a guardian does not have to be formally asked for approval of a deal made with his ward, since he says he approves of what is being done. Apparently, someone who had made a deal with a *pupillus* in the presence of his guardian later tried to back out of the deal arguing that it was invalid because the guardian had not been explicitly asked for his approval. The *regula* of D. 50.17.29 may reflect the argument that the deal was defective from the outset and could not be validated by lapse of time. If this is indeed so, the argument is an example of the *topos e contrario* by contrasting an invalid deal and a valid one. Legally, this argument would be weak because *interrogatio* of a guardian was not a constitutive requirement for the guardian's permission and because lapse of time was completely irrelevant in this context, but rhetorically it would be strong because it suggested that the invalidity of the deal could not be in any doubt.

Modestinus D. 50.17.195 Expressa nocent, non expressa non nocent. This *regula* only makes sense in the context of D. 35.1.52, of which it forms part as the last sentence, where Modestinus notes that sometimes explicit statements constitute an obstacle, although when omitted they can be tacitly understood and not present an obstacle. For instance, when Titius is given a legacy conditional on Maevius' consent, the legacy is invalid because a legacy cannot be made dependent on the will of a third party. But when the condition reads 'if Maevius goes up the Capitol', the legacy is valid because Maevius' consent is not a condition, even though it is left to Maevius' discretion to go up the Capitol and thus make the legacy due to Titius. By way of argument, Modestinus contrasts *expressa* with *non expressa* and *nocent* with *non nocent*, using the *topos e contrario*; he formulates the argument in general terms and calls it a saying, thereby suggesting that his view was widely accepted. In fact, the *regula* of D. 50.17.195 can only have held in this particular case because assigning it the status of a legal maxim in classical law, as has been done in modern literature, carries the somewhat perplexing implication that a foundational precept of Roman law is that it is generally better to conceal one's wishes in, say, a contract or a will.

Q. Cerv. Scaevola D. 50.17.88 Nulla intellegitur mora ibi fieri, ubi nulla petitio est. This *regula* forms part of D. 45.1.127. A *pupillus* had by means of a *stipulatio* promised someone a certain slave, but as his guardian had not authorised this transaction, only a natural obligation had been created. However, a third party had guaranteed its performance by means of a *fideiussio*. The *pupillus* did not deliver the slave in time, and then the slave died. The legal question was whether the *fideiussor* was liable towards the creditor. He probably was, but Scaevola, counselling the *fideiussor*, says he was not and uses a rhetorical stratagem to make his point, the *topos e consequentibus*: the *pupillus* had made a stipulation that was not enforceable in law and he could therefore not be too late. While there is no gainsaying this statement, it does not answer the legal question: it is a sophism. And to conceal its nature, Scaevola formulates this argument as a *thesis*.

Ulpianus D. 50.17.4 Velle non creditur, qui obsequitur imperio patris vel domini. Lenel inserted this *regula* in D. 29.2.6.4 between the first and second sentences. In this text, Ulpian discusses two different cases. The relevant case is the first one; it is about someone who mistakenly thought that he was in the power of his *pater familias* when, at the latter's instruction, he accepted an inheritance. It later turned out that at the moment of acceptance he had been *sui iuris*, probably because in the meantime his *pater familias* had died. A conflict arose, the legal question being whether he had acquired the inheritance. Ulpian contends he had not, neither for himself nor for the person who instructed him. In D. 29.2.6.4, Ulpian does not give an argument but the *regula* of D. 50.17.4 fits the bill perfectly: acquisition requires the will to acquire and because in this case the heir had been instructed to accept he was not regarded as willing to accept for himself. This logical reasoning, which today is qualified as the *modus tollendo tollens*, Cicero called the *topos a repugnantibus*. The *regula* also contains stylistic devices: the words *imperium* (instead of *iussum*) and *vel domini* amplify the argument, and the use of assonance in *imperio patris* gives the *regula* a semblance of permanence.

Papinianus D. 50.17.74 Non debet alteri per alterum iniqua condicio inferri. Lenel suggested that this *regula* formed part of the same *responsum* as Pap. D. 4.8.33. It turns on the following problem. Two people agree to submit their conflict to an arbiter, who must decide within a certain term but is allowed to extend this term. At some point, one of the parties for some reason moves to shorten the arbiter's decision term. The other party does not agree and Papinian supports him, stating that the arbiter cannot shorten the term when the parties to the conflict disagree on this point. D. 4.8.33 does not contain an argument, but D. 50.17.74 furnishes it: one party cannot impose an unfair condition on the other party. This argument is based on the contrast between fair and unfair, that is, on the *topos a repugnantibus* and it is worded in general terms, as a *thesis*.

Papinianus D. 50.17.75 Nemo potest mutare consilium suum in alterius iniuriam. Lenel combined this *regula* with D. 4.4.30. The case is rather complicated. A testator passes over his emancipated son, but he does bequeath him a legacy. When the testator dies, the son is still a *minor* and the legacy is not paid out to him. Sometime before he turns 25, the son claims *bonorum possessio contra tabulas* to get his intestate share of the inheritance, and when he reaches the age of 25 he also claims the legacy. The question is whether he can have it both ways. Papinian argues that by claiming the legacy the son is held to have abandoned his claim for *bonorum possessio contra tabulas*. In so arguing, Papinian uses the *topos a repugnantibus*: he contrasts the son's respecting and not respecting his father's will. Papinian then formulates his argument in general terms, now pointing up the son's change of mind. Papinian does not say that someone can change their mind as long as they do not harm someone else's interest, because that would make a rather weak argument. Instead, he turns it around and states that no one can change their mind to someone else's disadvantage. This is a powerful argument: it is short and it sounds fair.

6 *Qualitas* (Chapter 9)

The third *status*, *qualitas*, pertains to the question *quale sit* (How is it?), suits four *regulae*, and their arguments all derive from the *topos comparatio*.

Ulpianus D. 50.17.9 Semper in obscuris, quod minimum est sequimur. Lenel added this *regula* to D. 30.14, where Ulpian discusses the *ademptio* of a legacy in a will. In D. 30.14.1 he quotes a complicated case described by Papinian, in which the testator makes various bequests of unequal size to the same person, but then adds that only one of them is owed. The question then arises which bequest is owed. Papinian compares the different legacies and, possibly on the basis of the *topos in maiore minus inest* (*immi*), concludes that the smaller one should be paid. Ulpian converts this *ad hoc* argument into a general statement, a *thesis*.

Ulpianus D. 50.17.21 Non debet cui plus licet, quod minus est non licere. The tenor of this *regula* is similar to the last line of D. 40.7.3.15, where Ulpian describes the case of a slave who has been manumitted in his master's will on condition that he serve the instituted heir for five years. The heir at first refuses the slave's service, but he later changes his mind and the question then is whether the heir is still entitled to claim it. Ulpian says he is, provided he claims it within the term of five years, his argument being that although the slave can no longer serve the heir for five years, he can still serve him for a shorter time. Ulpian fashions this argument into a general rule that he who is entitled to more must also be entitled to less, implying that the smaller is contained in the larger: the *topos immi*. Attired as a *regula*, it suggests logic and law, but it is entirely based on rhetoric.

Gaius D. 50.17.113 In toto et pars continetur. Lenel inserted this *regula* between D. 3.3.46.7 and 48. In the Digest, the intervenient text D. 3.3.47 is a *responsum* by Julian. The case discussed by Gaius is whether one procurator is entitled to sue another for paying his debt to their joint principal when the principal has charged both by mandate to manage his business. In D. 3.3.46.7, Gaius argues that the procurator is entitled to do so because he is not less of a procurator because the other procurator is a procurator, too. He constructs this argument as the *regula* of D. 50.17.113 that 'The part is also contained in the whole' – in other words, he uses the *topos immi*. In D. 3.3.48, Gaius even specifies the wording of the *formula*. The case discussed by Julian in D. 3.3.47 is different in that he deals with procurators without a mandate from the principal, who could not sue each other without a special mandate. This suggests that the compilers erred when they split up Gaius' text and inserted Julian's and that Lenel hit the nail on the head when he included D. 50.17.113 after D. 3.3.46.7.

Ulpianus D. 50.17.156.1 Cui damus actiones, eidem et exceptionem competere multo magis quis dixerit. This *regula* is similar to the last sentence of Ulp. D. 43.18.1.4, where Ulpian discusses the relationship between the owner of a piece of land and a superficiary, a person who has the heritable right to use a building erected on that land, the *superficies*. The owner has an *actio in rem*, concerning both the *superficies* and the land. The superficiary can protect his use and enjoyment (*uti frui*) of the building by means of a praetorian interdict. Ulpian raises the following legal question: if the owner wants to bring suit against the superficiary, will the latter be granted a defence? Ulpian asserts that he must be granted an *exceptio in factum*, for 'It has been said that someone to whom we grant *actiones* is all the more entitled to an *exceptio*.' He formulates this argument on the basis of the *topos comparatio* and turns it into a general rule by using the term *actio* instead of interdict and by turning the *exceptio in factum* into an edictal *exceptio*. The compilers finished the job by changing *actio* into *actiones* and included the argument as a *regula* in D. 50.17.

7 *Ambiguitas* (Chapter 10)

The *'status' ambiguitas* turns on the question of how the meaning of a law or legal document must be construed when the wording admits of two different interpretations. It suits three *regulae*.

Pomponius D. 50.17.20 Quotiens dubia interpretatio libertatis est, secundum libertatem respondendum erit. Under the heading *De libertate relicta*, Lenel inserted this *regula* after D. 40.4.11 and D. 40.5.44, and by giving them separate numbers he implied that they were not connected – but we rather think they were. The problem Pomponius faced may have been the following one. A testator had instituted someone as his heir and to someone else had bequeathed a slave; in a *fideicommissum*, he had also requested that the slave be manumitted (D. 40.4.11 pr.). Somehow, the legatee did not acquire the slave; perhaps he had died before the heir accepted the inheritance. The legacy lapsed, and ownership of the slave passed to the heir upon his inheriting the testator's estate. The slave now claimed his freedom from the heir, but his new master refused to manumit him, arguing that the *fideicommissum* had not been entrusted to him (D. 40.5.44). Pomponius points to the ambiguity of the case: on the one hand, the testator had written down his intention that the slave be manumitted, but on the other hand, he had done so indirectly in a *fideicommissum* entrusted to the legatee. When faced with *ambiguitas*, Cicero advised to adopt the more useful, honourable, or compelling view, and that is what Pomponius does by stating that whenever there is any doubt over liberty in an interpretation, a reply in favour of liberty must be given. He formulated his opinion in general terms, as a *thesis*, and this may have moved the compilers to move it to D. 50.17.

Iulianus D. 50.17.64 Ea, quae raro accidunt, non temere in agendis negotiis computantur. Lenel added this *regula* to D. 28.2.13 pr. In this *responsum* Julian discusses the will of a testator who had included two conditional institutions of heirs, one for when a son would be born to him and one for when a daughter would be born, and who had unconditionally instituted his wife as heir. After his death, both a son and a daughter were born, probably twins. When he made his will, the testator did not take this possibility into account. How should the inheritance now be divided? The will is not clear on this point. Julian suggests that the inheritance should be divided among the son, wife, and daughter in the proportion of 4:2:1, and he argues that while formerly the will would have been regarded as broken, now *humanitas* favours its preservation. Legally, this was a weak argument since there was no reason to regard the will as invalid; it was only unclear. Julian therefore adds that someone who is managing his affairs cannot be expected to take into account situations that rarely occur (D. 50.17.64). This is not a legal rule but a rhetorical argument that dovetails nicely with D. 28.2.13 pr. And probably because it was formulated in general terms, as a *thesis*, the compilers moved it to D. 50.17.

Marcellus D. 50.17.192.1 In re dubia benigniorem interpretationem sequi non minus iustius est quam tutius. This *regula* is not only mentioned in D. 50.17 but also forms part of D. 28.4.3 pr., where Marcellus first describes the discussion that took place in connection with a *cognitio* procedure before the Emperor Marcus Aurelius, and he then quotes from a seemingly official report of that procedure, including the emperor's judgment. The case in question concerns a will in which the testator had erased the names of the heirs. After his death, the *fiscus* claims the inheritance because the heirs were considered unworthy to inherit. The heirs dispute this claim, asserting that they were still entitled to the *legata per praeceptionem* that had also been bequeathed to them. The case is a *res dubia* because it is unclear whether the testator, when he erased the names of the heirs, meant to invalidate the whole will or only the institution of the heirs. A clear case of *ambiguitas*. Marcellus refutes the various arguments put forward by the parties but, in the end, he concurs with the minority view using a rhetorical argument – in a doubtful matter, to follow the milder interpretation is no less just than safe – which he phrases in general words, as a *thesis*, to convince the emperor. (Which it does.)

8 D. 50.17.1 and the *regula Catoniana* (Chapter 11)

The twenty cases recapitulated above confirm that, in their original context, the *regulae* were topical arguments meant for a specific case but formulated in general terms. The next step was to ascertain whether this determination would also hold for the *regula* concept as it was introduced by the compilers in D. 50.17.1. This text by Paul is generally regarded as having been interpolated and as consisting of three contradictory sentences that should be read separately. We take the opposite view and we established that the three sentences that make up D. 50.17.1, far from having been interpolated, go together quite well. First, Paul describes the *regula* as a summary of someone's view of a conflict. He then states that the law cannot be inferred from that summary because it is not a normative rule; instead, the *regula* must follow the law. Finally, a *regula* provides a short description of the facts and is as it were a summary of the legal question, which means it will lose its function as soon as one fact of the case is changed. And that, we think, is precisely what happened when a *regula* was used as an argument in a case other than the one it had originally been invented for.

For palingenetic reasons, D. 50.17.1 is usually connected with the *regula Catoniana*, the oldest and most celebrated *regula* to have been preserved, and this compelled us to check whether our reading of D. 50.17.1 meshes with it. The *regula Catoniana* says that a legacy must be valid at the time when the will is drawn up (Cels. D. 34.7.1). In our view, it was used as an argument by an heir who refused to pay over a legacy left to a slave who was manumitted in the same will. This argument, though rhetorically and legally specious, may have been popular in legal practice. This fashionable-but-false premise is reflected in the Digest, where the *regula Catoniana* is mentioned about ten more times, yet in most cases it is declared non-applicable and in the remaining few cases the jurists disagree about its applicability. From this, we drew two conclusions. First, and contrary to traditional scholarly consensus, it is unlikely that the *regula Catoniana* was a normative rule, and second, it perfectly fits Paul's description of a *regula* in D. 50.17.1: (1) the *regula Catoniana* concerns the validity of a legacy, (2) far from being normative, the *regula Catoniana* is at variance with the Roman law of succession because it wrongly assumes that a legatee must be *capax* at the time of the making of the will, and (3) the *regula* 'loses its function as soon as it is falsified in any way', that is to say, it does not work in any other case than the one for which it has been invented. In short, like the other *regulae*, the *regula Catoniana* is a rhetorical argument meant for one specific case only but worded in general terms.

9 So Long to a Paradigm?

In the introduction to this book, we addressed the paradigm that has informed Roman law research and teaching for the past 200 years: the entrenched presumption that Roman law and rhetoric are two unrelated disciplines. When discussing modern Romanist literature on the *regulae* of D. 50.17, and on the *regula Catoniana* in particular, we could not help but notice time and again that this paradigm narrows scholarly appreciation of the work of the Roman jurists: the notion, let alone likelihood, of the Roman jurists using rhetorical arguments to substantiate their opinion on a knotty legal problem does not suit the modern image of Roman law as a science.

Possibly as a result, Romanist literature has hardly contributed to a balanced reading of the twenty *regulae* from D. 50.17 that we analysed. In half the cases, the *regula* in question has been connected with its original context, but in each case the conclusion arrived at has, without fail, been inspired by dogmatism and is therefore, we believe, inadequate.[1] Regarding four *regulae*, modern literature has made no connection with the original context,[2] and on six *regulae*,[3] there is no modern literature at all.[4] For several hundred years, research into the *regula Catoniana* has been obstructed by the precept that this *regula* is a normative rule even though it clearly clashes with Roman law.

Having argued, and we hope conclusively demonstrated, that title D. 50.17 contains a far from insubstantial number of *topoi* and *theseis* (where established scholarly tradition sees none) and that these rhetorical devices also turn up in the Digest outside that title, we think it likely that more are to be found in title D. 50.17 and elsewhere in the Digest. If Roman legal scholarship were to give rhetoric its due, future exegetical efforts might more readily recognise its role in Roman legal argumentation and thus lead to a more rounded understanding of the *responsa* of the Roman jurists. Time for a new paradigm? We think so.

1 This befell D. 50.17.4, 9, 10, 20, 29, 35, 88, 156.1, 180, and 192.1. A positive exception is Liebs' commentary on D. 50.17.35.

2 D. 50.17.7, 21, 31, and 64.

3 D. 50.17.13, 74, 75, 113, 167.1, and 195.

4 At least none that we could find.

Bibliography

Albertario, E. (1937), *Studi di diritti romano* V, Milan.

Alonso, J.L. (2001), *Estudios sobre la delegación, La doble atribución patrimonial* I, Santiago de Compostela.

Amelotti, M. (1966), *Il testamento romano attraverso la prassi documentale* I, *Le forme classiche di testamento*, Florence, repr. 1968.

Angelini, P. (1971), *Il "procurator"*, Milan.

Ankum, J.A. (1998), 'La forma dell'*acceptilatio* nella realtà giuridica di Roma nel periodo classico', in *Revue internationale des droits de l'antiquité* 45, 267–285.

Ankum, J.A. (2001), review of G.H. Potjewijd, *Beschikkingsbevoegdheid, bekrachtiging en convalescentie – een romanistische studie*, in *Savigny Zeitschrift* (rom. Abt.)118, 442–462.

Ankum, J.A. (2006), 'Der Ausdruck *favor libertatis* in den Konstitutionen der römischen Kaiser', in T. Finkenauer (ed.), *Sklaverei und Freilassung im römischen Recht, Symposium für Hans Joseph Wieling zum 70. Geburtstag*, Berlin-Heidelberg 1–17.

Apathy, P. (1975), *Animus novandi. Das Willensmoment beim römischen Schulderneuerungsvertrag*, Vienna-New York.

Arangio-Ruiz, V. (1936), review of G. Dulckeit, *Erblasserwille und Erwerbswille bei Antretung der Erbschaft*, in *Studia et documenta historiae et iuris* 2, 184–190.

Arangio-Ruiz, V. (1954), *La compravendita in diritto romano* II, Naples, repr. 1963.

Babusiaux, U. (2011), *Papinians* Quaestiones. *Zur rhetorischen Methode eines spätklassischen Juristen*, Munich.

Backhaus, R. (1981), *Casus perplexus. Die Lösung in sich widersprüchlicher Rechtsfälle durch die klassische römische Jurisprudenz*, Munich.

Backhaus, R. (1983), 'In maiore minus inest', in *Savigny Zeitschrift* (rom. Abt.) 100, 136–184.

Baldus, Chr. (1998), *Regelhafte Vertragsauslegung nach Parteirollen im klassischen römischen Recht und in der modernen Völkerrechtswissenschaft: zur Rezeptionsfähigkeit römischen Rechtsdenkens*, 2 vols., Frankfurt am Main.

Bauman, R.E. (1983), *Lawyers in Roman Republican Politics*, Munich.

Bayer, K. (1993), *Marcus Tullius Cicero, Topica: Die Kunst, richtig zu argumentieren*, Munich-Zürich.

Beek, L. ter (1999), *Dolus. Een semantisch-juridische studie*, Nijmegen.

Behrends, O. (1971), 'Die Prokuratur des klassischen römischen Zivilrechts', in *Savigny Zeitschrift* (rom. Abt.) 88, 215–299.

Behrends, O. and R. Knütel (edd.) (1990–2005), *Corpus Iuris Civilis: Text und Übersetzung*, 4 vols. Heidelberg.

Behrens, D. (1958), 'D. 50.17.1.', in *Savigny Zeitschrift* (rom. Abt.) 75, 353–361.

Bergh, G.C.J.J. van den (1971), 'Qui habet commoda ferre debet onera', in R. Feenstra, J.H.A. Lokin, N. van der Wal (eds.), *Flores legum* H.J. *Scheltema oblati*, Groningen, 21–44.

Bernasconi, S. (1976), 'Il legato del debito nel diritto romano', in *Studia et documenta historiae et iuris* 42, 23–98.

Beseler, G. (1920), *Beiträge zur Kritik der römischen Rechtsquellen* IV, Tübingen.

Beseler, G. (1929), *Juristische Miniaturen*, Leipzig.

Betti, E. (1935), review of G. Dulckeit, *Erblasserwille und Erwerbswille bei Antretung der Erbschaft*, in *Bullettino dell'Istituto di diritto romano* 43, 375–379.

Bianchini, M. (1967), *Studi sulla societas*, Milan.

Bluhme, F. (1820), 'Die Ordnung der Fragmente in den Pandectentiteln', in *Zeitschrift für geschichtliche Rechtswissenschaft* 4, 257–274, reprinted in *Labeo* 6 (1960) 50–96, 235–277, and 368–404. All references are to this reprint.

Bonner, S.F. (1977), *Education in Ancient Rome*, London.

Braet, A.C. (1997), 'Het enthymeem in Aristoteles' Rhetorica', in *Taalbeheersing* 19, 97–114.

Bretone, M. (2009), Ius controversum *nella giurisprudenza classica*, Rome.

Briguglio, F. (1999), *Fideiussoribus succurri solet*, Milan.

Bryen, A.Z. (2016), 'When Law Goes off the Rails: or, *Aggadah* Among the *iurisprudentes*', in *Critical Analysis of Law* 3:1, 9–29.

Brittain, Ch. (2001), *Philo of Larissa*, Oxford.

Broggini, G. (1966), 'La retroattività della legge nella prospettiva romanistica', in *Studia et documenta historiae et iuris* 32, 1–62.

Buchwitz, W. (2012), *Servus alienus heres. Die Erbeinsetzung fremder Sklaven im klassischen römischen Recht*, Vienna-Cologne-Weimar.

Buckland, W.W. (1908), *The Roman Law of Slavery*, Cambridge, repr. Northampton 1970.

Calero, M., (1988), 'Un famoso pleito sucesorio que decide Marco Aurelio', in *Labeo* 34, 18–42.

Cannata, C.A. (1991), 'Atto giuridico e rapport giuridico', in *Studia et documenta historiae et iuris* 57, 335–382.

Capogrossi Colognesi, L. (1998), review of R. Cardilli, *L'obbligazione di "praestare" e la responsabilità contrattuale in diritto romano*, in *Savigny Zeitschrift* (rom. Abt.) 115, 527–538.

Cardilli, R. (1995), *L'obbligazione di "praestare" e la responsabilità contrattuale in diritto romano*, Milan.

Castello, C. (1956), 'In tema di "favor libertatis"', in *Studia et documenta historiae et iuris* 22, 348–361.

Cervenca, G. (1965), 'Per lo studio della "restitutio in integrum" (problematicae prospettive)', in A. Giuffrè (ed.), *Studi in onore di Biondo Biondi* I, Milan, 599–630.

Ciulei, G. (1941), *Liber homo bona fide serviens*, Paris.

Corbett, E.P.J. (1990), *Classical Rhetoric for the Modern Student*, 3rd edition, New York-Oxford.

Crook, J.A. (1995), *Legal Advocacy in the Roman World*, Ithaca (NY).

Cunningham, G.J. (2018), *Law, Rhetoric, and Science: Historical Narratives in Roman Law*, thesis Glasgow http://theses.gla.ac.uk/id/eprint/41030. Date of last access 22nd March 2024.

Cunningham, G.J. (2020), 'The Place of Rhetoric in Late Republican Law: Some Thoughts on *Pietas* and the *Querela Inofficiosi Testamenti*', in B. Spagnolo and J. Sampson (eds.), *Principle and Pragmatism in Roman Law*, Oxford.

Daube, D. (1959), 'Zur Palingenesie einiger Klassikerfragmente', in *Savigny Zeitschrift* (rom. Abt.) 76, 149–264.

Dominik, W. (2017), 'The Development of Roman Rhetoric', in M.J. MacDonald (ed.), *The Oxford Handbook of Rhetorical Studies*, Oxford, 1–14.

Donatuti, G. (1940), *Lo statulibero*, Milan.

Dulckeit, G. (1934), *Erblasserwille und Erwerbswille bei Antretung der Erbschaft. Beiträge zur Willensproblem im klassischen römischen Erbrecht*, Weimar.

Ernst, W. (1999), 'Neues zur Sachmängelhaftung', review of E. Jakab, *Praedicere und Cavere beim Marktkauf*, in *Savigny Zeitschrift* (rom. Abt.) 116, 208–221.

Feldman, R. (2009), *The Role of Science in Law*, Oxford.

Finkenauer, Th. (2010), *Die Rechtsetzung Mark Aurels zur Sklaverei*, Mainz-Stuttgart.

Fiuris. *Archivio electronico per l'interpretazione delle fonti giuridiche romane* (2003), 2nd edition, Rome-Cagliari.

Flume, W. (1932), *Studien zur Akzessorietät der römischen Burgschaftsstipulationen*, Bonn.

Flume, W. (1996), 'Zu den römischen Bürgschaftsstipulationen', in *Savigny Zeitschrift* (rom. Abt.) 113, 88–131.

FIRA (1964) = V. Arangio Ruiz (ed.), *Fontes Iuris Romani Antejustiniani* III, *Negotia*, 2nd edition, Firenze 1943, repr. 1964 with an Appendix, 2nd repr. 1972.

Frezza, P. (1962), *Le garanzie delle obbligazioni* I, Padua.

Frier, B.W. (1985), *The Rise of the Roman Jurists*, Princeton.

Frost, M.H., (2005), *Introduction to Classical Legal Rhetoric. A Lost Heritage*, Aldershot-Burlington.

Fuhrmann, M. (1989), *Cicero und die römische Republik*, Munich-Zürich.

Fuhrmann, M. (2000), 'Die zivilrechtlichen Beispiele in Ciceros *Topik*', in Th. Schirren and G. Üding (eds.), *Topik und Rhetorik*, Tübingen, 51–66.

Fumagalli, M.B. (2008), *Riflessioni sulla lex Voconia*, Milan.

Georges, K.E. and H. Georges (1913), *Ausführliches Lateinisch-Deutsches Handwörterbuch*, 8th edition, Hannover, repr. 1976.

Giaro, T. (2007), *Römische Rechtswahrheiten: ein Gedankenexperiment*, Frankfurt.

Giodice Sabbatelli, V. (1993), *La tutela giuridica dei fedecommessi tra Augusto e Vespasiano*, Bari.

Giodice Sabbatelli, V. (2008), review of F.M. Silla, *La 'cognitio' sulle 'libertates fideicomissae'*, in *Iura* 57, 450–461.

Giomaro, A.M. and M.L. Biccari (2022), *Sulle* regulae iuris *fra I e III secolo: Paolo commenta Plauzio*, Palermo.

Giuffrè, V. (1965), *L'utilizzazione degli atti giuridici mediante "conversione" in diritto romano*, Naples.

Glare, P.G.W. (1968), *Oxford Latin Dictionary* I, Oxford.

Glare, P.G.W. (1969), *Oxford Latin Dictionary* II, Oxford.

Glare, P.G.W. (1982), *Oxford Latin Dictionary* VIII, Oxford.

Glynn Williams, W. (1983), *Cicero, The Letters to his Friends* II, Cambridge (Mass.)-London.

Guerle, H. de (1874), Lettres de M.T. Cicéron IV, Paris.

Harder, M. (1976), 'Commodum eius debet esse, cuius periculum est. Über die actio furti als stellvertretendes commodum beim Kauf', in D. Medicus and H.H. Seiler (eds.), *Festschrift für Max Kaser zum 70. Geburtstag*, Munich, 351–372.

Harke, J.D. (2014), *Argumenta Pomponiana*, Berlin.

Harries, J. (2006), *Cicero and the Jurists. From Citizen's Law to the Lawful State*, London.

Hartkamp, A.S. (1971), *Der Zwang im römischen Privatrecht*, Amsterdam.

Hausmaninger, H. (91968), 'Celsus und die *regula Catoniana*', in *Tijdschrift voor Rechtsgeschiedenis* 36, 469–488.

Hausmaninger, H. (1984), 'Zur Legatsinterpretation des Celsus', in *Iura* 35, 16–46.

Hendel, A.C. (2013), 'D. 28,4,3 Marcellus libro 29 digestorum. Zum Sicherheitsgedanken bei der benignior interpretatio', in *Savigny Zeitschrift* (rom. Abt.) 130, 419–431.

Heumann, H. and E. Seckel (1907), *Handlexikon zu den Quellen des römischen Rechts*, 10th edition, Graz, repr. 1958.

Honoré A.M. and A. Rodger (1972), 'The Distribution of Digest Texts into Titles', in *Savigny Zeitschrift* (rom. Abt.) 89, 351–362.

Honsell, H. (1969), *Quod interest im bonae-fidei-iudicium, Studien zum römischen Schadenersatzrecht*, Munich.

Horak, F. (1969), *Rationes decidendi. Entscheidungsbegründungen bei den älteren römischen Juristen bis Labeo*, Aalen.

Hubbell, H.M. (1971), *Cicero, Orator*, Cambridge (Mass.)-London.

Hubbell, H.M. (1949), *Cicero, De inventione, De optimo genere oratorum, Topica*, Cambridge (Mass.)-London, repr. 1976.

Humfress, C. (2007), *Orthodoxy and the Courts in Late Antiquity*, Oxford.

Impallomeni, G. (1963), *Le manumissioni 'mortis causa'. Studi sulle fonti autoritative romane*, Padua.

Jakab, E. (1997), *Praedicere und cavere beim Marktkauf. Sachmängel im griechischen und römischen Recht*, Munich.

Johnston, D. (1988), *The Roman Law of Trusts*, Oxford.

Jusztinger, J. (2017), 'Economic Significance of the Ancient Roman Superficies', in *Journal on European History of Law* 8, 98–102.

Kacprzak, A. (2012), *Tra logica e giurisprudenza*, Warsaw.

Kacprzak, A. (2016), 'Rhetoric and Roman Law', in P.J. du Plessis, C. Ando, and K. Tuori (eds.), *Oxford Handbook of Roman Law and Society*, Oxford, 200–213.

Kaiser, W. (2015), 'Justinian and the *Corpus Iuris Civilis*', in D. Johnston (ed.), *The Cambridge Companion to Roman Law*, Cambridge, 119–148.

Kaser, M. (1962), *Zur Methode der römischen Rechtsfindung*, Göttingen, repr. 1969.

Kaser, M. (1967), *Römische Rechtsgeschichte*, 2nd edition, Göttingen.

Kaser, M. (1971), *Das römische Privatrecht* I, 2nd edition, Munich.

Kaser, M. (1972), *Zur Methodologie der römischen Rechtsquellenforschung*, Vienna.

Kaser, M. (1973), 'Die Stipulationsklausel '*quanti ea res erit*', in *Savigny Zeitschrift* (rom. Abt.) 90, 184–219.

Kaser, M. and K. Hackl (1996), *Das römische Zivilprozessrecht*, 2nd edition, Munich.

Kasten, H. (1989), *Marcus Tullius Cicero an seine Freunde*, 4th edition, Munich-Zürich.

Kennedy, G. (1972), *The Art of Rhetoric in the Roman World*, Princeton.

Kennedy, G.A. (2002), 'Cicero's Oratorical and Rhetorical Legacy', in J.M. May (ed.), *Brill's Companion to Cicero. Oratory and Rhetoric*, Leiden-Boston-Cologne, 481–501.

Kleiter, T. (2010), *Entscheidungskorrekturen mit unbestimmter Wertung durch die klassische römische Jurisprudenz*, Munich.

Knütel, R. (1968), *Contrarius consensus. Studien zur Vertragsaufhebung im römischen Recht*, Cologne-Graz.

Knütel, R. (1971), 'Zum Prinzip der formalen Korrespondenz im römischen Recht', in *Savigny Zeitschrift* (rom. Abt.) 88, 67–104.

Knütel R. (1975), 'Der mehrfache Verfall von Kautionen', in *Savigny Zeitschrift* (rom. Abt.) 92, 130–161.

Knütel, R. (2006), 'Rechtsfragen zu den Freilassungsfideikommissen', in Th. Finkenauer (ed.), *Sklaverei und Freilassung im römischen Recht. Symposium für Hans Josef Wieling zum 70. Geburtstag*, Berlin-Heidelberg-New York, 131–151.

Kotlyar, I.A. (2021), 'Medieval juristic *regulae*: unity or disunity?', in *Tijdschrift voor Rechtsgeschiedenis* 89, 409–438.

Kreller, H. (1927) review of J. Lambert, *La règle Catonienne*, in *Savigny Zeitschrift* (rom. Abt.) 47, 436–439.

Kuhn, Th.S. (1996), *The Structure of Scientific Revolutions*, 3rd edition, London.

Kunkel, W. (1967), *Herkunft und soziale Stellung der römischen Juristen*, 2nd edition, Graz-Vienna-Cologne.

Lambert, J. (1925), *La règle Catonienne*, Paris.

Lambrini, P. (2006), *La novazione: pensiero classico e disciplina giustinianea*, Padua.

Leeman, A.D. (1963), *Orationis ratio*, Amsterdam, repr. 1986.

Leeman, A.D. and A.C. Braet (1987), *Klassieke retorica*, Groningen.

Leesen, T.G. (2010), *Gaius meets Cicero. Law and Rhetoric in the School Controversies*, Leiden.

Legier, H.J. (1966), 'Tacita condicio', in *Revue d'histoire de droit français et étranger* 44, 5–32.

Lehne, Chr. (2019), *Iurisperiti et oratores: eine Studie zu den römischen Juristen der Republik*, Vienna.

Lenel, O. (1889), *Palingenesia iuris civilis*, 2 vols., Leipzig, repr. Graz 1960.

Lenel, O. (1927), *Das edictum perpetuum*, 3rd edition, Leipzig, repr. Aalen 1956 and 1974.

Lesaffer, R. (2009), *European Legal History: a Cultural and Political Perspective*, Cambridge.

Levy, E. and E. Rabel (1931), *Index interpolationum quae in Iustiniani digestis inesse dicuntur* II, *ad libros digestorum* XXI – XXXV *pertinens*, Weimar.

Lewis, C.T. and C. Short (1879), *A Latin Dictionary*, New York, repr. Oxford 1969.

Liebs, D. (1970), '*Contrarius actus*. Zur Entstehung des römischen Erlassvertrags', in D. Liebs (ed.), *Sympotica Franz Wieacker, sexagenario Sasbachwaldeni a suis libata*, Göttingen, 111–153.

Liebs, D. (1982), *Lateinische Rechtsregeln und Rechtssprichwörter*, Munich.

Liebs, D. (2012), *Summoned to the Roman Courts: famous trials from antiquity*, Berkeley.

Linden, J. van der (1827), *De ware pleiter*, Amsterdam.

Lombardi, L. (1963), 'Aperçus sur la compensation chez les juristes classiques', in *Bullettino dell'Istituto di diritto romano* 66, 35–91.

Lovato, A. (2011), *Tra retorica e diritto: linguaggi e forme argomentative nella tradizione giuridica: incontro di studio, Trani, 22–23 maggio 2009: atti*, Bari.

Lübtow, U. von (1932), *Der Ediktstitel "Quod metus causa gestum erit"*, Greifswald.

Lübtow, U. von (1935), review of G. Dulckeit, *Erblasserwille und Erwerbswille bei Antretung der Erbschaft*, in *Savigny Zeitschrift* (rom. Abt.) 55, 403413.

MacCormack, G. (1985), '*Dolus* in Republican Law', in *Bullettino dell'Istituto di diritto romano* 3rd series 27, 1–38.

Manthe, U. (1997), 'Ein Sieg der Rhetorik über die Jurisprudenz. Der Erbschaftsstreit des Manius Curius – eine vertane Chance der Rechtspolitik', in U. Manthe and J. von Ungern Sternberg (eds.), *Grosze Prozesse der römische Antike*, Munich, 74–84.

Manthe, U. (2014), review of U. Babusiaux, *Papinians Quaestiones*, in *Savigny Zeitschrift* (rom. Abt.) 131, 4533–459.

Mantovani, D. (2015), review of V. Wankerl, *Appello ad principem*, in *Savigny Zeitschrift* (rom. Abt.) 132, 654–662.

Maschi, C. G. (1938), *Studi giuridici sull'interpretazione dei legati*, Milan.

May, J.J. and J. Wisse (2001), *Cicero, On the Ideal Orator*, Oxford-New York.

Mayali, L. (2015), 'The Legacy of Roman Law', in D. Johnston (ed.), *The Cambridge Companion to Roman Law*, Cambridge, 374–395.

Mayer-Maly, Th. (1966), 'Obligamur necessitate', in *Savigny Zeitschrift* (rom. Abt.) 83, 47–67.

Mayer-Maly, Th. (1960), 'Studien zur Frühgeschichte der Usucapio I', in *Savigny Zeitschrift* (rom. Abt.) 77, 16–51.

Medicus, D. (1962), *Id quod interest, Studien zum römischen Recht des Schadenersatzes*, Cologne-Graz.

Medicus, D. (1965), review of K.-H. Below, *Die Haftung für lucrum cessans im römischen Recht*, in *Savigny Zeitschrift* (rom. Abt.) 82, 392–398.

Medicus, D. (1969), 'Zur Funktion der Leistungsmöglichkeit im römischen Recht', in *Savigny Zeitschrift* (rom. Abt.) 86, 67–104.

Meer, J.A.J.M. van der (1996), *The lex Voconia: Made for Men. Mulier heres institui non potest*, Eijsden.

Miceli, M. (2008), *Studi sulla "rappresentanza" net diritto romano*, Milan.

Michel, J.H. (1966), 'L'influence de la lex venditionis sur les règles du contrat de vente', in *Revue internationale des droits de l'antiquité* 13, 325–340.

Mollá Nebot, M.ª A. S. (1993), *Extinción formal de las obligaciones verbales. La "acceptilatio"*, Valencia.

Mommsen, Th. (1856), *Römische Geschichte* III, Berlin, repr. 1933.

Mommsen, Th. and P. Krüger (1870), *Digesta Iustiniani Augusti*, 2 vols., Berlin, repr. 1962 (editio maior).

Mommsen, Th. and P. Krüger (1872), *Corpus Iuris Civilis* I, Institutiones, Digesta, 12th edition, Berlin 1911, repr. 1973 (editio stereotypa).

Montañana Casani, A. (2000), 'La veuve et la succession héréditaire dans le droit classique', in *Revue internationale des droits de l'antiquité* 47, 415–448.

Müller-Eiselt, K.P. (1982), *Divus Pius constituit. Kaiserliches Erbrecht*, Berlin.

Nelson, H.L.W. (1981), *Überlieferung, Aufbau und Stil von Gai Institutiones*, Leiden.

Nörr, D. (1965), 'Zur sozialen und rechtlichen Bewertung der freien Arbeit in Rom', in *Savigny Zeitschrift* (rom. Abt.) 82, 67–105.

Nörr, D. (1972), 'Spruchregel und Generalisierung', in *Savigny Zeitschrift* (rom. Abt.) 89, 18–93.

Nörr, D. (1974), *Rechtskritik in der römischen Antike*, Munich.

Nörr, D. (1977), 'Cicero als Quelle und Autorität bei den römischen Juristen', in F. Bauer, K. Lare and F. Wieacker (eds.), *Beiträge zur europäischen Rechtsgeschichte und zum geltenden Zivilrecht. Festgabe für Johannis Sontis*, Munich, 33–52.

d'Ors, A. et al. (1968), *El Digesto de Justiniano*, I, Pamplona.

d'Ors, A. et al. (1972), *El Digesto de Justiniano*, II, Pamplona.

d'Ors, A. et al. (1975), *El Digesto de Justiniano*, III, Pamplona.

Otto, K.E., B. Schilling and K.F.F. Sintenis (1830–1833), *Das Corpus iuris civilis (Romani) ins Deutsche übersetzt*, Leipzig, repr. Aalen 1984–1985.

Palazzolo, N (1968), *Dos praelegata. Contributo alla storia del prelegato romano*, Milan.

Palma, A. (1992), *Humanior interpretatio. 'Humanitas' nell'interpretazione e nella normazione da Adriano ai Severi*, Turin.

Pastori, F. (1962), *La superficie nel diritto romano*, Milan.

Pastori, F. (1987), 'Sulla struttura della "actio de superficie"', in F. Pastori et al. (eds.), *Studi in onore di Arnaldo Biscardi* VI, Milan, 325–353.

Paulus, Chr. (1992), *Die Idee der postmortalen Persönlichkeit im römischen Testamentsrecht*, Berlin.

Pérez Simeón, M. (1998), 'Si quis pro centum ducenta per notam scripsisset', in *Revue internationale des droits de l'antiquité* 45, 797–816.

Pérez Simeón, M. (2001), *Nemo pro parte testatus pro parte intestatus decedere potest*, Barcelona.

Pergami, F. (2012), *Quod initio vitiosum est non potest tractu temporis convalescere. Studi sull'invalidità e sulla sanatoria degli atti negoziali nel sistema privatistico romano*, Turin.

Perrin, B. (1914), *Plutarch, Lives* II, with an English translation, Cambridge (Mass.)-London.

Pescani, P. (1974), Il piano del Digesto e la sua attuazione', in *Bullettino dell'Istituto di diritto romano* 77, 221–405.

Plessis, P.J. du (2010), *Borkowski's Textbook on Roman Law*, 4th edition, Oxford.

Plessis, P.J. du (2013), *New Frontiers: Law and Society in the Roman World*, Edinburgh.

Potjewijd, G.H. (1998), *Beschikkingsbevoegdheid, bekrachtiging en convalescentie – een romanistische studie*, Deventer.

Quadrato, R. (1983), *Sulle tracce dell'annullabilità: "quasi nullus" nella giurisprudenza romana*, Naples.

Querzoli, S. (2013), *Scienza giuridica e cultura retorica in Ulpio Marcello*, Naples.

Rainer, J.M. (2014), *Römische Rechtsgeschichte: ein Studienbuch*, 11th revised edition, Munich.

Reggi, R. (1958), *Liber homo bona fide serviens*, Milan.

Reimundo, B. (1983), *La sistematizacion de la indignidad para suceder según el derecho romano clásico*, Oviedo.

Reinhardt, T. (2003), *Cicero's Topica*, Oxford, repr. 2005.

Reynolds, L.D. and N.G. Wilson (1991), *Scribes and Scholars. A Guide to the Transmission of Greek and Latin Literature*, 3rd edition, Oxford.

Riccobono, S. (1929), review of J. Stroux, *Summum ius summa iniuria*, in *Gnomon* 5, 65–87.

Riposati, B. (1947), *Studi sui 'Topica' di Cicerone*, Milan.

Robbe, U. (1937), *I postumi nella successione testamentaria romana*, Milan.

Rodger, A. (1984), 'Roman Gifts and Rain-Water', in *The Law Quarterly Review* 100, 77–85.

Rodger, A. (1988), 'The Palingenesia of Paul's Commentary on the actio aquae pluviae arcendae', in *Savigny Zeitschrift* (rom. Abt.) 105, 726–728.

Rossi, G. (2003), 'Rhetorical role models for 16th to 18th century lawyers', in O.E. Tellegen-Couperus (ed.), *Quintilian and the Law*, Leuven.

Rubinelli, S. (2009), *Ars Topica*, New York.

Sacconi, G. (1971), *Ricerche sulla delegazione in diritto romano*, Milan.

Sanguinetti, A. (1999), 'La promessa del fatto altrui nella riflessione dei giuristi romani', in *Studia et documenta historiae et iuris* 65, 151–210.

Scarano Ussani,V. (1987), *L'utilità e la certezza. Compiti e modelli del sapere giuridico in Salvio Giuliano*, Milan.

Schanbacher, D. (1987), *Die Konvaleszenz von Pfandrechten im klassischen römischen Recht*, Berlin.

Schanbacher, D. (1992), 'Zur Bedeutung der Leistungszweckbestimmung bei der Übereignung durch *traditio* und beim Leistungsversprechen durch *stipulatio*', in *Tijdschrift voor Rechtsgeschiedenis* 60, 1–27.

Schiavone, A. (2012), *The Invention of Law in the West*, Cambridge (Mass.)-London.

Schieder, Chr. (2011), *Interesse und Sachwert*, Göttingen.

Schmidlin, B. (1970), *Die römischen Rechtsregeln*, Cologne-Vienna.

Schmidlin, B. (1976), 'Horoi, pithana und regula – zum Einfluss der Rhetorik und Dialektik auf die juristische Regelbildung', in *Aufstieg und Niedergang der römischen Welt* II, 15, 101–130.

Schmidlin, B. (1976), 'Regula iuris: Standard, Norm oder Spruchregel? Zum hermeneutischen Problem des Regelverständnisses', in D. Medicus and H.H. Seiler (eds.), *Festschrift für Max Kaser zum 70. Geburtstag*, Munich, 91–109.

Schulz, F. (1936), *Principles of Roman Law*, Oxford.

Schulz, F. (1946), *History of Roman Legal Science*, Oxford, repr. 1967.

Schwarz, A.B. (1951), 'Das strittige Recht der römischen Juristen', in *Atti Verona* 2, 121–148 = *Festschrift Fritz Schulz* 1, Weimar, 201–225.

Sciarrino, E. (2007), 'The Elder Cato and Gaius Gracchus: Roman Oratory before Cicero', in W.J. Dominik and J. Hal (eds.), *A Companion to Roman Rhetoric*, Oxford, 54–66.

Scott, S.P. (1932), *The civil law, including the Twelve Tables, the Institutes of Gaius, the Rules of Ulpian, the Opinions of Paulus, the Enactments of Justinian, and the Constitutions of Leo, translated from the original Latin, edited and compared with all accessible systems of jurisprudence ancient and modern* I–XVII, Cincinnati, repr. New York 1973.

Serangeli, S. (1982), *Studi sulla revoca del testamento in diritto romano* I, Milan.

Shuckburgh, E.S. (1912), *The Letters of Cicero, the whole extant correspondence in chronological order* IV, London.

Silla, F.M. (2008), *La 'cognitio' sulle 'libertates fideicommissae'*, Padua.

Sitzia, F. (1977), *Ricerche in tema di "actio aquae pluviae arcendae" dalle XII tavole all'epoca classica*, Milan.

Solmsen, F. (1929), *Die Entwicklung der aristotelischen Logik und Rhetorik*, Berlin.

Spagnolo, B and J. Sampson (eds.) (2020), *Principle and Pragmatism in Roman Law*, Oxford.

Spruit, J.E. (1994), with R. Feenstra and K.E.M. Bongenaar (eds.), *Corpus iuris civilis. Tekst en Vertaling* II, Digesten 1–10, Zutphen-The Hague.

Spruit, J.E. (1996), with R. Feenstra and K.E.M. Bongenaar (eds.), *Corpus iuris civilis. Tekst en Vertaling* III, Digesten 11–24, Zutphen-The Hague.

Spruit, J.E. (1997), with R. Feenstra and K.E.M. Bongenaar (eds.), *Corpus iuris civilis. Tekst en Vertaling* IV, Digesten 25–34, Zutphen-The Hague.

Spruit, J.E. (2000), with R. Feenstra and F.B.J. Wubbe (eds.), *Corpus iuris civilis. Tekst en Vertaling* V, Digesten 35–42, Zutphen-The Hague.

Spruit, J.E. (2001), with R. Feenstra and F.B.J. Wubbe (eds.), *Corpus iuris civilis. Tekst en Vertaling* VI, Digesten 43–50, Zutphen-The Hague.

Stagl, J.F. (2007), 'Die Ausgleichung von Vorteil und Nachteil als Inhalt klassischer "aequitas"', in D. Mantovani and A. Schiavone (eds.), *Testi e problemi del giusnaturalismo romano*, Pavia, 675–713.

Stagl, J.F. (2009), *Favor dotis, Die Privilegierung der Mitgift im System des römischen Rechts*, Vienna-Cologne-Weimar.

Stagl, J.F. (2013), 'Durch Rede zum Recht am Beispiel von Quint. decl. 360 (Making Law through Discussion: the Example of Quint. Decl. 360)', in *Journal on European History of Law* 4, 2–9.

Stagl, J.F. (2014), 'Glanz der Rhetorik und Finsternis der Logik in einer Entscheidung Mark Aurels (Marcell. D. 28.4.3 Pr.-1)', in R. Van den Bergh (ed.), *Meditationes de iure et historia: essays in honour of Laurens Winkel*, Pretoria, 862–871.

Stagl, J.F. (2020), 'El "favor libertatis": una "institución particular". A propósito de Marcell. D. 28.4.3 pr.-1', in *Revista General de Derecho Romano* 34, 1–31.

Stagl, J.F. (2023), *Der Tempel der Gerechtigkeit. Zur Morphologie und Hermeneutik der Pandekten*, Paderborn.

Stein, P. (1966), *Regulae Iuris: From Juristic Rules to Legal Maxims*, Edinburgh.

Stein, P. (1978), 'The Place of Servius Sulpicius Rufus in the Development of Roman Legal Science', in O. Behrends and M. Diesselhorst (eds.), *Festschrift für Franz Wieacker zum 70. Geburtstag*, Göttingen, 175–184.

Stein, P. (1999), *Roman Law in European History*, Cambridge.

Stoll, H. (1924), 'Die formlose Vereinbarung der Aufhebung eines Vertragsverhältnisses im römischen Recht', in *Savigny Zeitschrift* (rom. Abt.) 44, 1–85.

Stroux, J. (1926), 'Summum ius summa iniuria, Ein Kapitel aus der Geschichte der interpretatio iuris', Leipzig-Berlin, repr. in *Römische Rechtswissenschaft und Rhetorik*, Potsdam 1949, 9–66.

Sturm, F. (1971), review of G. Sacconi, *Ricerche sulla delegazione in diritto romano*, in *IURA* 22, 260–269.

Tafaro, S. (1971), review of H. Honsell, *Quod interest im bonae-fidei-iudicium. Studien zum römischen Schadenersatzrecht*, in *Index* 2, 359–376.

Tafaro, S. (1984), *Regula e ius antiquum in D. 50.17.23: ricerche sulla responsabilità contrattuale* I, Bari.

Tafaro, S. (1998), *Il giurista e l'"ambiguità": ambigere ambiguitas ambiguus*, Bari.

Talamanca, M. (1958), *Ricerche in tema di "compromissum"*, Milan.

Talamanca, M. (1965), 'Sul concorso fra legato e manumissione', in A. Giuffrè (ed.), *Studi in onore di B. Biondi* II, Milan, 313–382.

Talamanca, M. (1995–1996), '"Adscriptio partium" e "pollicitatio condicionis": il problema della assenza del relato nel testamento "per relationem"', in *Bullettino dell'Istituto di diritto romano* 98–99, 571–730.

Tellegen, J.W. (1982), *The Roman Law of Succession in the Letters of Pliny the Younger* I, Zutphen.

Tellegen, J.W. (1988), 'Gaius Cassius and the *Schola Cassiana* in Pliny's Letter VII 24.8', in *Savigny Zeitschr"ift (rom. Abt.)* 105, 263–311.

Tellegen, J.W. (1994), '"Res corporalis" et les codfications modenes du droit civil', in *Labeo* 40, 35–55.

Tellegen, J.W. (2003), 'The Reliability of Quintilian for Roman law: on the *causa Curiana*', in O.E. Tellegen-Couperus (ed.), *Quintilian and the Law*, Leuven, 191–200.

Tellegen, J.W. (2010), 'The Immortality of the Soul and Roman Law', in C. Russo Ruggeri (ed.) *Studi in onore di Antonino Metro* VI, Milan, 297–321.

Tellegen, J.W and Tellegen-Couperus, O.E. (2000), 'Law and Rhetoric in the *causa Curiana*', in *Orbis Iuris Romani* 6, 171–202.

Tellegen, J.W and Tellegen-Couperus, O.E. (2004), 'Mommsen en Themis', in *Rechtsgeleerd Magazijn Themis* 165, 70–75.

Tellegen, J.W and Tellegen-Couperus, O.E. (2007), 'Achieving Justice by Twisting the Truth', in F. Milazzo (ed.), *Studi per Giovanni Nicosia* VIII, Milan, 231–254.

Tellegen, J.W. and T.G. Leesen (2016), 'Cicero's Topica and Trebatius Testa', in C.L. van Blom and E.J.M.F.C. Broers (ed.), *Ad fundum, Liber Amicorum Olga Tellegen-Couperus*, Oisterwijk, 109–129.

Tellegen-Couperus, O.E. (2003), 'A clarifying *sententia* clarified: on *Institutio Oratoria* VIII.5.19', in O.E. Tellegen-Couperus (ed.), *Quintilian and the Law*, Leuven, 213–221.

Tellegen-Couperus, O.E. (2006), review of M.H. Frost, *Introduction to Classical Legal Rhetoric. A Lost Heritage*, in *Rhetorical Review* 4, 7–12.

Tellegen-Couperus, O.E. (2021), 'Quintilian and the Law', in M. van der Poel, M. Edwards and J.J. Murphy (eds.), *The Oxford Handbook of Quintilian*, Oxford, 259–277.

Tellegen-Couperus, O.E. and J.W. Tellegen (2013), '*Artes Urbanae:* Roman Law and Rhetoric', in P.J. du Plessis (ed.), *New Frontiers: Law and Society in the Roman World*, Edinburgh, 31–50.

Tellegen-Couperus, O.E. and J.W. Tellegen (2016), 'Reading a Dead Man's Mind. Hellenistic Philosophy, Rhetoric, and Roman Law', in P.J. du Plessis (ed.), *Cicero's Law: Rethinking Roman Law of the Late Republic*, Edinburgh, 26–49.

Thomas, Ph. (2014), '*Ars aequi et boni*, legal argumentation and the correct legal solution', in *Savigny Zeitschrift* (rom. Abt.) 131, 41–59.

Thomas, Ph. (2016), 'A Barzunesque View of Cicero: From Giant to Dwarf and Back', in P.J. du Plessis (ed.), *Cicero's Law, Rethinking Roman Law of the Late Republic*, Edinburgh, 11–25.

Trofimoff, H. (1994), 'Les sources doctrinales de l'ordre de presentation des articles 1156 à 1164 du Code Civil sur l'interpretation des contrats', in *Revue historique de droit français et étranger* 72, 203–233.

Tuori, K. (2007), *Ancient Roman Lawyers and Modern Legal Ideals: Studies on the Impact of Contemporary Concerns in the Interpretation of Ancient Roman Legal History*, 2nd edition, Frankfurt.

Vaughn, J.W. (1985), 'Law and Rhetoric in the Causa Curiana', in *Classical Antiquity* 4, 208–222.

Viehweg, Th. (1974), *Topik und Jurisprudenz*, 5th edition, Munich.

Voci, P. (1963), *Diritto ereditario romano* II, *Parte speciale: Successione intestata, Successione testamentaria*, 2nd edition, Milan.

Voci, P. (1967), *Diritto ereditario romano* I, *Introduzione. Parte generale*, 2nd edition, Milan.

Wacke, A. (1973), 'Zur Lehre vom *pactum tacitum* und zur Aushilfsfunktion der *exceptio doli*', in *Savigny Zeitschrift* (rom. Abt.) 90, 221–261.

Wacke, A. (1995), 'Verbotene Dahrlehnsgewährung an Hauskinder', in *Savigny Zeitschrift* (rom. Abt.) 112, 239–329.

Wacke, A. (1997), 'Die Konvaleszenz der Verfügung eines Nichtberechtigten', in *Savigny Zeitschrift* (rom. Abt.) 114, 197–232.

Wacke, A. (2000), '*Ex post factum convalescere* im römischen und modernen Recht', in M. Zabłozka, J. Krzynówek, J. Urbanik, and Z. Słuzewska (eds.), *Au-delà des frontières. Mélanges de droit romain offerts à Witold Wołodkiewicz*, Warsaw, 1025–1052.

Wagner, H. (1974), review of G. Sacconi, *Ricerche sulla delegazione in diritto romano*, in *Savigny Zeitschrift* (rom. Abt.) 91, 452–465.

Waldstein, W. (1975), 'Konsequenz als Argument klassischer Juristen', in *Savigny Zeitschrift* (rom. Abt.) 92, 26–68.

Waldstein, W. (1986), *Operae libertorum. Untersuchungen zur Dienstpflicht freigelassener Sklaven*, Stuttgart.

Wankerl, V. (2009), *Appello ad principem. Urteilsstil und Urteilstechnik in kaiserlichen Berufungsentscheidungen (Augustus bis Caracalla)*, Munich.

Watson, A. (1967), *The Law of Persons in the Later Roman Republic*, Oxford.

Watson, A. (1971), *The Law of Succession in the Later Roman Republic*, Oxford.

Watson, A. (1974), *Law Making in the Later Roman Republic*, Oxford.

Watson, A. (1985), *The Digest of Justinian*. Latin text edited by Theodor Mommsen with the aid of Paul Krüger. English translation edited by Alan Watson, 4 vols., Philadelphia.

Wenger, L. (1953), *Die Quellen des römischen Rechts*, Vienna.

Wesel, U. (1963), 'Vispellio', in *Savigny Zeitschrift* (rom. Abt.) 80, 392–394.

Wesener, G. (1995), 'Nichtediktale Einreden', in *Savigny Zeitschrift* (rom. Abt.) 112, 109–150.

Wieacker, F. (1967) 'The *causa Curiana* and Contemporary Roman Jurisprudence', in *The Irish Jurist* 2, 151–164.

Wieacker, F. (1967), review of P. Stein, *Regulae iuris: From Juristic Rules to Legal Maxims*, in SZ 84, 434–454.

Wieacker, F. (1988), *Römische Rechtsgeschichte* I: *Einleitung, Quellenkunde Frühzeit und Republik*, München.

Wieacker, F. (2006), *Römische Rechtsgeschichte* II: *Die Jurisprudenz vom frühen Prinzipat bis zum Ausgang der Antike im weströmischen Reich und die oströmischen Rechtswissenschaft bis zur Justinianischen Gesetzgebung*, Munich.

Wieling, H.J. (1972), *Testamentsauslegung im römischen Recht*, Munich.

Woess, F. von (1911) *Das römische Erbrecht und die Erbanwärter*, Berlin.

Wolf, J.G. (2013), review of U. Babusiaux, *Papinians Quaestiones*, in *Tijdschrift voor Rechtsgeschiedenis* 81, 275–281.

Wollschläger, Chr. (1970), *Die Entstehung der Unmöglichkeitslehre*, Cologne-Vienna.

Wubbe, F.B.J. (2001), review of G.H. Potjewijd, *Beschikkingsbevoegdheid, bekrachtiging en convalescentie – een romanistische studie*, in *Tijdschrift voor Rechtsgeschiedenis* 69, 373–381.

Yates, F.A. (1966), *The Art of Memory*, London.

Zandrino, L. (2010), *La delegatio nel diritto romano: profili semantici ed elementi fattispecie*, Naples.

Ziegler, K.H. (1971), *Das privaten Schiedsgericht im antiken römischen Recht*, Munich.

Ziegler, K.H. (1992), 'Papinians Beitrage zum privaten Schiedsgericht', in *Savigny Zeitschrift* (rom. Abt.) 109, 533–538.

Zimmermann, R. (1996), *The Law of Obligations. Roman Foundations of the Civilian Tradition*, Oxford.

Zulueta, F. de (1946), *The Institutes of Gaius*, I, Text with critical notes and translation, Oxford.

Index of Sources

www.ingramcontent.com/pod-product-compliance
Lightning Source LLC
Chambersburg PA
CBHW071322230926
51849CB00002B/292
* 9 7 8 9 0 0 4 7 1 1 0 1 3 *